To Mary, Mother of God
and Queen of Martyrs.

To Don Bosco,
great catechist.

To all the young Pilgrims
visiting the Catacombs of St. Callixtus.

My warmest thanks to Anna Maria Page Antoldi,
who shared the role of Maecenas
to the second English edition.

First English Edition: May 1993.
Second English Edition: January 2000.
Third English Edition: May 2006.

Front cover

Front cover represents Jesus, the Good Shepherd, carrying the delivered soul into Paradise. The Catacombs of St. Callixtus are a cemetery where everything speaks of life. (Photo: Vatican Museums).

Photos

– Díaz Sánchez Martín: p. 11,21, 23, 48, 75.
– Kandulna Joseph: p. 18, 153.
– Marzi Franco: p. 28, 29, 30, 32, 34, 51, 86a, 135.
– Mazzoleni Danilo: p. 25.
– Pavia Carlo: p. 108, 150, 152.
– Reekmans Louis: p. 97b, 103.
– Archives of the Catacombs of St. Callixtus:
  p. 20, 172, 174, 177, 179, 187.
– Centro Elicotteri Carabinieri (Ten. Col. Frasca Nunzio):
  p. 7, 8, 14-15, 27, 41, 89.
– Edizioni Regoli: p. 128.
– Pontifical Commission for Sacred Archaeology (PCAS):
  p. 42, 53, 67, 69, 76a, 80, 81, 84, 104, 116, 120, 122,
  124a, 131b, 132, 139, 143, 170, 180, 186.
– All the other photos: Elle Di Ci (Pera Guerrino).
– Reconstruction of the frescoes (Fabris Severino):
  p. 43, 44, 82b, 110b, 112b, 119, 124b, 147b, 166.

All drawings in chapters XII and XIII
belong to inscriptions
of the "Callixtian complex".
Cf. ICUR, IV.

ISBN 88-209-1902-8

ANTONIO BARUFFA

THE CATACOMBS OF ST. CALLIXTUS

History – Archaeology – Faith

Translation
by
WILLIAM PURDY

PUBLISHED BY L.E.V.
VATICAN CITY

Preface to the third Italian edition

The public's favourable reception to the first edition of my book: "Le Catacombe di San Callisto. Storia – Archeologia – Fede" *continued with the second, which was sold out in two years.*

This left me with the problem of whether to limit myself to a simple re-printing or make a revised edition. Some scholars advised me not to increase the size of the volume so as to allow the text to be easily read.

However, it seemed to me unsuitable to reprint the book as it was, without taking advantage of literary criticism and the recent developments in scholarly research.

Hence, out of respect for my readers and for greater historical accuracy, I decided to update the volume. Without increasing the number of pages, paragraphs have been modified to permit greater precision on some topics.

The main novelty in this third edition are the photographs, which I have notably increased, improving some reproductions and adding new subjects, in order to gain a better knowledge of the iconography and epigraphy of the catacombs. I have arranged them so that the reader may quickly identify the monuments described.

I have already had occasion to thank those whose skill and friendship have helped me with this book. I want now to add grateful mention of Prof. Giovanni Cecchin, former lecturer at the University of Turin and visiting fellow *of Princeton University N. J., and of Vincenzo Fiocchi Nicolai, Professor of Topography at the Pontifical Institute of Christian Archaeology and member of the Pontifical Commission for Sacred Archaeology. They read the book thoroughly and made valuable comments.*

A. B.

Rome, The Catacombs of St. Callixtus, 14th October 1991.
Memorial day of the martyr Pope St. Callixtus I.

Preface to the second Italian edition

Critics have given a warm welcome to my book: *"Le Catacombe di San Callisto. Storia – Archeologia – Fede"*. I was surprised to see several reviews in both the national press and in specialized publications. The readers also seemed favorable to it, since the first edition was quickly sold out.

Various considerations have suggested a second edition. The book was just published when Professor Louis Reekmans of the University of Louvain released a weighty study of one area of the Catacombs of St. Callixtus: *"Le complexe cémétérial du pape Gaius dans la Catacombe de Callixte"*. Its contributions are of such scholarly importance that they cannot be overlooked.

I may add that in the meantime I have received many letters, not only expressing satisfaction with the work, but wanting to know more about the persons and topics dealt with in the book. It seems right, as far as possible, to meet these requests.

Thus the book retains its simple style, and has six more chapters; some have been divided into two for easier reading, while others have been re-worked so as to lay out the material more logically, as suggested by colleagues and readers. I have added some more topographical plans, making the routes clearer; there are more photographs as well.

I am deeply grateful to Rev. Prof. Ugo Casalegno, a friend and fellow student since boyhood, for helping me revise the language of the manuscript.

A. B.

Rome, Catacombs of St. Callixtus, 29th June 1989.
Feast of SS. Peter and Paul.

Foreword

Anyone reading the title of this book at a glance, might think that it is just another guidebook to Rome's most famous underground cemeteries added to those already published in the recent past. But a look at the contents shows that it is something different and in many ways new. Both in the originality of some chapters and in its main purpose the book is addressed primarily to non-specialists and above all to young people.

For example, some parts concentrate on a general summary of the history of the catacombs, while others are particularly dedicated to the many inscriptions, sometimes freely translated, but always adhering to the spirit of the texts. The documentary evidence which the author offers for the veneration of St. Cyprian in the Cemetery of St. Callixtus, in the light of the relations between the Church of Rome and Carthage in the first centuries, as well as the new details of the homage paid by the modern popes during their visits to their tombs, and the "extraordinary adventure" of Giovanni Battista de Rossi which culminated in the discovery of that catacomb, is very interesting.

The survey of the inscriptions deserves special mention, because among the thousands published in the fourth volume of the "Inscriptiones Christianae Urbis Romae" (ICUR), those which have been chosen contain noteworthy formulas or attract interest by revealing human feelings, faith, sorrow, family affection. For the most part humble people, though inwardly rich, through these inscriptions, tell us much about themselves, which otherwise we would never have known.

It should be made clear, however, that Prof. Antonio Baruffa's book, though up-to-date in scholarship, avoids a language which is used only by specialists or students. He instructs simply but effectively; he takes the reader by the hand and explains all the particulars of the catacombs with words easily understood by everybody, aiming at clearing every possible doubt and anticipating possible questions. Prof. Baruffa has undoubtedly profited by the experience of his many years as a guide at St. Callixtus as well as from his work as lecturer in Christian archaeology at the Pontifical Salesian University in Rome.

Avoiding the many controversies which have risen among scholars in the last century concerning the Catacombs, the author has limited himself to the established data, offering a summary of many studies and leaving aside hypotheses and questions yet to be solved. It would have been out of place here to deal with such problems.

The fascinating itinerary in subterranean Rome winds through the ancient "areas" and the most significant evidence found in the Catacombs of St. Callixtus, whether it contains frescoes, sculptures, inscriptions or venerated sepulchres. The book draws the readers' attention to much that would otherwise escape them, and here the priestly sensibility and the catechetical and pastoral concern of Fr. Baruffa, rich in ministerial experience, especially with the young, is felt. The presentation of the subject, though scholarly,

is not dry but rather brings the catacomb to life, so that readers, despite the distance of so many centuries, will feel brought back to an age in early history which was rich in faith and will rediscover values and feelings which actively engage them. They will be inspired to imitate such shining examples of Christian life.

The book includes chronological tables and clear maps of the catacomb as well as a series of coloured photographs which are excellent visual aids.

After a first draft of the book, the author has enriched his material, and has gratefully welcomed suggestions from many distinguished scholars (much more distinguished than the present writer).

To conclude, let me say that this guidebook on the Catacombs of St. Callixtus is so worthily presented as to need no preface; I have gladly written these few words to wish good fortune to Fr. Baruffa's book. I have known him since the days when we attended the Pontifical Institute of Christian Archaeology.

"Ad maiora" then: may readers so value these pages as to repay the effort the writer has so happily put into them.

DANILO MAZZOLENI

Rome, 7ᵗʰ August 1988.
Memorial of St. Sixtus II.

7

Introduction

Among the places that a pilgrim or tourist coming to Rome includes in his programme as deserving a visit are the catacombs. They are always fascinating and for many they are a genuine invitation to explore the roots of Christianity.

Thousands visit them every year: family or parish groups, school parties or individuals. Few visitors have precise ideas about the catacombs, most of them know little of archaeology or of early Church history.

Every day, the guides to the catacombs are asked many questions. "When did the catacombs begin?"... "How were they dug?"... "Why did the emperors persecute?"... "Did the Christians live down there?"... "What importance can the catacombs still have today?"...

There is no lack of valuable studies on these early Christian cemeteries, but they are nearly always for archaeologists or analyse the monuments from a strictly scientific point of view.

Wishing therefore to help visitors who are not specialists, I set out to write a book in clear and simple language: historically accurate, well illustrated and bearing in mind the sort of question just referred to.

In particular I want to offer this work to the many young people who come to the Catacombs of St. Callixtus. In their search for the authentic, they will find here a real help in re-discovering the faith of the Church of the first centuries. Facing it honestly, they will be stimulated to reflect on their way of life. In this they will also be helped by the consistent Christian witness of so many people of their own age.

This book is written without great pretensions. It proposes to follow the visitors step by step, so that they may realise the historical and religious importance of the catacomb. It should also revive long afterwards the memory and emotions left by a never-to-be forgotten visit to this "sanctuary of the martyrs".

This guidebook has fifteen chapters. The first is general, giving a brief history of the Christian catacombs of Rome from their origins down to our own time. The other chapters deal with the Catacombs of St. Callixtus "area by area".

The criterion followed in this underground journey is at once historical, topographical and catechetical. If the historical-topographical description is obvious and relatively easy, the catechetical is more difficult and very fascinating when we understand the message offered by the early Christians through the images and inscriptions. In fact it would be hard to separate the historical and archaeological elements from the catechetical at St. Callixtus without repeating oneself. The crypts of the martyrs are very important for a catacomb. It is an indisputable fact that this early Christian cemetery developed largely because of them. Saint Callixtus preserves a fair number of them. I have tried to give the right prominence to each. Since these catacombs are the official cemetery of the Church of Rome (κοιμητήριον κατ' ἐξοχήν) the Crypt of the Popes is of great importance in our description.

The architectonic aspect deserved proper consideration. Anyone visiting the catacombs for the first time is strongly impressed by the imposing excavations and wants to have detailed explanations.

Yet what most makes the Catacombs of St. Callixtus live for us today, even after sixteen centuries, are their paintings and inscriptions. The former are not numerous and, given the perishable materials with which they were executed, they tend to deteriorate steadily.

The inscriptions, on the other hand, are more plentiful and richer in variety and content. They are the most valuable first-hand historical documents, a direct expression of the thought and faith of the first Christian communities in Rome. Hence I have thought it suitable to comment on a small selection of the most significant inscriptions found in the "Callixtian complex".

This task called for checking all the data and for evaluating, as far as possible, every statement, cutting down to a minimum what is merely hypothetical.

To have listed my sources fully would have meant weighing down every page with notes. This might have satisfied scholars, but would have made things harder for the ordinary readers.

Instead, I wanted to give them a way of approaching Christian archaeology and of getting to know a catacomb without becoming bored and tired.

Moreover, a possibly easy risk for an archaeologist might be that of presenting a monument in a cool detached manner. I do not deny that there can be benefits in this approach, particularly at the level of pure scholarship.

Nonetheless, given the pastoral and catechetical scope of this guidebook, I have tried to bring to life a part of the history of the origins of Christianity. I have approached a world which in many respects can never be repeated, and I have sought to communicate its feelings, its state of mind, and its faith. These at least were my aims. I leave it to the reader to judge how far I have succeeded.

An appendix follows which presents the written testimonials of some leading figures who have made St. Callixtus famous, such as the martyrs buried within this catacomb: St. Fabian, St. Cornelius, St. Sixtus II. I have also described the visits made to these underground crypts by some popes and other illustrious pilgrims.

I conclude with an account of the great Giovanni Battista de Rossi, who, forty years after his first explorations, recalled his discoveries in the St. Callixtus Cemetery. It was these findings in this important early Christian cemetery that allowed de Rossi to identify the catacomb and bring some order to the names of other sites of subterranean Christian Rome.

Pope Paul VI, visiting the Catacombs of Domitilla and St. Callixtus on 12th September 1960, in his homily at the basilica of SS. Nereus and Achilleus, said:

"The catacombs are a reminder of a long history of persecution suffered by the Church in the first centuries. At the same time they are the image and the record of a religious intimacy which is extremely beautiful and fertile, of a tranquil and humble profession of faith which is an example for all time, of an unconquerable conviction that Christ is truth, salvation, hope, victory.

We have come to drink at the springs, we have come to honour these tombs, humble yet glorious, to draw from them admonition and strength. We have come to sense through our present experience the flow of a tradition which is not unmindful and unfaithful but always identical, always strong, always fertile.

We have come to renew ourselves with ancient examples of Christian virtue, to draw inspiration and vigour to imitate them today. We have not come to feel outdated or old but to become young and genuine in the profession of a faith, which the years do not wear out but fortify".

If these simple pages can help the young, the believer, the tourist to rediscover the roots of his faith, they will give the writer the satisfaction that his work has not been done in vain.

A. B.

Rome, Catacombs of St. Callixtus, 15th August 1988.
Feast of the Assumption of Our Lady.

I owe many thanks to those who have offered observations and suggestions during the writing of these pages:

— Prof. Umberto Fasola B., Secretary of the Pontifical Commission for Sacred Archaeology and Professor emeritus of Topography of the cemeteries and of ancient Rome.

— Antonio Ferrua S.J., Professor emeritus of Classical and Christian Epigraphy.

— Jos Janssens S.J., Professor of Christian Archaeology at the Pontifical Gregorian University.

— Danilo Mazzoleni, Professor of Classical and Christian Epigraphy at the Pontifical Institute of Christian Archaeology and associate Professor of Christian Archaeology at the University of Rome ("La Sapienza").

— The warmest gratitude to my Provincial, Rev. Angelo Viganò, who has the credit for the publication of this book.

I.
The Story
of the Catacombs

1. A YOUNG ARCHAEOLOGIST

In 1849 Giovanni Battista de Rossi, an enthusiastic 27-year-old archaeologist, entered a vineyard between the Appian Way and the Ardeatina in search of Christian antiquities. His expert eye fell on a broken strip of marble, which had been used as a step. It bore the inscription "[...] NELIVS · MARTYR". He at once guessed the missing part of the name. He completed it as CORNELIVS and realized that it was a significant part of the marble inscription of the martyred Pope Cornelius, who died at Civitavecchia in 253 and was buried some years later in a *hypogeum* near the Cemetery of Callixtus.

From that day a question persisted in the mind of the great archaeologist: could the Catacombs of St. Callixtus, the official cemetery of the 3rd century Church of Rome, be found beneath that vineyard?

To be certain he would have to begin excavations, but first the land would have to be acquired. He went to Pope Pius IX and told him of his discovery. He said he was convinced that he had at last found the Catacombs of St. Callixtus which, according to the ancient documents, had contained the Crypt of the Popes and the grave of St. Cecilia. The Pope willingly agreed to his proposal and bought the vineyard.

Excavations proved de Rossi right and, in the space of a few years, he uncovered no less than six crypts of saints and martyrs: the Crypt of the martyred Pope St. Cornelius, of the martyrs Calocerus and Parthenius, the famous Crypt of the Popes, that of the martyr St. Cecilia, the Crypts of Pope St. Gaius and of the martyred Pope St. Eusebius.

Thus began the locating and the study of "subterranean Christian Rome", consisting of about sixty Christian catacombs, large and small, in and about Rome.

2. THE CATACOMBS THROUGH THE CENTURIES

The history of the Christian catacombs in Rome can be divided into several main periods.

First and Second Centuries

During the first century the Christians in Rome had no cemeteries of their own. Most of them were buried in common cemeteries in the open and with the pagans. For example St. Peter was buried in the necropolis on the Vatican Hill, under the present basilica, and St. Paul in the necropolis along the Via Ostiense.

Other Christians, however, who owned private property, buried their dead in family tombs above ground.

After the middle of the 2nd century some cemeteries dug on the estates (villas, orchards, fields) of noble and rich families of converts were put at the disposal of their brethren in the faith. The latter were too poor to buy tombs. Thus excavation had its origin.

To this period belong those catacombs which are named after their proprietors, such as Priscilla, Domitilla, Praetextatus, the Crypts of Lucina...

The Third Century

As the Christians grew in numbers, some catacombs were acquired by the Church of Rome and administered by it. We know for certain that the Catacombs of St. Callixtus were dependent on the Church from the beginning of the 3rd century. In fact a contemporary writer, the Roman Hippolytus in his *Philosophúmena* (Confutation of All Heresies) relates that Pope Zephyrinus (199-217) appointed deacon

THE SEVEN ECCLESIASTICAL REGIONS
WITH THEIR PARISHES (TITULI)
AND THEIR CEMETERIES (CATACOMBS)

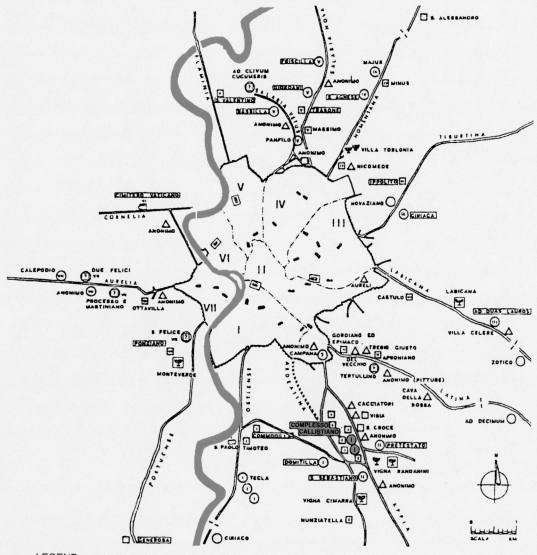

LEGEND

☐ Community catacombs and their probable inclusion in one on the seven ecclesiastical regions

○ Community catacombs with pre-Constantine nuclei.

△ Private *hypogeum*.

⊙ Probable location of catacombs not yet found.

♈ Jewish catacombs.

⊻ Jewish catacombs lost or utterly fallen down.

▭ Titular churches of the seven ecclesiastical regions

⬭ Certain or probable building interventions of pope St. Damasus.

〰 The Aurelian Walls.

PONTIFICAL COMMISSION
OF SACRED ARCHAEOLOGY
TECHNICAL BUREAU.
Drawing by G. Fiorenza
(from a map
by Fr. U. Fasola, Rome, 1985).

Callixtus as custodian and administrator of the catacomb.[1]

During this period, the martyred Pope St. Fabian († 250) divided the city of Rome into seven ecclesiastical regions. To each of these regions probably more than one catacomb was assigned for Christian burials. The city at the time had well over a million inhabitants and the Christians according to reliable estimates, numbered a few tens of thousands.

The Fourth Century

With the Edict of Milan, promulgated by Constantine and Licinius in February 313, Christians were no longer persecuted. The catacombs then finally became the property of the Church. The faithful continued to be buried there out of devotion to the martyrs, who had been buried there in great numbers.

Over the tombs of most venerable martyrs of the faith, churches or small basilicas were built. Pope St. Damasus (366-384) was especially distinguished for his devotion to the martyrs.

"St. Damasus — as D. Mazzoleni writes — composed about 50 verse inscriptions for saints and martyrs. For his activity, and for his intensive explorations for venerable tombs, giving them monumental form, Pope Pius XI in 1926 proclaimed him patron of Christian archaeology.

During his pontificate, in fact, he commissioned much restoration work in the catacombs: he built new staircases, widened galleries, opened *lucernari* (shafts for light). His full scale plan transformed these places into centres for the veneration of the martyrs, arranged like a crown around Rome, and its goal aimed at a continual presence of pilgrims".

St. Damasus' untiring work in favour of the veneration of the martyrs led to some large scale restructuring of several parts of the catacombs.

"The cemetery areas in the neighbourhood of these burials were altered, sometimes defying all the laws of statics, overloading walls and ground with new rooms even behind the venerable tombs, called *retrosanti*.

For the less fortunate, new enclosures, needed because of the growing Christian population, were added further away. That is why some catacombs, such as those named after Callixtus, Praetextatus, Domitilla, Priscilla, took on colossal proportions" (U. Fasola).

Smaller ones were dug near these large underground cemeteries intended for the Christian people and controlled by ecclesiastical authority, which Prof. Antonio Ferrua calls *di diritto privato* (the exclusive property of one or of a few families).

At the begining of the 5th century, after the "sack of Rome" by the Visigoth Alaric (410), the custom of burial within the catacombs ceased. Open-air burial resumed, above the grounds of the very catacombs, and much later, within the city walls.

From the Fifth
to the Ninth Centuries

During this long period the catacombs were regarded as sanctuaries of the martyrs, and many pilgrims visited them simply to pray at those tombs.

"To make prayer easier for the groups gathered at the martyrs' tombs, underground rooms were created, galleries were widened and small basilicas were excavated.[2] Liturgical assemblies, on the other hand, took place in the grandiose 'cemeterial basilicas' above ground. Their floors were filled with tombs, and sepulchres were built in the walls, while a ring of family mausoleums surrounded them" (U. Fasola).

Modern excavations document how much the tombs of the martyrs were venerated. Many requests were made in order to have a sepulchre alongside these champions of the faith; but this was granted mostly to those worthy of it, who led holy and innocent lives. At least this was the norm ...

"Moreover, the burial in places so widely visited was not only an honour but also a very useful way of keeping the memory of the dead person alive and enjoying at the same time the altogether special intercession of the martyrs" (J. Janssens).

The devotional graffiti (invocations or records of rites carried out, scratched on the plaster by pilgrims) and the compilation and drawing up of some *Itineraries* are characteristic of this early period. These were a great help to de Rossi for identifying the tombs of martyrs in the catacombs.[3]

But times got worse. The Goths seriously damaged these holy places during the siege of Witigis in 537-538

and that of Totila in 545-546, as did the Lombards under Aistulph in 735.

In the 8th century the popes, no longer able to provide adequate protection for the catacombs and lacking the means for the continual renovation and maintenance of the cemetery basilicas, began to transfer the relics of the martyrs and saints within the city. These "translations" continued also in the first decades of the 9th century.

On the two preceding pages: Aerial view of the "Callixtian Complex" enclosed by the three roads: the Appian Way (on the right), the Via Ardeatina and the Vicolo delle Sette Chiese (on the left).

I. On the right of the internal avenue of cypresses and starting at the botton:

- The Istituto Salesiano San Callisto (where the guides live).
- The Istituto Salesiano San Tarcisio (former Trappist monastery called "Santa Maria delle Catacombe di San Callisto"), situated after the crossroads of two avenues.
- The "Quo Vadis?" Church (at the end of the avenue).
- In the background: the Aurelian Walls and the Porta Appia or Porta di San Sebastiano.

II. On the left of the internal avenue of cypresses:

- The historic centre of the Catacombs of St. Callixtus (at the crossroads of the two internal avenues).
- The so-called "Basilica Anonima dell'Ardeatina" and the "Basilica circiforme" (as a circus) of Pope St. Mark († 336), situated at the extreme edge of the field near to the Via Ardeatina.

From the later Middle Ages to the sixteenth Century

Once the transfer of the bodies of martyrs was completed, the catacombs were finally abandoned. Landslides and vegetation obstructed and hid their entrances. Within a few decades most of the sanctuaries and cemeteries were forgotten, traces of their existence lost. Hence the catacombs remained largely neglected during the late Middle Ages.

Not only was the location of most of the catacombs forgotten, but great confusion arose about their names. There remained a clear record of only three of them: St. Sebastian on the Appian Way, St. Lawrence (called also of Cyriaca) on the Tiburtina, and St. Pancras on the Aurelia. But also in the Middle Ages only a very small part of them could be visited.

Seventeenth and Eighteenth Centuries

Following the long period of abandonment in the Middle Ages, it was the archaeologist of Maltese origin Antonio Bosio (1575-1629) who began to re-discover and study the catacombs. He alone located some thirty of them. Giovanni Battista de Rossi called him "the Christopher Columbus of subterranean Rome".

Not having at his disposal the precious *Itineraries*, whose value was appreciated only two centuries later by de Rossi, Bosio confused the names of the catacombs. However, he left us a fundamental work, *Roma Sotterranea* (Subterranean Rome), a unique source of information and observations collected throughout his career.

When Bosio died, a long dark period began for the catacombs. The archaeologists of the time abandoned the scientific methodology of the great explorer. Ignorant of the translation of the martyrs which had taken place in the 8th and 9th centuries, they were convinced that many of the bodies of these witnesses to Christ were still buried in the catacombs. They even claimed to identify martyrs tombs based on the evidence of objects or decorations which they misinterpreted. For example this occurred with the little perfume bottles found inside the *loculi*; these were mistaken for vessels containing the blood of martyrs. The palm leaves scratched or painted on the marble slabs sealing the tombs were interpreted as symbols of martyrdom.

With these arbitrary premises, it was easy for them (so they thought) to presume where the martyrs' burial places could be found. Sadly, this kind of method did enormous damage to the cemeteries since thousands of still sealed tombs[4] were opened and false relics began to circulate.

Prominent in the destruction and sacking of the catacombs between the end of the 18th century and the beginning of the 19th were the "corpisantari", a vile and unscrupulous gang which searched for the bodies of martyrs. They went through underground cemeteries and carried off whatever could make them earn a profit.

As if this were not enough, the vine growers who owned the land above the catacombs, went down into the galleries to take away materials for their farm buildings. In this way vast underground areas took on the desolate aspect the visitor sees today: tombs opened, marble slabs broken, frescoes damaged beyond repair.

The Nineteenth Century and Giovanni Battista de Rossi

The 19th century marks the beginning of great enthusiasm for the study of Christian antiquities. This resumption and renewal began with de Rossi's teacher, Fr. Giuseppe Marchi S. J. (1795-1860).

A devoted archaeologist, Marchi's method "systematically traces the various types of Christian monuments, goes back to its origins and classifies, precisely illustrates the stages of his enquiry, makes use of absolutely new and rigorous critical methods" (P. Testini).

Nevertheless, it was not until the middle of the 19th century that the catacombs regained their ancient splendour. We owe the setting out of new guidelines to Giovanni Battista de Rossi (1822-1894), who is considered the founder and pioneer of Christian archaeology.

It was he who was destined to undertake the arduous task of beginning the scientific exploration of the catacombs.

Within half a century he made numerous discoveries, re-ordering the entire topography of Bosio's *Roma Sotterranea*. He planned a detailed study of every single catacomb, but the task was so huge that he was able to illustrate, scientifically, only St. Callixtus and the "Generosa alla Magliana".

His works, the three volumes of *Roma Sotterranea Cristiana* and the *Bullettino di Archeologia Cristiana* (1864-1894), still remain an inexhaustible source for the study of Christian archaeology. De Rossi wanted to collect all the epigraphs of Christian Rome in a number of books; he was able to finish only two volumes. The first contains all the dated epigraphs then known. The second is the critical edition of the mediaeval collections of palaeochristian epigraphs. These are for the most part inscriptions in verse. To encourage the work of excavation and conservation in the catacombs, Pius IX, who was a great friend of de Rossi, founded in 1852 the Commission for Sacred Archaeology (CDAS). Now Pontifical Commission for Sacred Archaeology (PCAS).

In 1925 Pius XI established the Pontifical Institute of Christian Archaeology (PIAC).

The purpose of this Institute, the only one of its kind, is to reinforce Christian archaeological studies and promote scholarly research.[5]

3. THE TERM "CATACOMBS"

The pagans called their cemeteries by the Greek word "necropolis", which means the "city of the dead". The Christians preferred the word "cemetery", which they coined from the Greek verb *koimáo*, to sleep. The word clearly reflects the Christian faith in the resurrection. For them, the cemetery was only a place of sleep, where they awaited the final resurrection of their bodies. This also explains why the Christians loved to call the day of a martyr's death *dies natalis*, the day of birth into heaven, into true life. Hence began the Christian usage of commemorating saints and martyrs in the liturgical calendar on the day of their death, since this was considered "the day of their spiritual birth in heaven".

The term "catacombs" was not used by the early Christians, but appeared later in the Middle Ages.

The Romans applied the term *Catacumbas* to a locality on the Appian Way. Going out of Rome, opposite the Circus of Maxentius before you reach the tomb of Cecilia Metella, you pass a hollow, a depression in the ground. In ancient times it was much more marked than it is now. The zone was called "Catacumbas", which means "near the hollow". Some scholars maintain that "the name was suggested by the presence of a series of 'pozzolana' quarries from which came the blocks of tufa for building the city walls" (M. Guarducci).

Here began what are today known as the Catacombs of St. Sebastian, known in ancient documents as the *Cymiterium Catacumbas ad sanctum Sebastianum via Appia*, named after the locality in which they were found.

In the Middle Ages, the term "catacombs" was no longer confined to the Cemetery of St. Sebastian, but was extended to all the cemeteries which were discovered, with the specific sense of "underground cemetery".

Thus from the name of a zone on the Appian Way the term "catacombs" came to indicate all the palaeochristian cemeteries.

4. WERE THE CATACOMBS PLACES OF REFUGE?

Christian cemeteries or catacombs were ordinarily protected by Roman law, as was the necropolis. The law in fact established and considered every sepulchre as a "sacred place" regardless of the religion to which the deceased belonged. But in spite of this law, it is known that Christian cemeteries were not always protected and were at times also confiscated.

A very common and still deeply rooted belief is that catacombs were mysterious places, unknown to the authorities of the time. Some still imagine that the Christians hid there day and night to avoid arrest. These ideas are quite mistaken, and have been spread by certain novels and pseudo-historical films. The catacombs were simple underground cemeteries, so well known to the authorities that they were confiscated at least twice. The first time came by order of emperor Valerian in 258 and lasted two years. He forbade Christians to enter their cemeteries and hold prayer meetings. During this period, Pope Sixtus II was caught by surprise while presiding at a liturgy in the area of St. Callixtus and was put to death. It was August 6th, 258.

The second confiscation was decreed by Diocletian in 303 and lasted seven years. Maxentius restored the catacombs to the Church before he was defeated by Constantine at the battle of the Milvian Bridge on October 28th, 312.

In the first three centuries, the Christians had no basilicas or churches in the city, therefore common prayer, the Eucharist and the sacraments took place in a few places reserved for worship and in private houses called *domus ecclesiae*, house churches. Some rich Christians set aside a hall or room where their brethren in the faith could come together for Mass and prayer.

Nevertheless, meetings for funerals and devotional services for the martyrs in the catacombs were frequent. Only rarely, during the periods of violent persecution, did the Christians use the catacombs as places of momentary refuge, and then only to take part in the Eucharist.

5. THE REAL REASON FOR THE PERSECUTIONS

It is commonly believed that the first three Christian centuries were a period of persecution. This needs to be properly understood. Not all the emperors persecuted the Christians, and there were periods of relative tranquillity. Other emperors persecuted the Christians only for a short time.

In the first two centuries, apart from limited occasions, life for the Christians in Rome was peaceful enough. In the 3rd century, however, the Roman authorities set out to destroy the Christian organization, striking at its hierarchy: the pope, bishops, presbyters and deacons.

Why was the Roman government, generally open and tolerant towards the other religions, so intransigent at times towards Christianity? Juridical pretexts for persecution were many: treason, sacrilege, impiety, hatred of the human race, unlawful association considered dangerous to the State, and disloyalty to the emperor by refusing to sacrifice before his statue ...

The real motive was much simpler. Other religions stooped to compromise and adapted themselves to the official cult. Moreover, they were presented rather as a private affair, supplying some inner need of the individual's belief in a higher power or need of purification, without the slightest social significance.

The religion preached by Christ was very different. It strongly rejected the official cult of the emperor and aspired to renew the whole person from within, that is, in heart and mind. This was the only way to change society.

Now, to preach openly that everyone, even a slave, is our brother or sister, that we are all children of God and equal before Him, that we shall be judged by the love we show even to our enemies, that what we do not need belongs to the poor and that they should not be exploited, and that justice must be the aim of those who

have power... none of these ideas were conceivable by the Roman authority. These truths were gradually recognized after centuries of Christianity. They were superior to the mentality of that age and could not be accepted by the Roman government, for they would have undermined the structure of the Roman empire. Rome in fact favoured slavery, the exploitation of the provinces, the destruction of human dignity for hundreds of thousands of persons.

Hence the violent opposition of the State towards Christianity in so far as it was seen as the most dangerous enemy. Hence also the real motive for persecuting the Church, its organization and its members.

6. THE IMPORTANCE OF THE CATACOMBS

The importance of the catacombs may be summed up in the words of de Rossi's illustrious pupil, Orazio Marucchi: "The catacombs can be regarded as the cradle of Christianity and the archives of the primitive Church. Their paintings, sculptures and inscriptions provide the most valuable material for illustrating the usage and customs of the early Christians and the history of the persecutions they suffered.

Moreover, they enable us to show how identical was the faith lived in the first centuries with the Act of Faith, or Credo, that we profess today. This has great value for us because these monuments, the catacombs, belong to the first centuries of Christianity".

Prof. Ferrua is more explicit about the Credo: "It is undeniable that Christian archaeology can give, for some truths of the Catholic faith, proofs in the proper sense, for instance judgement and reward after death, the communion of saints, the efficacy of prayer of the living for the dead and vice versa, the existence of purgatory, the cult of the holy martyrs, the coming of St. Peter to Rome and his pre-eminence in the Church, the very ancient use of sacraments, such as Baptism and the Eucharist".

---

[1] Some scholars identify this Roman Hippolytus with the learned St. Hippolytus.

[2] *Hypogea:* excavated completely underground.

[3] The great archaeologist called these *Itineraries* "the topographical key to the suburban tombs of the martyrs and popes".

[4] De Rossi wrote: "To their system of ransacking every sepulchre we owe the devastation of the walls and the opening of the *loculi*".

[5] Both the Institute and the Commission have their headquarters near St. Mary Major on Via Napoleone III, 1.

II.
The Catacombs
of Saint Callixtus

Historical and Archaeological Information

1. THE APPIAN WAY

The Appian Way, known as the "Queen of roads" *(Regina Viarum)* in ancient Rome, was lined on both sides with the splendid funerary monuments of the best known Roman families. The road dates back to 312 B.C., and was built by the "censor" Appius Claudius (called the Blind), from whom it took its name.

Today, very little remains of these ancient monuments along the Appian Way. The most massive tombs have survived because their concrete base has withstood the wear and tear of time, and has offered nothing to plunderers.

The Appian Way began at the Porta Capena, in the first city wall known as that of "Servius Tullius", close by the Circus Maximus. Passing through the "Porta Appia", also known as "Porta San Sebastiano" (St. Sebastian Gate), in Aurelian walls, the road reached Santa Maria Capua Vetere in the southern province of Campania. At a later stage it was prolonged as far as Benevento, Canosa, Taranto and Brindisi.

Along this celebrated road, which still preserves in some areas the stone slabs of its ancient road bed, the Roman legions first passed for the conquest of Southern Italy, and then of the East.

The Apostles Peter and Paul came to Rome by this famous road. We read in the *Acts of the Apostoles:* "... We came to the town of Puteoli. We found some believers there who asked us to stay with them a week. And so we came to Rome. The believers in Rome heard about us and came as far as the towns of Market of Appius *(Appii Forum)* at Three Inns *(Tres Tabernae)* to meet us. When Paul saw them, he thanked God and was greatly encouraged. When we arrived in Rome, Paul was allowed to live by himself with a soldier guarding him" (28,14-16)[1].

Just beyond the small church "Quo Vadis?" the Appian Way "gently climbs a ridge created by a flow of lava, which came down at the time when the volcanoes of Frattocchie were active and reached almost as far as Porta San Sebastiano. The ground at this point becomes higher than the plain of Latium" (L. Quilici).

Precisely along this ridge, between the second and third mile[2] from the "Servian Walls", which date back to the Republican age, began some of the most extensive underground Christian cemeteries of Rome, as well as private *hypogea*[3] and two Jewish catacombs.

Among these cemeteries, on the right of the Appian Way as you leave Rome, are the Catacombs of St. Callixtus, "the most magnificent and gigantic of the underground cemeteries, not only of the Appian Way but of all the suburban regions. Fr. Marchi called it the colossal region of subterranean Rome" (de Rossi).

2. THE "CALLIXTIAN COMPLEX"

By this generic term we mean the vast area between the Appian Way, the Ardeatina and the Vicolo delle Sette Chiese. Fifteen of these thirty hectares are taken up by catacombs. The galleries of the "Callixtian complex" with their four levels reach a length of almost twenty kilometres. The tombs are numerous, and reach perhaps a half a million.

This complex developed from different points over the centuries. Some have even been joined to one another. Here are the names: the Crypts of Lucina, the Cemetery of St. Callixtus, the Cemetery of St. Soter, the Cemetery of SS. Mark, Marcellianus and Damasus (called also of Basileus) and the Cemetery of Balbina.

Of all these, the ones that concern us most are the Crypts of Lucina and the Catacombs of St. Callixtus, which formed a single cemetery from the second half of the 4th century. The Catacombs of St. Soter, of Basileus and of Balbina are independent cemeteries. The last two were reached from the Via Ardeatina.

3. THE ORIGIN OF THE CATACOMBS OF ST. CALLIXTUS

Pope John XXIII said: "The Catacombs of St. Callixtus are the most august and celebrated of Rome", and de Rossi labelled them unquestionably "the Catacombs preeminently, the first cemetery of the community of Rome, the glorious burial place of the popes of the 3rd century".

The Crypts of Lucina

The first underground nucleus originated from an open-air cemetery belonging, in de Rossi's opinion, to the noble family of the *Caecilii*, from which descended the celebrated martyr St. Cecilia. Below the ground in this area, after the middle of the 2nd century, a *hypogeum* began to develop called the "Crypts of Lucina", named after the noble woman who, according to tradition, buried there the martyr Pope St. Cornelius. This *hypogeum* never grew large. It remained substantially within the boundaries of the private property above.

The "First Area"

In the same period, starting from the same burial area above ground, two more *hypogea* were dug, and they were properly called the "First Area", because, together with the Crypts of Lucina, they make up the very nucleus of the Catacombs of St. Callixtus. It is exactly in this "First Area" that the most sacred memorials of this cemetery will be located in the course of the 3rd century: the Crypt of the Popes, that of St. Cecilia, and the *Cubicula* of the Sacraments.

The two above-mentioned *hypogea* were excavated almost contemporaneously, parallel to one other, each having its own staircase. Staircase A is now called the Staircase of the Martyrs (see map on p. 50). Both staircases were covered with a double layer of stucco and were painted with red and brown linear decorations with star-shaped blue flowers, parts of which can still be seen on Staircase B. Later on the two *hypogea* were connected by a series of transverse galleries forming a "grid".

Above the archaeological area of the Catacombs of St. Callixtus.

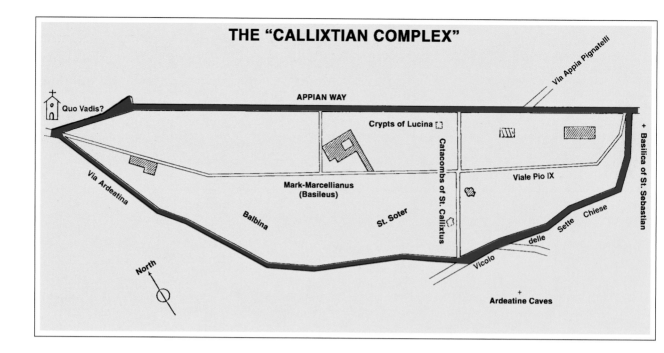

THE "CALLIXTIAN COMPLEX"

Gallery L, which at first was the only access to the Crypt of the Popes, had a light-shaft but no connecting passages. They went on digging it only during the period of religious peace, when the main staircase, called the *damasiana*, was constructed.

The "First Area" ran between an ancient sandpit and a country lane which joined the Appian Way with the Ardeatina. According to Roman law the underground excavations had to correspond to the boundaries of the property above ground which, as de Rossi demonstrates, measured 30 metres wide by 75 metres long.[4] So the "First Area" began from a very humble origin!

The Catacombs of St. Callixtus, like the other great cemeteries of the early Christians, were not excavated all at once, but came from the fusion of several *hypogea* built independently in different times. Each had its own staircase and initially they had just some galleries and a few *cubicula:* the "First Area" or the Area of the Popes and St. Cecilia, the Area of SS. Gaius and Eusebius, the Western Area, the Liberian Area, the Crypts of Lucina ...

4. THE NAME: CATACOMBS OF ST. CALLIXTUS

The names of the catacombs arose for different reasons, stemming from particular circumstances or from the customs of the times.

In most cases they took the name of the donor of the land and so we have the Catacombs of Praetextatus, of Domitilla, of Commodilla, of Pamphilus, of Pontianus, of Calepodius, of Priscilla ...

Other times they took the name from the best-known martyr or martyrs buried there. Thus we have the Catacombs of St. Sebastian, St. Agnes, SS. Mark and Marcellianus, SS. Marcellinus and Peter.

Sometimes the name is given by the locality in which they are situated: *ad ursum pileatum* (near the place where there was a statue of a bear with a hood), *ad duas lauros* (near the two laurel bushes), *ad clivum cucumeris* (near the water-melon slope), *ad septem palumbas* (near the place of the seven doves), or "catacumbas" (near the pits, that is at St. Sebastian on the Appian Way).

The only exception are the Catacombs of St. Callixtus, which took their name from the martyred Pope St. Callixtus (217-222) who, before becoming Pope, was their faithful guardian and administrator for almost twenty years.

St. Callixtus was born into a family of Christian slaves, so he knew from childhood what slavery was. Subsequently he was emancipated and took service

On the following page: Pagan funerary monument near the Cripts of Lucina (3rd century A.D.).

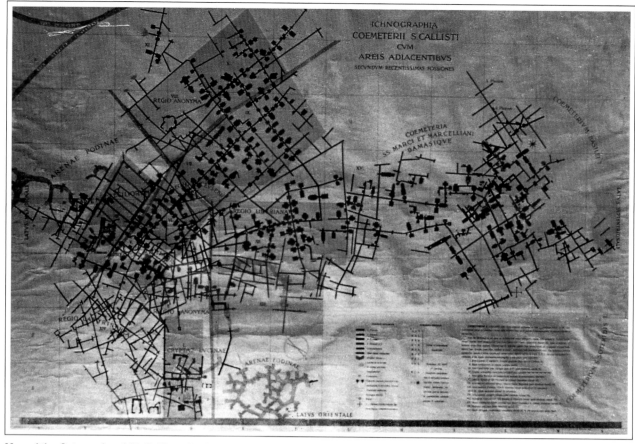

Map of the Catacombs of St. Callixtus by Giovanni Battista de Rossi.

with a banker, Carpophorus, but proved to have little business acumen.

Accused by the Hebrews of intolerance towards them, he was condemned to hard labour in the mines of Sardinia. Thanks to the intervention of Marcia, a woman of Christian sympathies and a favourite of emperor Commodus (180-192), Callixtus was freed along with other fellow-believers. Pope St. Zephyrinus wanted him as his collaborator and ordained him deacon.

At the beginning of the 3rd century the so-called "First Area" was somewhat developed and the proprietor gave it to the Christian community, that is to the Church of Rome. Pope Zephyrinus put his first deacon, Callixtus, in charge of it.

In effect the deacon was the overseer of the corporation of *fossores* — diggers assigned to the excavations — and also had the task of providing graves for all Christians, particularly the poor and the slaves.

St. Zephyrinus' decision to put Callixtus in charge of the communal cemetery shows the clergy taking steps to help the faithful. St. Justin and the apologist Tertullian relate that the needs of the faithful were financed from public offerings: to help the poor and destitute families, to assist old people, widows, those who had been shipwrecked, condemned to pay a fine, exiled, imprisoned, and to bury the dead ...

At the death of Pope Zephyrinus, Callixtus was elected to succeed him. The opposing faction headed by the presbyter Hippolytus, put up hard resistance. Callixtus suffered much from this schism in the Church of Rome and also from the continued attacks on his reputation.[5]

During his pastoral activity he distinguished himself for his organizing talent. He was a strenuous defender of orthodoxy (protection of the faith from errors) and full of zeal and charity in reconciling heretics.

After five years of pastoral service he died a martyr in Trastevere following a popular riot. The moment was too dangerous for him to be buried in the cemetery on the Appian Way and he was interred in the nearby Catacombs of Calepodius on the Aurelia Antica.

24

5. BRIEF HISTORY OF THE CATACOMBS OF ST. CALLIXTUS

"Among all the cemeteries of the Church of Rome, that of Callixtus on the Appian Way is the most famous and the best remembered" (de Rossi).

The history of the Catacombs of St. Callixtus is part of the general history of the Christian catacombs of Rome, already looked at in the first chapter. As the official cemetery of the Church, it developed considerably in the 3rd and 4th centuries.

It was among the most visited from the 8th to the 9th centuries. Then came the translations of the relics of the martyrs and saints inside the city walls. Throughout the late Middle Ages it was completely abandoned, so that no one knew exactly where it was.

Not until 1432 do we find a hint of a visit. A signature in charcoal was found on the wall of a *cubiculum*, written by a certain John Lonck, perhaps a Scottish pilgrim. These were occasional visits, limited to a few galleries. Only occasional landslides opened holes for access. But none of those rare visitors knew that they were in the Cemetery of St. Callixtus.

At that time the Catacombs of St. Callixtus became confused with those of St. Sebastian. The names of the pious visitors were for the most part those of friars from the nearby convent of St. Sebastian.

In 1475 it was the turn of Pomponius Laetus (1428-1498) and his fellow-members of the "Roman Academy of Antiquaries". They were scholars fond of pagan classicism and their visits certainly had no devotional purpose ...

The real exploration began a century later with Bosio, but even this learned man could not identify the catacomb, nor discover the tombs of the martyrs because of the massive piles of debris under which they were buried.

There then followed centuries of darkness for the Catacombs of St. Callixtus, during which the continual opening of *loculi* caused irreparable damage. Finally the moment of rediscovery came through the work of de Rossi, who zealously explored, studied and restored the cemetery, and made the greatest and most interesting discoveries. In 1849 he found part of the funerary inscription of St. Cornelius. In 1852 he found the tomb of this Pope and that of the martyrs Calocerus and Parthenius. In 1854 there came to light the two most

The Eastern Trichora.

**The martyr Pope St. Callixtus I.
(Gilded glass.
From the National Library, Paris).**

sacred memorials of these catacombs, the Crypt of the Popes and that of St. Cecilia. In 1856, the Crypts of Pope St. Gaius and of the martyr Pope St. Eusebius.

6. THE DOCUMENTARY SOURCES

By "sources" we mean the ancient historical and liturgical documents which offer precious evidence about the Catacombs of St. Callixtus.

Chronologically, the first work dates back to the first half of the 3rd century. Written in Greek by Hippolytus, a contemporary of Pope Callixtus, the work is entitled *Philosophúmena*. In chapter IX we read that pope Zephyrinus "made deacon Callixtus head of the administration of the cemetery" (εἰς τὸ κοιμη-τήριον κατέστησεν). Here we have the official cemetery of the Church of Rome, which will later take the name: "Catacombs of St. Callixtus".

In the *Liturgical Calendar* of 354 of the Church of Rome, which is to be found in the *Chronographus*, compiled by Furius Dionysius Filocalus, are listed the names of the popes *(Depositio Episcoporum)* and martyrs *(Depositio Martyrum)* buried "in Calisti", in the Cemetery called St. Callixtus.

The *Liber Pontificalis* is a historical source which relates the biographies of the popes, written by persons in ecclesiastical circles from the 6th century onwards.

About Pope Callixtus, we read that "he enlarged the Cemetery on the Appian Way where many bishops and martyrs rest", and also that "the Cemetery is named after Callixtus".

The tombs of martyrs became the key places for pilgrims to visit and so it became necessary to use guidebooks, called *Itineraries*, most of which were the work of priests from France and Germany.

The most important of them is the *Notitia Ecclesiarum Urbis Romae...* [6] dating from the first half of the 7th century: it contains a list of the catacombs and gives the names of all the martyrs and saints buried in the Cemetery of St. Callixtus and also offers useful topographical information.

Also in *De locis sanctis Martyrum...*, dating back to the middle of the 7th century, "the saints and martyrs buried *in coemeterio Calisti*" are recorded.

We find the Catacombs of St. Callixtus mentioned in the following documents as well:

— The *Index of Oils:* they are lists of oils collected by presbyter Giovanni di Monza from the lamps found near the tombs of saints and martyrs. These oils, kept in ampullae, were presented to Queen Theodelinda at the beginning of the 7th century.

— The *Einsiedeln Itinerary:* it dates from the early 9th century. "The appearance of this itinerary", wrote de Rossi, "was like the dawn which lit up Christian topography along the Appian and Ardeatina roads". The itinerary was discovered by the Benedictine Jean Mabillon (1632-1707) in the Swiss monastery of Einsiedeln.

— The *Notitia portarum, viarum, ecclesiarum...:* it is a guidebook compiled in the 12th century by William of Malmesbury, based on an earlier document of the 7th century.

The *Mirabilia Urbis*, with an "Index Coemeteriorum" of the 12th century.

The reader may welcome two passages from these *Itineraries*. They deal with the Catacombs of St. Callixtus.

a) From *Notitia Ecclesiarum...*

This itinerary, after dealing with the martyrs of the Catacomb of Praetextatus, reads: "On the same road (the Appian Way) you will come to St. Cecilia (that is, to the Catacombs of St. Callixtus). Here are to be found an innumerable multitude of martyrs: first the martyred Popes Sixtus and Dionysius, the martyr Flavian, the virgin martyr St. Cecilia. Eighty martyrs lie there below *(deorsum)*. Zephyrinus, Pope and confessor, lies above ground *(sursum)*. Eusebius, Pope and martyr, lies farther off in a crypt *(longe in antro)*. Cornelius, Pope and martyr, lies farther off in another crypt *(longe in antro altero)*. Afterwards you will reach (the church of) St. Soter, whose body lies to the North *(ad aquilonem)*".

b) From *De locis sanctis Martyrum...*

"Near the Appian Way, in the eastern part of the city is the church of the martyr St. Soter, where he is buried with many martyrs, and near the same road is the Church of St. Sixtus, Pope, where he rests. There lie also the virgin Cecilia and SS. Tarcisius and Zephyrinus in one mausoleum *(in uno tumulo)*. There SS. Eusebius and Calocerus and Parthenius lie in separate tombs *(per se singuli iacent)*. In that place there rest also eight hundred martyrs. Then, not far, in the Cemetery of St. Callixtus, sleep (i.e. their bodies are deposited) Cornelius and Cyprian in a church".

Thanks to these *Itineraries* de Rossi was able to reconstruct the whole topography of the catacombs.

He fixed their location and their placenames precisely, indicating each catacomb with its proper name. Furthermore, he was guided by those valuable documents in his excavations, and they were also for him a great help in the identification of the tombs of the martyrs.

---

[1] The *Appii Forum* and *Tres Tabernae* were two places on the Appia between Velletri and Terracina. The first was 60 kilometres from Rome, the second 50.

[2] A Roman mile was 1478 metres.

[3] The term *hypogeum* comes from Greek and is commonly used to designate underground burial places of very limited extent.

[4] "In fronte P(edes) C, in agro P(edes) CCL". The "Roman foot" was 29,6 centimetres.

[5] Hippolytus' attacks on Callixtus reveal a source gravely marred by the passionate hostility of the author" (E. dal Covolo).

[6] The translation of the titles of these Itineraries:
 – The list of the churches of the City of Rome...
 – The holy places of the martyrs.
 – The list of the gates, roads and churches...
 – The marvels of the City of Rome with its "Index of Cemeteries".

Aerial view of the historic centre of the Catacombs of St. Callixtus.

III.
Above ground

1. PAGAN AND CHRISTIAN BURIALS

It is well known that in antiquity Rome had no communal cemeteries as it does now. The law forbade burial or cremation within the confines of the *pomerium*, that is, within the inhabited area, the perimeter of which did not always coincide with the city walls. The Laws of the XII Tables categorically stated: "You shall not bury or burn a corpse in the city".[1]

Outside the *pomerium* one could build a tomb where one liked, as long as one could afford the costs. Generally, the Romans chose a place of burial along one of the roads leading out of the city.

There were also burial places belonging to particular categories of people or to associations, such as the "priestly colleges" or those of magistrates, imperial freedmen, sailors and craftsmen ...

Though there is enough archaeological evidence in Rome of cemeteries common to pagans and Christians, nonetheless the early Christian cemeteries, also called catacombs, developed from the strong desire of Christ's faithful to keep their tombs apart from those of the pagans. The latter in fact, up to the end of the 2nd century, generally preferred to cremate their dead, while the Christians preferred burial. These cemeteries were dug outside the city in compliance with the Roman law. Thus the catacombs were located in the vicinity of the pagan tombs, which, in most cases as we have seen, lined the consular roads (Appian Way, Latina, Salaria ...).

On the following page:
Entrance to the Catacombs
of St. Callixtus.

2. THE AREA OF OPEN-AIR BURIAL

This above ground area for burials, extant before the excavation of the Crypts of Lucina and the so-called "First Area", was carefully explored by de Rossi. Graves occupied the ground. These tombs could contain several corpses laid one above the other. From the 5th century onwards this area was much used for burials.

It is now difficult for us to have an exact idea of all the monuments which were located on the "Callixtian complex" at the end of the 5th century. It included churches, funeral monuments, mausoleums, which were built over or beside the martyrs tombs.

The topographical documents, for example, tell us of the basilica of St. Cornelius, which Pope St. Leo the Great (440-461) had built near Cornelius' tomb, of the church of St. Soter, of the basilica of SS. Mark and Marcellianus, of the anonymous one discovered in 1960, of the basilica of St. Mark and of the mausoleum of St. Damasus.

If we add to them the tombs, columbaria, sepulchres and pagan mausoleums along the Appian Way and the Ardeatina, the scenery must have been really imposing and awe-inspiring.

Unfortunately the destruction and vandalism wrought by the barbarians (Goths and Lombards), farmers and the ravages of time have had their detrimental effect on all these ancient memorials.

3. THE TOMB OF THE YOUNG MARTYR TARCISIUS

In this open area, St. Callixtus probably erected the tomb of his predecessor St. Zephyrinus. We know little of this Pope. He was a Roman, and he defended the Church by promoting sound doctrine and fighting heresies.

Dying St. Tarcisius, holding the Eucharist to his breast (Eastern Trichora, modern sculpture).

Zephyrinus was the first pope to be buried in the Cemetery of St. Callixtus. The *Liber Pontificalis* says that his grave "was in his cemetery near that of Callixtus". The expression, in my view, is to be understood in the sense that Zephyrinus was buried in a tomb or mausoleum above ground, near the "First Area".

Decades later, perhaps during the persecutions of Decius (249-251) or Valerian (253-260), Tarcisius, the martyr of the Eucharist, was buried beside the tomb of Zephyrinus. These open-air tombs were abandoned when the relics of Pope St. Zephyrinus and St. Tarcisius were transferred into the city. Time completed the ruin of that mausoleum. Today it is impossible to locate their precise burial place, but following the indications of the ancient pilgrim guides, the *Itineraries*, they must have been either in the present little church called the Eastern *Trichora*, or in the adjoining flower beds.

Pope Damasus commemorated the martyrdom of young Tarcisius with a poem inscribed above his tomb. It has come down to us. Here is the most interesting passage:

"Tarsicium sanctum $\overline{XPI}$ (Christi) sacramenta gerentem cum male sana manus premeret vulgare profanis, ipse animam potius voluit dimittere caesus prodere quam canibus rabidis caelestia membra".

"When a wicked group of fanatics flung themselves on Tarcisius — who was carrying the Eucharist — wanting to profane the sacrament, the boy preferred to give up his life rather than yield up the Body of Christ to those rabid dogs". ICUR, IV, 11078.[2]

According to tradition, young Tarcisius, during a period of persecution, was carrying the sacrament to

Christians in prison or at their homes. On the way he met a small group of scoundrels who tried to snatch the Body of Christ from his hands. The heroic boy chose to lose his life rather than give way to them.

Later iconography (pictures, statues) represents him dying while clutching the Eucharist to his breast.

4. THE TRICHORAE

Of all the small early Christian basilicas and mausoleums which stood in the "Callixtian complex", two monuments only have survived, thanks to the restorations by de Rossi and his successors. They are known as *trichorae*, so called from the three small apses which form part of their layout.

To distinguish one from the other, the one near the Via Ardeatina is the Western *Trichora*, the other near the entrance to the catacomb is the Eastern *Trichora*.

When de Rossi discovered them in 1844, the western one had been turned into a country shed, the eastern into a wine cellar. They have now become two small churches, but originally they must have been two "memorial cells": the one a small basilica over the tomb

of a martyr and the other a family mausoleum near highly venerated tombs.

The Western Trichora

"It was restored — as S. Carletti writes — at the beginning of the 20th century and retains the ancient masonry from ground level up to the springs of the arches: practically as far as the point at which the building, originally covered by a cupola according to de Rossi's hypothesis, was cut for the reconstruction of the vault. But the surviving masonry cannot be precisely dated, since the system of rows of bricks alternating with thick layers of cement was widely used from the 3rd century onwards.

Excavations by the Pontifical Commission for Sacred Archaeology in 1979-1980 in that same area have revealed the presence of a martyr's tomb, placed within a central mound with a *fenestella confessionis*,[3] and surrounded by a number of devotional graves.

During these same excavations, eight mausoleums were discovered, connected with the *trichora*. They were family tombs built there with the desire to be under the

The Western Trichora with its apses.

The interior of the Eastern Trichora. Here we now find the grave of Giovanni Battista de Rossi.

protection of the venerated martyr, whose name archaeologists have not yet found. While keeping the archaeologists' zone accessible, the surroundings have been now converted into a room for meetings and gatherings for prayer, according to the suggestions of Pope Paul VI during the Holy Year of 1975. The Pope wanted the religious ceremonies of the Jubilee to stress the spiritual atmosphere of the primitive Christian world, which the catacombs and their monuments and tombs of the martyrs evoke. Throughout that Holy Year the *trichora* witnessed religious ceremonies, which bore great spiritual fruit. To perpetuate the memory of this a bronze bust of that great Pope, the work of M. Galbiati, has been placed inside it, together with an artistic lamp, the gift of Paul VI himself and a Latin inscription composed by Fr. Antonio Ferrua".

The Eastern Trichora

History

From the report on the excavations made by Mons. Wilpert at the beginning of the 20th century, we learn that this primitive building or little basilica was raised

on foundations of basalt. These square foundations were intended to give the building the greatest possible solidity. The reason for this was that galleries and cubicles lay beneath.

The building of the *trichora* belongs therefore to the period of religious peace, the time when, following the mass conversions of pagans, cemeterial burial was greatly increasing.

We do not know who the builder was, but we do know that it was restored by Leo III (795-816). To this Pope's time we may also attribute the frescoes, whose few remains were vaguely visible at the beginning of the 20th century. Probably they depicted the saints and martyrs of the catacomb with the figure of Christ in the centre. Above the dado, there was a decoration of marble.

The little basilica or mausoleum did not even contain a tomb, which could have indicated some type of veneration. All the tombs of this *trichora* have been destroyed. In any case they could not have been many. More numerous were the sarcophagi lining the walls, but only fragments of these survive.

One of these represents Christ saving Peter from sinking in the Sea of Galilee (*Matthew* 14, 24-35). Of this scene, only two known examples images are extant in all palaeochristian art.

The *trichora* was lengthened in modern times and the addition is still there, but its date is not known. The original entrance, now walled up, was on the left side. Near this door was a staircase which led down to Gallery I. This staircase also is modern and was constructed when Gallery I and a part of Gallery B had been used as wine cellars (see map on p. 50).

The sarcophagi

Along its interior walls the *trichora* still has a good number of fragments of sarcophagi, belonging to the mausoleums from the open-air cemetery, which were found in the excavations. Mons. Wilpert set out these fragments in groups according to their content. They all refer to biblical scenes.

The Magi Kings (Eastern Trichora).

Eucharistic bread (Eastern Trichora).

Dolphins tied to the trident.

Dolphin twisted around the trident.

From the Old Testament we find: Adam and Eve, Noah and the ark, Abraham's sacrifice, the crossing of the Red Sea, the three young men in the fiery furnace, Jacob blessing Ephraim and Manasseh (*Genesis* 48, 1-22) ...

From the New Testament: the Epiphany, the miracles of Jesus, the multiplication of the loaves and fishes, the healing of the blind man and of the woman with an issue of blood, the raising of Lazarus. Also episodes concerning SS. Peter and Paul, Philip catechizing Queen Candace's eunuch (*Acts* 8, 26-40), pastoral scenes and portraits of loved ones ...

Ulysses and the Sirens

As de Rossi states, "the symbolic creativity of the early Christians sought, as far as possible, allusions to the Gospel stories even in pagan sculptures, carved with quite different intentions by the artists. It is obvious and widely-accepted that Christians under-

Bust of Giovanni Battista de Rossi (Eastern Trichora).

What are we to make of these images?

The composition as a whole alludes, undoubtedly, to the moral situation of early Christians facing the seduction of the pagan world. The youngster learns the true doctrine which will fortify him against the enticements of vice.

That this is the right interpretation we are convinced by St. Maximus, bishop of Turin (380-423 circa). Indeed this Father of the Church stresses the symbolism even more. In Ulysses' ship he sees the Church, and in the mast, to which the king is tied, he discerns the cross from which the crucified Lord teaches the faithful to close their ears to the call of the senses.[5]

The second sarcophagus fragment comes from the Crypts of Lucina and was found in Gallery B. It portrays a trident raised between two mythological animals: a seahorse and a winged horse. Beside the trident a name is carved: Lollia, a Christian woman.

The trident was used by the early Christians as a symbol of the cross. In fact, in an inscription in this cemetery, we find it carved between two fishes: the cross, therefore, as a fountain of life for Christians. Sometimes, instead of the trident we find the anchor between two fishes. Here too the symbolism is the same, because the anchor was a clear allusion to the cross.

The inscriptions

In the highest part of the *trichora* walls, some early Christian inscriptions from the cemetery above ground can be seen. Among these are lines from a fragment which record the martyrdom of Pope Sixtus II *(Dum populi rector...)*.

The poem was composed by an imitator of Pope Damasus and belongs to the middle of the 5th century. It was probably found on the spot where Sixtus was beheaded. The fragments belong to a later copy, perhaps dating back to the 7th century.

Also on the left side we find a marble bust of G. B. de Rossi, placed there in 1892 to mark his seventieth birthday.

In visiting or describing this catacomb we often come across inscriptions, frescoes, paintings and sculptures. It will be useful, therefore, to say a few words about the general characteristics of early Christian epigraphy and iconography.

stood pastoral and agricultural scenes, personifications of the seasons, dolphins and marine monsters swimming in the waves as being parables and not to be taken literally.

Much more difficult and elusive is the hidden meaning that the ancient believers attributed in their minds to certain scenes which bear no relation to the parables of the Gospel or to Christian symbolism".

Take for example two sarcophagus fragments: the first is found on the left wall of this *trichora*. It is a plaster cast, whose original is to be found in the "Torretta".[4]

The name of the dead person is carved at its centre as a monogram: Tyrannio. On one side Ulysses with the Sirens is represented. The King of Ithaca, tied to the ship's mast by two of his companions, is listening to the deceitful song of the Sirens. A third companion is rowing. None of these latter can hear the song, because their ears are sealed with wax.

On the other side we see a young man seated, listening to a philosopher lecturing. The pupil wears the pallium or cape and holds a book in his hands.

5. PALAEOCHRISTIAN EPIGRAPHY

As D. Mazzoleni writes, "the many thousands of Christian inscriptions of the first centuries (more than fifty thousand) are the key to discovering a practically unknown world, because they are a mine of data about otherwise unknown details concerning communities in centres, large or small, of the ancient world: from Rome to Corinth, from Carthage to Eumenia in Phrygia. This is valuable and first-hand material, for it is a direct expression of the 'people of God' without intermediate agency, without distortion of facts or ideas.

Christian epigraphy, however, does not consist only of dedications of churches, of inscriptions relating to martyrs or popes, or of prayers or biblical quotations. For the most part it concerns epitaphs (slabs with funerary inscriptions) of believers from all social classes, who express, as best as they can, sincere human feelings in the colloquial language of the day, with irregular and careless writing, often with grammatical inaccuracies. Very often, we sense even today the affection, faith, hope, grief and pain present in the words of the persons who commissioned those funerary inscriptions.

If some of those crude drawings, often scratched beside the inscriptions, may make us smile, very touching however are the expressions with which parents mourn the untimely death of their little ones, or a husband recalls the wife he loved so much...

Christian epigraphy is a relatively new science (little more than a century old), as its foundations and method were essentially defined by the 'father' of Christian archaeology, Giovanni Battista de Rossi. The object of study includes all written examples on every sort of material (except manuscripts and coins) dating from the first centuries of Christianity. Its chronogical period goes from the second half of the 2nd century — the oldest surviving texts belong to this early period — up to the pontificate of Pope Gregory the Great (590-604).

If some epigraphs look interesting for their intrinsic poetry, others abound in precious elements indicating the language spoken by the people of late antiquity, along with their religious conceptions, their affections, their ideas concerning the mystery of death. At the same time, a modern investigator can reconstruct many aspects of the life of the early Christian community, thus gaining a knowledge of its social composition, the level of education of its members and so on...

From these brief indications, we come to realize how appropriate Prof. Antonio Ferrua's definition of epigraphy is: truly it becomes the 'eye of archaeology'".

The Inscriptions in the Catacomb

In this catacomb many *loculi* are anonymous. Only for a modest number do we know who was buried in them. The inscriptions are in Greek or Latin, according to the place of origin of the deceased.

The name could be scratched on the plaster which held the marble slab or the tile of the tomb; it could also be written on the slab or tile itself in black with charcoal or in red with minium or red lead. But most often it was carved on the enclosing slab. Very rarely was it written in mosaic.

At first, the epigraphic formulary was very simple: a name, and sometimes the date of burial. The anniversary of the burial was very important for Christians, as on that day they gathered at the tomb to carry out the so-called *refrigerium*, a rite in honour of their loved ones. In this rite, prayers for the eternal repose of the soul of the relative were followed by a frugal meal, as though the dead person were present.

During the 3rd century the texts of the inscriptions were enriched with specifically Christian elements. Symbols (the fish, the anchor, the dove...) began to appear, as well as expressions such as *in pace, in Christo* (in peace, in Christ).

In the 4th century, words of good wishes, of prayer, of sorrow, appear carved in the marble. After so many centuries these expressions tell us of a dialogue between the living and the dead, united in one hope and in the certainty of a better life: "Rest in Christ", "May your spirit be among the saints", "I am in peace", "I pray for you"... The tomb itself is named with words which evoke the idea of a temporary rest before the final resurrection: "the house of peace", "of sleep"...

A valuable though not frequent element on the slabs is the date on which the person died. The years were indicated by the consulates. Here is an example:

... DIT · DEP(ositio) VI[I] ID(us) IVL(ias) · POST (umio) QVI(eto) ET VELD(umniano) CO(n)S(ulibus)

"Deposition of.. seven days before the Ides of July (9th of July) under the consulate of Postumius Quietus and Veldumnianus".

Postumius Quietus and Veldumnianus were consuls in 272 under emperor Aurelian, the builder of the great walls around Rome. The stone was found in 1974 in an area of the Catacombs of St. Callixtus during an excavation. We have here "a Christian inscription of the 3rd century, one of the first, and perhaps the oldest, of the dated inscriptions in St. Callixtus" (A. Ferrua).

6. PALAEOCHRISTIAN ICONOGRAPHY

The tombs of the martyrs, the *cubicula* and even the *arcosolia*,[6] were sometimes decorated with mosaics, but more often with fresco paintings. The colours were applied to the last layer of plaster while it was still wet *(a fresco)*. The calcium, combining chemically with the carbon dioxide of the air formed a thin crystalline skin of calcium carbonate, which fixed and protected the painting.

The colours used were vegetable or mineral, such as ochre or cinnabar (vermilion), or artificial, such as ceruse (white lead) or lampblack. These colours can be classified, according to the terms used by Pliny, as "austere" (moderate tones) or "florid" (lively tones).

Christian iconography first emerges between the end of the 2nd century and the beginning of the 3rd and is almost exclusively funerary. At first, the repertoire of subjects is limited to those which most effectively and immediately express faith in Christ's work of Salvation.

Among the images represented in the catacombs, mostly chosen from the Bible, two figures predominate: the Good Shepherd, symbolizing Christ the Saviour, and the "Orante" (from the Latin *orare*, to pray), representing the soul in divine peace.

The Good Shepherd

No passage in the Gospel left so deep an impression on the minds of the first Christians as the parable of the lost sheep (*Luke* 15, 3-7), or the speech in which Jesus presents himself as the Good Shepherd (*John* 10, 1-16), and this because no text explained better the price paid by Christ for the salvation of mankind.

In fresco paintings as well as sculptures, Jesus, the Good Shepherd, is represented in the splendour of his youth. The head is slightly turned to one side. He wears a short tunic down to his knees and tied at the hips by a belt. The right shoulder is completely bare, while the feet are covered by long sandals. From one shoulder hangs a haversack for food. On his back he carries a lamb which he holds firmly by its legs.

The symbolism of this well-known depiction is quite clear: the figure of the Good Shepherd represents Christ the Saviour, while the lamb alludes to the soul saved by Him.

The Good Shepherd, whether represented in frescoes, sarcophagi, or marble slabs, is the most repeated image in the catacombs of Rome. Sometimes the Good Shepherd appears alone, carrying the lamb, but in most cases he is with the flock (the blessed souls) in a garden (Paradise) filled with trees and flowers and gladdened with the chant of birds.

The "Orante"

"This figure, with arms outstretched, appeared in Christian art, together with the Good Shepherd, not as a depiction of a particular dead person, nor as an image of the living praying for the dead, but as the soul in the state of bliss after death. The 'Orante' personifies the Christian at peace in the beatific vision" (L. de Bruyne).

An "Orante" between two sheep.

Crypts of Lucina: The Good Shepherd (sepulchral slab of Apuleia Crysopolis).

The main idea expressed in early Christian art

The fundamental concept, therefore, expressed in early Christian art is Christ the Saviour and the soul in divine peace. The Good Shepherd and the "Orante" are the main themes on which the iconography of the first centuries is based. All the other figures, drawings and scenes express this plan of salvation, which might be outlined as follows:

— *The work of salvation prepared by God* in the Old Testament, depicted with scenes of Adam and Eve after the Fall, of Noah in the ark, of Daniel in the lions' den, of Susannah accused by the elders, of Jonah, of the three youths in the fiery furnace in Babylon, of Moses striking the rock...

— *The work of salvation fulfilled by Christ* in the New Testament (Gospels), expressed in the Christological scenes: the manger, the adoration of the Magi, the Baptism of Jesus, his miracles (the paralytic, the man born blind, the woman with an issue of blood, the resurrection of Lazarus, the banquet scenes alluding to the Eucharist, the multiplication of the loaves and fishes, scenes of the passion...).

— *The work of salvation continued by the Church* during the apostolic and post-apostolic period: Christ the Teacher with the apostles, Christ consigns the law to Peter, scenes concerning SS. Peter and Paul ...

— *Salvation achieved in the after life:* SS. Peter and Paul leading the dead into paradise, Martyrs accompanying the dead person to judgement, the souls in eternal peace paying homage to Christ, the crowning of the apostles who acclaim Christ...

Besides biblical episodes, early Christian art also used allegorical figures (the seasons), scenes from everyday life (trades and banquets), also just ornamental themes, such as baskets of flowers and fruit, *putti* (baby angels), grape harvesters, leaves, stylized plants, palm branches, birds, vases, geometrical patterns borrowed from Hellenistic-Roman decorations.

7. THE SYMBOLS NEAR THE ENTRANCE STAIRCASE

On the walls of the underground cubicles, the Christians depicted various symbols, and more often they carved them on the marble slabs which sealed the tombs. In the small garden next to the entrance, some modern copies of the original symbols found in the catacombs can be seen. It will help to have a thorough description of them.

The term "symbol" refers to a sign or image of a concrete material object, intended to evoke a spiritual idea or reality. We may compare it to a modern slogan: it is concise enough to summarize a whole train of thought. It reveals and it conceals; it speaks to those who can read it.

As D. Mazzoleni points out, "widely used in literature and liturgy, the symbol had an important place in early Christian art because of its capacity to link up visible images to the invisible world, and make clear in essential terms the fundamental concepts of the new religion.

Christian symbolism is based not on a vast repertory, but on two crucial points in the life of the believers in the earliest communities: the catechesis or teaching to the catechumens in preparation for Baptism, and the one given to them after Baptism, which accompanies them throughout their lives.

Yet it may be asked why the tufa walls of the catacombs were chosen to express in graphic form concepts not always connected with death and resurrection. When Christians came to pray at the tomb of their loved ones, those symbols recalled to them the fervent time of their catechumenate, the sacraments they had received, and the principal truths of the faith. Those symbols were a visible reminder of the faith they professed, a pledge of eternal life". Here is a list of them:

— *The fish:* in Greek is written ΙΧΘΥΣ (Ichthús). Arranging these Greek letters vertically, an acrostic is created: "Jesus Christ, Son of God, the Saviour".[7]

F	Ἰησοῦς	Jesus
I	Χριστός	Christ
S	Θεοῦ	God's
H	Υἱός	Son
	Σωτήρ	Saviour

The fish, symbol of "Jesus Christ, Son of God, the Saviour".

ΙΧΘΥΣ (Ichthús = fish), the popular acrostic signifying "Jesus Christ, Son of God, the Saviour".

— The *Good Shepherd* with a lamb on his shoulders. He symbolizes Christ the Saviour and the soul saved by him.

— The *Orante* stands for the soul which already lives in God's divine peace.

— The *monogram of Christ* is made of two letters of the Greek alphabet, the **X** (chi) and the **P** (ro), which interweave forming a ☧. They are the first letters of the Greek word Christòs, Christ.

— *Alpha and Omega* (**A-Ω**): the first and last letters of the Greek alphabet. They indicate Christ, the beginning and the end of all things. We read in the *Revelation:* "I am the alpha and the omega, the first and the last, the beginning and the end" (22, 13). Hence the name "the apocalyptic letters".

— *The anchor:* its fundamental meaning is hope in the promise of a future life. In the *Letter to the Hebrews* we read: "We have this hope as an anchor for our lives. It is safe and sure, and goes through the curtain of the heavenly temple into the inner sanctuary" (6, 19).

But this does not exhaust the symbolism of the anchor. As the anchor gives security to the ship, so hope assists the believer to reach the harbour of eternity with serenity. For a Christian death is not the end of everything, but the 'passage' to another, blessed life. Further, the anchor made allusion to the cross in a discreet and veiled manner.

— *The dove with the olive branch in its beak:* it is a symbol of the soul in eternal peace.

— *The horse:* it alludes to the strenuous fight that a Christian must endure against earthly passions to reach his eternal reward.

— *The cock:* it is the herald of the new day. It recalled the early Christians to the symbolism of light; and hence it was an invitation to resuming the praise of God and good works, as opposed to the night with its darkness of evil and sin.

The monogram of Christ.

A bird quenching its thirst.

The anchor.

The dove with the olive twig.

**A bird pecking grapes,
a symbol of the soul
nourishing upon the Eucharist.**

**The dove holding a crown with its bill,
symbol of the soul
that has attained its eternal reward.**

Small boat.

— *The hare:* this animal, searching for a safe refuge, is an image of the believer who fears the snares of evil.

— *The palm and the crown:* the martyrs by shedding their blood merited Christ's reward of eternal life. In St. John's vision described in the book of *Revelation*, they carry the palm: "After this I looked, and there was an enormous crowd – no one could count all the people! They were from every race, tribe, nation, and language, and they stood in front of the throne and of the Lamb, dressed in white robes and holding palm branches in their hands ... These are the people who have come safely through the terrible persecution. They have washed their robes and made them white with the blood of the Lamb. That is why they stand before God's throne and serve him day and night in his temple. He who sits on the throne will protect them with his presence" (7,9. 14-15). St. Gregory the Great comments: "Just as in the games the winner was given the palm, so it will be given to the Christian who during life has conquered the devil and the passions". Sometimes we find palm leaves carved on the marble slabs simply as ornament or used as punctuation between words. The true significance of the palm is inferred from the context. In *I Corinthians*, St. Paul says: "Surely you know that many runners take part in a race, but only one of them wins the prize. Run, then, in such a way as to win the prize. Every athlete in training submits to strict discipline, in order to be crowned with a wreath that will not last; but we do it for one that will last for ever. That is why I run straight for the finishing-line; that is why I am like a boxer who does not waste his punches. I harden my body with blows and bring it under complete control, to keep myself from being disqualified after having called others to the contest" (9, 24-27). The palm and the crown soon passed into Christian iconography and epigraphy as symbols of victory and of the supreme prize offered by God to the Christians: Paradise.

— *The vase overflowing with water:* it is a symbol of refreshment or solace. The soul now enjoys the blessed life and can thus satisfy its thirst for God.

— *A bushel or vessel full of grain:* it represents the Christian's good works.

— *The ship and the lighthouse:* the ship sailing for harbour over which shines the lighthouse is a symbol of the Christian who, illuminated by faith aims securely towards the port of salvation, the heavenly fatherland.

— *The phoenix:* the fabled bird of Arabia, hence called the Arabian phoenix, beautiful and unique, said to be re-born every thousand years from its ashes. For the early Christians it stood for the resurrection of the body and the birth to a new divine life.

— *The peacock:* apart from its highly decorative use in fresco paintings, it symbolizes the immortality of the soul. It was so interpreted also in the pagan world. Its flesh was believed to be incorruptible.

— *Orpheus:* a mythical figure dear to classical antiquity, always portrayed with a lyre. His melodies and songs charmed the wild beasts. For the Christians he was a symbol of Christ, who with his teachings in the Gospel transforms the human heart.

— *The cross with bent arms:* according to some this would indicate the glorious cross, the means by which Christ conquered the world. The short lines at the ends of the arms of the cross would represent rays of glory.

According to others, however, they were simply a decorative motif already common elsewhere in pre-Christian art: 卍 - 卐 .

---

[1] *Hominem mortuum in Urbe ne sepelito neve urito.* Cf. Cic. De Legibus, II, 23, 58.

[2] St. Damasus calls the martyr Tarsicius. I prefer the spelling, now more common, Tarcisius. The initials ICUR signify: *Inscriptiones Christianae Urbis Romae.* i.e. Christian Inscriptions of the City of Rome. Volume IV contains all the epigraphs from the "Callixtian complex" from no. 9367 to 12888 brought to light before 1964.

[3] Meaning an opening in the mound which allowed pilgrims to see and touch the martyr's tomb.

[4] See map on p. 22.

[5] Homily XLIX: *De cruce Domini,* which begins with the words *Saeculi ferunt fabulae Ulyssem...,* cf. PL, LVII, 339-340.

[6] Cf. p. 45.

[7] Acrostic is a word from Greek, meaning "word formed from the first letters of every verse or paragraph".

The Abbey of "Santa Maria delle Catacombe di San Callisto" (nowadays the "Istituto Salesiano San Tarcisio").

IV.
Underground excavation

Before describing the different areas of this cat-acomb, it is necessary to explain some general ideas about the excavations and the various types of burial. This will make it easier to understand the catacomb and the visit will become more interesting.

1. THE REASONS FOR UNDERGROUND EXCAVATION

We must not imagine that the catacombs were the one and only burial places in the Christian world of the first three centuries; rather they belonged to certain cities and regions of the Roman empire: Rome, Naples, Syracuse, Malta, Tunis... Just to cite the more im-portant cities. In all other parts of the empire the dead were buried above ground in mausoleums or in simple graves.

Why did Christians dig the catacombs? For various reasons. First of all they rejected the custom of cremation, and preferred inhumation, just as Christ was buried. Further, Christ's exhortation to care for the poor (*Luke* 11, 41) induced the early Christian communities and individual believers to solve the problem of burial for their brethren by donating land for burial, in a spirit of charity and love.

The problem of space also played a part in the development of the catacombs. The areas above ground owned by the Christians in the 2nd and 3rd centuries were not extensive. Had they used only the open-air cemeteries, the burial space available would have quickly been exhausted.

In antiquity, a tomb was sacred and inviolable; even after years, no other person could be buried in the same grave occupied by another. So the choice of excavations solved the problem, allowing the ex-ploitation of space underground.

There were other reasons for this choice. Above all, the sense of community. The early Christians wished to be together, even in the "sleep of death". Furthermore, such out of the way areas favoured community prayer and the use of symbols and other manifestations of their faith.

The depth of excavations also gave greater security for the tombs, particularly in times of persecution, when surface graves were more exposed to vandalism and violation.

The economic factor should not be underes-timated. This kind of burial was more economical, and suited a Church whose number of believers grew continually, especially among the very poor.

2. THE ANCIENT DIGGERS

The catacombs were the exclusive work of a specialized guild of workers, called *fossóres*, from the Latin *fódere*, to dig. Their work was lengthy, and required patience; with a pick and shovel, they dug by the dim light of oil lamps. Baskets or sacks were used to remove the dirt.

Some *fossores* painted the walls and even executed the inscriptions. From the 4th century onwards the Church authorized them to sell tombs. Unfortunately, abuses did occur.

In the larger catacomb complexes, excavation went on for more than three hundred years, from the middle of the 2nd century until the first decade of the 5th. Some areas — in particular those of the Popes, of St. Miltiades, of SS. Gaius and Eusebius, of the Crypts of Lucina — were excavated during persecutions, others during periods of religious peace.

On the following page:
Burial in the catacomb and "fossores" at work.

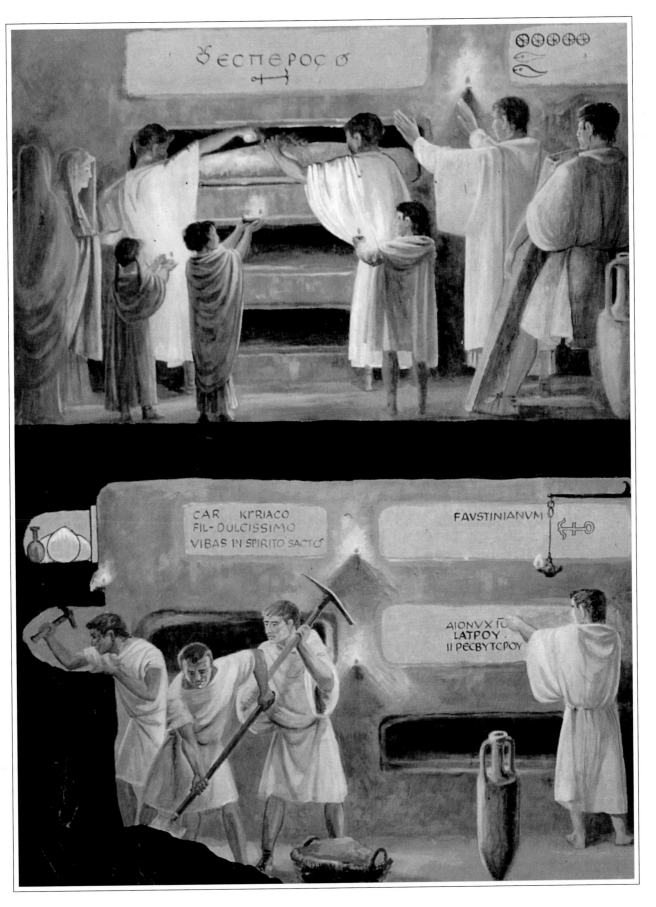

43

3. THE SUBTERRANEAN GALLERIES

The catacombs were preferably dug in a kind of tufa called "cappellaccio" (bad hat) in Roman dialect, rather than in other types of tufa, such as the "terroso" (earthy) or the "litoide" (rocky), the latter being particularly suitable for the roofs of the galleries. Tufa is a volcanic rock which abounds in the subsoil of the Roman country side. The galleries were dug *ex novo* in the virgin tufa. Frequently the Christians made use of galleries in abandoned quarries.[1]

The catacombs are dug on different floors or levels (half-floors), and in some cases they spread out on four floors or five levels. The first floor may be three to eight metres in depth, depending on the slope in which it is excavated. The second floor is generally between ten and fifteen metres down, the third about twenty metres, the fourth still deeper. However, there are some exceptions to these general figures.

The maximum depth, as evidenced in one zone of the "Callixtian complex", is about thirty metres. The various levels are reached by a series of steep staircases dug in the tufa or built of masonry.

Normally the galleries of the Catacombs of St. Callixtus are about three metres high. The "First Area" is an exception to the rule. Here we are very close to the tombs of the martyrs (the Crypt of the Popes and of St. Cecilia) and the Christians sought a burial place close to those glorious tombs, which created some more problems.

The older *loculi*, therefore, are the highest ones. When space was exhausted, the gallery was simply dug deeper, to make new tombs along the walls. Hence there was normally no need of ladders for burying the dead. The short stairs in Gallery A and B were only made necessary following these further deepenings (see map on p. 50).

However, requests for places in the "First Area" grew to the point that a first and a second extensions were not enough. Thus in the late 4th century the *fossores* decided, contrary to all custom, to re-open the *loculi* already occupied. They transferred the bones to a sandpit, near the Crypt of St. Cecilia, on the third floor. This sandpit contains no less than fourteen layers of bones. It is reached by a stairway which begins in Gallery H.

4. TYPES OF BURIAL

The loculus

In the walls of an intricate network of galleries, which form a real maze, there are rows of tombs called *loculi*.

This type of rectangular tomb would accomodate normally only one corpse, though there are many that would hold two or more.

The bodies were placed in the *loculus* not in a coffin but simply wrapped in a sheet or shroud. The corpse might have been sprinkled with lime, more often with scents. Sometimes a small vessel of those perfumes was placed in the tomb.

After the burial the *loculus* was closed with tiles, bricks or thin marble slabs, which were secured with plaster or mortar (composed of lime and sand or "pozzolana").

Ordinarily an oil lamp was placed beside the tomb. This is similar to the affectionate custom we still have of taking flowers or candles to the tombs of our loved ones. It was actually in the round holes that we see beside the *loculi* that the terracotta lamps or the glass phials of perfume were placed.

The "a mensa" tomb

This is a more spacious *loculus*. Its enclosing slab was not laid vertically but horizontally, giving it the aspect of an altar table. Above it a sort of rectangular niche was dug. Table-tombs are typical, though not frequent, in the 2nd century and in the first half of the 3rd.

The forma

This is a tomb dug in the floor of a crypt, of a *cubiculum* or of a gallery. It was closed with marble slabs or, more often, with large tiles. *Formae* were very numerous near the tombs of martyrs.

On the preceding page:
Axonometric view of the various levels of the Catacombs of St. Callixtus.

The arcosolium

It is a different and more beautiful tomb with an arch above it, *solium sub arcu*. As with the table-tomb, the sealing slab was laid horizontally.

The *arcosolium* could contain one corpse or an entire family group. Many are painted or decorated with mosaics. It is a typical tomb of the 3rd and 4th centuries.

The sarcophagus

This kind of burial was rather rare in the catacombs, because it was costly. Sarcophagi were made with terracotta, local stone, or most often with marble.

The term comes from the Greek verb *sarkophaghéin*, to eat flesh. The name probably has its origin in a legend. It was said that a particular type of stone from Lydia (present-day Turkey), from which coffins were made, was able to accelerate the decomposition of corpses.

Most Christian sarcophagi were carved on the front (or even on all four sides) with representations inspired by the Bible.

The cubiculum

In the catacombs there are also numerous small rooms called *cubicula*. They are square or polygonal, with a vault ceiling, and may also be decorated with small columns dug into the tufa.

They house *loculi* or *arcosolia* for one or more related family.

Some *cubicula* served associations or guilds, (i.e. bakers, coopers...). In most cases their use was similar to that of family mausoleums in our present cemeteries.

The crypt

In the catacombs we also find bigger rooms, called crypts. Under Pope Damasus, many of the martyrs' burial places were converted into crypts (small underground churches) with paintings, mosaics or other architectonic decorations. I shall come back to them when describing the Crypts of the Popes and of St. Cecilia.

5. THE IDENTIFICATION OF TOMBS

The Christians buried in the catacombs were largely poor and of humble origin. Very many were slaves, and this explains why so many tombs are nameless.

Even in death, they were welcomed as brothers in the Christian community and, in cemeteries under the Church's jurisdiction, they were given decent burial without payment.

Other graves had some small marks of identification. They were often insignificant objects, such as a little oil lamp, a coin, a brooch, a glass phial, a shell, a jewel, a toy, or a particular sign like the loaves inscribed with a cross or the monogram of Christ ... Tombs in which the sealing stone carries the name of the dead person are extremely rare.

6. THE TOMBS OF CHILDREN AND ADULTS

In the galleries we find rows of small tombs, dug particularly near the junctions, so as not to endanger the solidity of the structure at those points with large openings.

These small tombs were for new-born babies and children. Their number demonstrates the high infant mortality of the time. Tertullian tells how the Christians, out of charity, collected the tiny bodies of the new-born from the refuse heaps and gave them decent burial.

We may wonder why the graves of adults were often decidedly small. Excavation was cut to the minimum, as the dirt had to be disposed of with baskets on shoulders, but also the people in the Roman period were notably shorter than they are today.

7. OPEN AND EMPTY TOMBS

The tombs in all the galleries are now open and empty. We have already seen that systematic opening went on from the second half of the 17th century to

On the following page:
Gallery D in the "First Area".

the beginning of the 19th, with the aim of finding presumed bodies of martyrs. The bones, confusingly, were broken into tiny fragments.

It should also be noted that dampness and the passing of time tend to pulverize bones. In any case, all the bones found in these galleries were collected in an ossuary. The rest, reduced to fragments, can still be seen in many of the *loculi* of this vast cemetery.

Only in the most recently discovered catacombs, such as Pamphilus, Novatian, and the one in Via Latina, can we see galleries with tombs still closed. No *loculus* has been opened; they have been left intact to preserve their original state.

8. THE IMPRESSIONS OF A 4th CENTURY STUDENT

Visitors or pilgrims, going down into the catacombs for the first time, are deeply moved by these awe-inspiring sites. The same occurred to St. Jerome (circa 340-420), a 4th century young scholar, who later became secretary to Pope Damasus.

"When I was still a boy at school in Rome, I used to go out on Sundays to the tombs of the apostles and martyrs, with friends of my own age who shared the same convictions.

We often visited the galleries dug deep into the ground. On both sides, the walls contained the bodies of the dead, and everything was so dark that it seemed to fulfil the prophetic words: they go down alive into *sheol*. Rarely, a little light entered from above as though from a crack rather than a window, to temper the horror of this darkness; feeling my way slowly through that deep blind night, I thought of Virgil's phrase: '*Horror ubique animos simul ipsa silentia terrent*',[2] that is, 'Fear and silence, everywhere present, terrify the soul'".

---

[1] The Roman catacombs are not connected to each other and so do not form a single network of underground galleries. In antiquity, in fact, it was forbidden by law to dig galleries under a public road.

[2] "Dum essem Romae puer, et liberalibus studiis erudirer, solebam cum ceteris eiusdem aetatis et propositi, diebus dominicis sepulcra apostolorum et martyrum circuire, crebroque cryptas ingredi, quae in terrarum profunda defossae, ex utraque parte ingredientium per parietes habent corpora sepultorum, et ita obscura sunt omnia, ut propemodum illud propheticum compleatur: 'Descendant ad infernum viventes' (*Ps*. 55, 16); et raro desuper lumen admissum, horrorem temperet tenebrarum, ut non tam fenestram, quam foramen demissi luminis putes; rursumque pedetentim acceditur, et caeca nocte circumdatis illud Virgilianum proponitur: 'Horror ubique animos, simul ipsa silentia terrent' " (*Aeneid*. lib. II, 755). (Cf. *PL* XXV, 375).

Surface area above the Catacomb of Basileus (on the right) and of Balbina with the Anonymous Basilica (on the extreme left).

V.
The Area of the Popes and of St. Cecilia

The Crypt of the Popes

This is the famous "First Area" identified by de Rossi. It consists of two floors, of which the first is very limited and was excavated at a later period, while the second varies in depth from 10 to 12 metres.

1. THE ENTRANCE STAIRCASE

This leads directly to the second floor, to the Area of the Popes and of St. Cecilia. This is the older level, excavated during the period of persecution. The present, modern staircase is over the one which had been built in the 4th century under Pope Damasus in order to allow the pilgrims an easier access to the martyrs' tombs.

Many fragments of the sealing stones of *loculi* are attached along the walls of the first stretch of the stairway. On the landing where the stairway turns at a right angle, there is a statue of the Good Shepherd, a replica of the famous 4th century one now in the Vatican Museums.

At this point there are some tombs. Further down, on the left, there are two pagan sarcophagus lids, which originally belonged to the surface area. The lower one has charming scenes of *putti* performing acrobatics on horses.

Near the bottom of the stairs on the right is an inscription dating back to the time of Diocletian:

colleague Maximian. The Roman date tallies with August 26th, 290 A.D. (ICUR, IV, 9546).

On the left, the mutilated epigraph of a certain Agrippina reveals the true meaning of death for a Christian: the day of death is called the "day in which she entered into the light".

> ...DIA · AGRIPPINA REDD(idit)
> (c)VIVS · DIES · INLVXIT
> ...DE · POSITA · IDIBVS

..."Agrippina gave up (her soul to God)
Entered into the light...
Buried on the ides of "[1]...

2. THE SKYLIGHT

At the foot of the stairs, one of the many *lucernaria* (skylights) in the vault of the roof can be seen. These were opened preferably along the galleries, or at their crossings above the staircases, and in the roof of a crypt or of a *cubiculum*.

> VIBIV(s) FI(r)MVS R(ecessit) VII KA(lendas) SEP(tembres)
> DI(o)C(letiano) IIII ET MAX(imiano) (III) CO(n)S(ulibus)

It records one Vibius Firmus, who died seven days before the Kalends of September, under the fourth consulate of emperor Diocletian and the third of his

They are wide shafts, usually square in cross-section and reaching the surface. During the period of excavation they served for pulling out the earth.

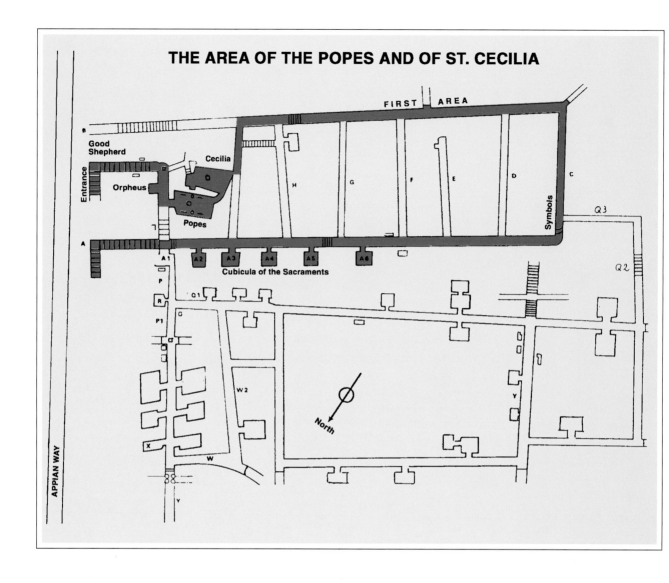

THE AREA OF THE POPES AND OF ST. CECILIA

When the work was finished they remained open as a vent for air and light.

Sections of the walls lined with bricks, and not plastered, are restoration work done by de Rossi, as is indicated in the marble plaques with the date in Roman numerals and the letters C.D.A.S. (Commissione di Archeologia Sacra, the Commission for Sacred Archaeology).

3. THE GRAFFITI

At the foot of the stairs on plastered masonry walls (now protected by glass) begins a series of graffiti scratched by pilgrims at the time when the martyrs were still buried in the catacombs.

The graffiti were scratched with an iron point on the plaster of the walls, or on the mortar sealing the *loculi*, and occasionally also on the marble slabs.

There are two different kinds of graffiti: "devotional" (called also "proscimeni", from the Greek *proskiménoi*), which appear on the walls of basilicas, *cubicula* and plastered galleries; and "sepulchral", carved in the mortar sealing the *loculi* while it was still fresh, with a deeper groove.

While the sepulchral graffiti confine themselves to recording the name and date of burial, the age and the usual invocation of peace, the devotional ones vary much more in content. They are particularly frequent near the tombs of martyrs. They are testimony to the passage of pilgrims who, from the 4th century, visited the Roman catacombs to invoke the protection of the martyrs for the living and the dead.

Felicio priest, a sinner

The graffiti left by priests are particularly interesting. Most often they are mere signatures followed by the abbreviation $\overline{\text{PRB}}$, *presbyter*, priest. Quite often this is followed by the words *indignus peccator*, unworthy sinner. The graffito of a priest Felicio is seen scratched on the outer wall of the Crypt of the Popes: *Felicio $\overline{\text{PBR}}$ peccator*, Felicio priest, a sinner (ICUR, IV, 9524).

Such phrases may strike us as being false humility, but it was not. They came from a deep awareness of the teachings of the Gospel.

The priest pilgrims knew perfectly well that man can approach God only when he realizes his own limitations and recognizes that he is a sinner.

Only with this sincere humility can he ask pardon and regain God's friendship. This is the first step towards cleansing one's conscience and with the sacrament of penance this process of reconciliation is completed.

To admit oneself a "sinner" was, at the time, anything but empty rhetoric, and to visit the places sanctified by those who had given testimony to their loyalty to God with their blood, was something which strengthened one's faith.

Devotional graffiti are also often useful for identifying a venerated tomb. A pilgrim carved these statements not out of a general interior disposition, but out of devotion to a particular martyr. He or she wanted to make a tangible and lasting request for the martyr's intercession before the throne of God. The martyr was an immediate and shining example of faithfulness, as well as an effective advocate.

"Jerusalem, city and ornament of God's martyrs"

Continuing along the short gallery on the right, a gate leads into *cubiculum* L2, named "Orpheus".[2] The mythical figure is depicted on the vault ceiling, seated on a rock. He is dressed in eastern attire and holds a lyre. Two sheep lie beside him. The picture is also enlivened by other surrounding figures: peacocks, sea monsters, ornamental and floral motives. Orpheus, as I have said, is a symbol of Christ. The paintings date back to the early 3rd century.

The series of graffiti in Greek and Latin on the left wall of the Gallery L read: "O St. Sixtus, remember in your prayers Aurelius Repentinus..."; "O holy Souls, remember Marcianus, Successus, Severus and all our brethren" (ICUR, IV, 9521, 9522).

They are names of pilgrims during the period of persecution. Other names belong to the age of Constantine, and even to presbyters of the 8th and 9th centuries.

All these invocations show that we are very close to a sanctuary of martyrs, as indicated also by a Latin graffito, which is written in Greek script: *Gerusale*

Graffiti by pilgrims on the entrance wall in the Crypt of the Popes dating from the 4th to the 9th centuries.

civitas et ornamentum martyru(m) d(e)i... That is: "O Jerusalem, city and ornament of God's martyrs" (ICUR, IV, 9524). This unidentified pilgrim compared that sanctuary to the heavenly Jerusalem, that is, to Paradise.

4. THE DISCOVERY OF THE CRYPT OF THE POPES

"An inner voice told me that here below..."

Describing his discovery of the Crypt of the Popes, de Rossi writes: "Much as I had tried to penetrate every corner of the vast necropolis, as far as the earth and the ruins allowed, nowhere had I seen such imposing constructions, or such a mass of debris thrown down from above, as in the immediate neighbourhood of the Eastern *Trichora*. Instinct therefore told me that here, beneath me, were the Crypts of St. Sixtus and St. Cecilia...

In March 1854 we began to clear the earth out of a gallery which led towards the Crypt of St. Eusebius, which was still blocked with debris.

To make this easier, architect Fontana thought it would be a good idea to open one of the skylights very close to the *trichora*. At first I disliked this idea, foreseeing a useless delay in the search for the Crypt of St. Eusebius, but very soon I saw a magnificent arched doorway leading into an exquisite room.

The reader may imagine how eagerly I examined every fragment of marble which came to light under the blows of the pick. From day to day I awaited the solution of the chief topographical problem of underground Rome, which I had been studying for five years: the location and discovery of the Crypt of the Popes and that of St. Cecilia...

When the diggers reached the floor and the threshold of that doorway, I saw the outer walls of the crypt covered with graffiti in Greek and Latin, written by ancient visitors to that illustrious *hypogeum*. This fortuitous clue assured me that I was standing before the noblest and most venerated crypt in the cemetery. The clue became a certainty when I deciphered those difficult, minute and badly worn writings...

Repeatedly I saw the name of St. Sixtus invoked. But according to the ancient *Itineraries*, in the area where Sixtus was buried, also Pontianus, Antherus,

Lucius, Stephen and Eutychian, were to be found, that is, nearly all the popes of the 3rd century. And nearby, the tomb of St. Cecilia was to be located as well.

When the crypt was cleared of the debris I found myself in a room adorned with marble columns, which lay broken among the ruins. The side walls contained opened *loculi*, without inscriptions. The wall facing us had a bigger sepulchre. In front of this was a marble step with four square holes marking the place of four small pillars which had supported a table, perhaps an altar ...

These brief indications were more than enough to confirm that the crypt I was describing was the nerve-centre of the whole Cemetery of St. Callixtus ...

The barbarian devastations were no less thorough here than in the other historic crypts. The pillagers, breaking in through the light shaft and through a hole made in the wall facing us, took possession of an infinity of marbles, not leaving even a simple fragment attached to the highest of the *loculi*.

But the last layer of the ruins proved rich in broken stones belonging to the crypt. Luckily for us, these sacrilegious, or rather utterly ignorant robbers took no notice of the smallest bits of marble. Thus, I was able to recognise and pick out four inscriptions of the 3rd century popes. Piecing the fragments together I could read the names of Antherus, Fabian, Lucius and Eutychian. I also found the remains of a splendid inscription of Pope Damasus which had escaped the pillage". (R.S.C., I, p. 252-256).

The presence of so many *loculi* of popes in one place is something found nowhere else in subterranean Rome. The reason is very simple. We know how jealously the apostolic Churches preserved the tombs of their bishops; this had become the best way for establishing their apostolic origin.

Tertullian wrote: "Show us the origins of your Church, list for us the succession of your bishops, take us by a direct line to the apostle or disciple who founded your episcopal see".

The Churches of the first centuries of Christianity spared no pains to recover the bodies of their Pastors who had died in exile. Think of the translation to

On the following page:
The Crypt of the Popes (3rd century).

Rome of Pope Pontianus from Sardinia, of Pope Cornelius from Civitavecchia and of Pope Eusebius from Sicily.

5. ORIGIN OF THE CRYPT OF THE POPES

The Crypt of the Popes, discovered as we have seen by de Rossi in 1854, was labelled by him as "the little Vatican, the central monument of all Christian cemeteries".

It originated towards the 2nd century as a private *cubiculum*. When the "First Area" became directly dependent on the Church of Rome, it was thought suitable to transform that *cubiculum* into the burial place of the Popes.

In its lower part the crypt had four niches containing sarcophagi, and twelve *loculi*, six on each side. In front of the end wall, a table-tomb ("a mensa") was built.

Reconstruction of the Crypt of the Popes by Mario Maresca (from the film "The Catacombs of Rome", Ars Mar Film, 1987).

Before the opening of the light-shaft, which partly destroyed the ancient roof that was probably decorated, a little window had been opened beside the door, to let a little light into the crypt from the light-shaft of the short Gallery L. Because of this window, the door of the crypt is not at the centre of the wall but slightly to the left.

6. FIVE ORIGINAL SEPULCHRAL INSCRIPTIONS

It is quite certain that six popes were buried in this crypt. It is highly probable that three others were too. The other graves contained eight members of the ecclesiastical hierarchy (bishops or deacons).

In clearing the crypt, de Rossi found the original marble slabs, broken and mutilated, of four popes: Antherus, Fabian, Lucius and Eutychian. The burial inscription of Pope Pontianus was discovered by Mons. Wilpert in 1909, during the excavations in the Crypt of St. Cecilia. Part of it was found in the well of the crypt,

at a depth of eight metres. The name of the five popes were written in Greek, following the official usage of the Church in the 3rd century.

There are some peculiarities in the lettering. The small omega (ω) is preferred to the capital (Ω) and the final sigma of their names is the (C) instead of the classical sigma (Σ). This is usual from the end of the 2nd century onwards.

The names of the five popes, with some biographical notes on each, follow here in chronological order.

The Pope and martyr Saint Pontianus

empire for three years without ever visiting Rome. Reacting against the religious policy of his predecessor, Maximinus, who was hostile to Christianity, issued an edict of persecution against the hierarchy (bishops, priests, deacons) of the various Churches.

His most illustrious victim was Pope Pontianus, who was exiled to Sardinia and condemned to hard labour in the mines, *ad metalla*. While in exile, Pontianus abdicated on 28th September 235, in order to avoid making difficulties for the Church during his absence.

The unhealthy climate, the work in the mines and the treatment probably hastened his end.

ΠΟΝΤΙΑΝΟC · ΕΠΙCΚ(οπος) · Μ(ά)ΡΤ(υς)
Pontianus · Bishop · Martyr

St. Pontianus (230-235) was a Roman. He had a relatively calm pontificate during the reign of Alexander Severus, an emperor with a lively moral sense and benevolent towards the Christians. Things changed for the Church with the accession of Gaius Julius Verus Maximinus (235-238), called "the Thracian" after his birthplace (Thrace) in the Balkan Peninsula.

This emperor, a rough soldier who remained fundamentally a barbarian, governed the Roman

When he died, the Church considered him a true martyr. A few years later, Pope Fabian had his body brought back from Sardinia and it was given honourable burial in the Crypt of the Popes at St. Callixtus.

His marble slab is broken into six pieces (ICUR, IV, 10670). According to the custom of the time, St. Pontianus was called "bishop" not pope. This detracts nothing from his primacy: the bishop of Rome was

Crypt of the Popes: Sepulchral inscription of the martyred Pope St. Pontianus († 235 ca.).

regarded from the beginning as the successor of St. Peter and the vicar of Christ. The title *papa*, father, became exclusive to the bishop of Rome during the 4th century. The abbreviation MPT means martyr, and was added to the slab some decades later. The same thing happened to Pope Fabian.

Pope Saint Antherus

ΑΝΤΕΡωC · ΕΠΙ(σκοπος)
Antherus · Bishop

Historical sources do not tell us much about Pope Antherus, who was of Greek origin. Both the *Liber Pontificalis* and the *Liberian Catalogue* offer uncertain and contradictory information.

Antherus succeeded St. Pontianus as Pope on 21st November 235, following a vacancy of nearly two months. His pontificate was very brief only 43 days! He was not executed, and he may have died while in prison, on 3rd January 236, immediately after being sentenced by emperor Maximinus.

Antherus actually died before his predecessor, St. Pontianus. He was the first of the nine popes to be buried in this crypt, as the translation of St. Pontianus took place later. His tomb was very modest, a simple *loculus* excavated in the tufa.

His epitaph has survived in three fragments, and is the oldest existing inscription which recalls not only a Roman pope, but a member of the clergy too (ICUR, IV, 10558).

The Pope and martyr Saint Fabian

ΦΑΒΙΑΝΟC · ΕΠΙ(σκοπος) · Μ(ά)ΡΤ(υς)
Fabian · Bishop · Martyr

St. Fabian's epitaph is also mutilated. De Rossi found five fragments of it, enough to give us the Pope's name, his rank of bishop and the abbreviation MPT for "martyr" (ICUR, IV, 10694).

St. Fabian (236-250) was a Roman and was elected pope on the death of St. Antherus. His pastoral ministry of 14 years coincided with a period of religious peace promoted by emperors Gordian III (238-244) and Philip the Arabian (244-249).

Fabian set to work at once to restore the organization and administration of the Church, seriously jeopardized by Maximinus' persecution.

He divided Rome into seven ecclesiastical regions, each with its *tituli* (parishes) and its "catacombs" (cemeteries).[3] St. Fabian's reorganization of the Roman Church was imposing, and attracted so much attention, that it upset new emperor Decius (249-251), an Illyrian (Dalmatian).

Quintus Messius Gaius Trajan Decius, a cultivated person of a well-to-do family, was a rigid conservative, anxious to restore the ancient Roman traditions, including religion. He set out systematically to uproot Christianity, which he judged to be politically dangerous. He issued an edict which required every subject to sacrifice to the official State divinities before the local authorities and commissions set up for the purpose. By threats, imprisonment, torture, confiscations, he tried to force into idolatry all who refused to obey. But on the Church hierarchy the death penalty was imposed. Pope Fabian was one of the first victims. He was brought to trial before the emperor himself but he outspokenly refused to sacrifice to the gods. He was condemned to die at once by decapitation. It was 20th January 250 A.D. According to St. Cyprian, after his execution Decius said: "I would rather have a rival in the empire than a bishop in Rome".

Through its persecution, the Church of the first three centuries followed Jesus her Master in the *via dolorosa*. Many Christians, following Pope Fabian's example, testified to their faith in Christ by shedding their blood. This blood, as Tertullian said, was the seed of new Christians: "Crucify us, torture us, put us to death, annihilate us. Your injustice is the proof of our innocence. Your harvest of blood only increases the numbers in our ranks. The blood of the martyrs is the seed of new Christians". Indeed, Jesus himself had told

his faithful not to fear death: "Whoever loses his life for my sake will find it" (*Matthew* 16, 25).

Unhappily, alongside the numerous champions of the faith there were many apostates, called *lapsi*. The painful question of the *lapsi* was to trouble the peace of the Church in the following years.[4]

In 251 Decius died fighting the Goths, the first Roman emperor to be killed in battle. His edict against Christians was not only a political mistake but proved to be a resounding failure as well. It may be regarded as the last act of persecution which sought to strike the Christians without naming them. From Nero to Decius, Christianity was considered an "unlawful superstition", and had been tolerated or fought ambiguously. From then on, persecution or recognition took place openly.

Pope Saint Lucius I

> ### ΛΟΥΚΙϹ [ἐπίσκοπος]
> ### Lucius [bishop]

The epitaph of St. Lucius (253-254) has survived in a very mutilated state. De Rossi found only two fragments which carry his name. No doubt, next to the name was the title "bishop" (ICUR, IV, 10645).

Lucius' pontificate was short: eight months in all. Elected at the death of St. Cornelius, he was soon exiled, like his predecessor. The emperor Trebonianus Gallus (251-253) sent him to Civitavecchia (Centumcellae).

Gaius Vibius Trebonianus Gallus, a general elected by the legions at the death of Decius, was at first tolerant towards Christians, but very quickly he changed his policy. In 252 a plague raged through the empire. Propitiatory sacrifices were at once ordered to get rid of that calamity. Naturally the Christians did not take part. Their absence aroused the hatred of the pagans. There were protests and riots in several parts of the empire. The emperor then promulgated an edict condemning bishops, priests and deacons to exile. Pope Lucius was banished from Rome, thus paying for his loyalty to God.

Shortly afterwards, in August 253, Trebonianus Gallus was killed in a rebellion at the hands of his soldiers. When Valerian succeeded him, Pope Lucius was called back to Rome and welcomed with great joy by the faithful.

The circumstances in the capital, however, were not peaceful, because of the schism of Novatian, a priest who refused to pardon the *lapsi*. In this delicate situation Lucius showed great balance and moderation. He ordered the *lapsi* to be forgiven, but only after an adequate period of penance.

Pope Saint Eutychian

> ### ΕΥΤΥΧΙΑΝΟϹ · ΕΠΙϹΚ(οπος)
> ### Eutychian · Bishop

As for St. Eutychian's (275-283) epitaph, de Rossi was rather lucky. Among the debris in the Crypt of the Popes he found about a dozen fragments which revealed his complete name, as well as the title "bishop" in abbreviated form (ICUR, IV, 10616).

The letter Χ in Eutychian's name has an I interwoven with it (✷). This needs explaining. Either the stonecutter was distracted and mistakenly left out

Crypt of the Popes: Sepulchral inscription of Pope St. Eutychian († 283).

the X while having already carved the I, or he was carving a K in place of the X. Realizing his mistake, he tried to rectify it as best as he could, but the vertical line of the letter I was already carved and could not so easily be disposed of.

St. Eutychian was pope for eight years. There were no persecutions in his time, but the Church of Rome was not without problems: the continual threat of heresies, the question of the *lapsi*... Little is known of this Pope's life and activities. Unfortunately the archives of the Church of Rome were destroyed during the tremendous persecution of Diocletian. St. Eutychian was from Luni in Liguria (Italy) and was the last of the nine popes to be buried in this crypt. He died the year before Diocletian was nominated emperor.

7. OBSERVATIONS ON THE EPITAPHS OF THE POPES

As regards the form of their lettering the inscriptions of the Crypt of the Popes have many similarities. It may be argued that they are the work of a single family of stonecutters, who passed on their skill from father to son or from master to pupil.

According to ancient custom, the letters were first painted in red by a process largely similar to the one still used today. The whole surface of the slab was coloured and then rubbed with pumice, so that the colour remained only in the hollows of the letters. This work was mostly done before the slab was set in place, but in the inscriptions of St. Pontianus and St. Antherus it was done afterwards, because the red is still visible under the sealing plaster.

8. THE TITLE "MARTYR"[5]

Very few sepulchral inscriptions carry the glorious title "Martyr", because those with that title suffered destruction more than others and for various reasons.

In Pope Damasus' time, when the tombs of the martyrs were embellished, the original inscriptions may have been removed and placed elsewhere. Those which remained in place were later exposed to the threat of the barbarian invasions (Goths and Lombards) and easily perished. Lastly, it must be presumed that they were destroyed at the time when the relics were transferred. The cult of relics was then prominent, but history at that time proceeded with categories somewhat different from ours.

The custom of inscribing the honorific title "Martyr" on the sepulchral slab goes back to 258, as is clear from the inscription of Felicissimus and Agapitus, deacons of Pope Sixtus II, buried in the neighbouring

Cemetery of Pretextatus. Not long afterwards, this title came to be added to the inscriptions on the tombs of well-known martyrs. But it could not be cut on the tombstones of all the other martyrs, especially the oldest, because all knowledge of them was lost and the tombstones carried only names.

This explains why the martyrs named in the *Itineraries* are so few and why these documents often contain only general expressions, such as "many saints, many martyrs, very many other martyrs, countless multitudes of martyrs...".[6]

Their exact number is sometimes given. The highest figures mentioned are 80, 260, 365, 800. Such figures may perhaps be a repetition of the numbers given by the guides, who, taking the pilgrims around the sanctuaries, were prone, as is their custom, to exaggerate.

9. THE MARTYR POPE SIXTUS II

For Sixtus II (257-258) the literary sources are again not generous with information. He seems to have been a Greek, elected pope on 30th August 257. St. Cyprian calls him "a good and peace loving priest". But if information about his life and pastoral activity is scarce, the news about his martyrdom is precise and detailed.

To account for the causes leading to his glorious end, it is worth considering his pontificate in its historical context.

Emperor Valerian

Publius Licinius Valerian Augustus (253-260), a learned man of noble birth, has passed into history as one of the fiercest persecutors of Christianity. In the first three years of his reign he was tolerant. Suddenly, in August 257, he issued an edict ordering persecution against the Christians, perhaps influenced by his financial adviser, the Egyptian Macrianus.

The edict prescribed that ecclesiastics should make sacrifice under pain of exile. For the average Christian, disregard of the imperial edict meant capital punishment. Entrance to the cemeteries (catacombs) and other religious meetings were prohibited. The Church's properties were confiscated.

Here is an excerpt from Valerian's edict forbidding access to the cemeteries:

"The most sacred emperors (Valerian and his son Gallienus) command that there shall be no meetings (of Christians) in any place, and that they shall not frequent cemeteries (catacombs).

If anyone fails to observe this beneficial precept he shall be beheaded".[7]

**Crypt of the Popes:
The sign for martyr,
in Greek "MPT"
(detail of Pope
St. Fabian's epitaph).**

A second edict, even more frightening, was issued in 258 under the consuls Tuscus and Bassus.

The emperor laid down that ecclesiastics were to be punished with immediate death if they should refuse to sacrifice. Christians of high rank were to be deprived of their rank in society and wealth and, if they still persisted in their faith, they were to be killed. Matrons (women of noble rank) were condemned to exile, and the freedmen of the imperial palace were sent to forced labour.

The persecution did not last long. In 260 Valerian was defeated by King Sapor and died a prisoner in Persia after being deeply humiliated as a man and as a soldier.

This persecution was also a failure and marked the beginning of the end of paganism. But it stressed an important new fact: for the first time the State *recognized the organization of the Church as such*, although it outlawed and persecuted its hierarchy and confiscated its property. Moreover, the persecution showed a precise intention of attacking those Christians who had influence in society and of removing them from their key positions in the empire.

In the past, the Christians had been accused of shunning public life, and the policy of Marcus Aurelius (161-180) and the Severan emperors (193-235) had been to try to assimilate them into the State. Valerian, along with the pagan high society and the Senate, saw the problem from a different standpoint. There was now fear of the "Christianization" of the State and so war was declared against it.

The martyrdom of Sixtus II

Sixtus II was one of the first victims of Valerian's second edict and may be considered the real martyr of the Roman catacombs. In fact, while he was conducting a religious service in the Cemetery of St. Callixtus, Sixtus was surprised by Valerian's soldiers. After a very hasty trial he was beheaded there on that same day, the 6th of August 258.

News of the martyrdom of Sixtus II spread immediately throughout the Christian world. Less than a month after his execution, St. Cyprian wrote to his colleague Successus: "You should know that Sixtus was killed in the 'cemetery' on August 6th and with him four deacons"[8]. The Catacombs of St. Callixtus were known as the "cemetery", because it was the official cemetery of the Church of Rome.

The veneration of St. Sixtus spread rapidly in antiquity and his name was inserted in the Roman canon along with those of St. Cornelius and St. Cecilia. A rather long vacancy followed Sixtus' death, because on the day he was beheaded six deacons were also executed and a seventh, Lawrence, was burnt alive four days later on the Via Tiburtina.

It is known, that in the first centuries of the Church the bishop of Rome was preferably chosen from among the deacons rather than from the presbyters. Deacons had a better knowledge of ecclesiastical organization and were close collaborators of the pope.

During the interim period, from 6th August 258 to 22nd July 259, the Church of Rome was governed by a council of presbyters.

10. POPE SIXTUS II'S TOMB

The tomb of the founder of the cubiculum

Facing us in the wall of the Crypt of the Popes there are two tombs almost equal in size. The lower one is the usual primitive sepulchre, "a mensa". It was cut into the tufa, decorated with marble and topped with a slab laid horizontally. Above it was the usual four-cornered niche, decorated with a double layer of stucco and painted red lines.

In order to reinforce the front side of the tomb, a thin masonry wall was built with two small lateral pillars. Traces of mortar can still be seen on this wall. This shows that it bore an inscription in marble, probably from the very beginning.

This tomb was the principal one in the *cubiculum* which later became the "Crypt of the Popes". Here was buried the "founder" of the *cubiculum* and, to all appearances, he was a member of the *Caecilii* family, though excavation has not yielded any fragment of his epitaph so far.

The tomb of Pope Sixtus II

The niche above the table-tomb was modified in the middle of the 3rd century to provide for a second sepulchre. The two side walls were decorated with marble slabs and the wall opposite the entrance was widened to make room for the sarcophagus of the martyred Pope. An inscription must have been fixed on the front of it, as had been done for the earlier popes (Pontianus, Antherus, Fabian...), but it has never been found.

11. THE CRYPT OF THE POPES BECOMES A SHRINE

In the 4th century, when the veneration for the martyrs grew, this burial place was transformed into a small underground church. The door was heightened and widened and under the entrance arch a monogram in red was painted, which has now almost completely vanished.

In the roof, two light-shafts were opened. The central one lit the crypt, while the left-hand one shed light directly on the altar. The narrow window beside the door, which had hitherto given light to the burial place, was bricked up to reinforce the entrance wall. On the wall to the right a small niche was opened for lamps.

Two spiral columns rested on high bases which still remain in place. These columns supported an architrave which carried, according to the ancient usage, lamps, crosses and ornamental wreaths.

In front of Sixtus II's tomb St. Damasus built an altar of which only the base survives. As the *Liber Pontificalis* relates, Sixtus III (432-440) placed a marble slab above the entrance door on the inside wall of the crypt. This tablet contained the names of the popes and of other members of the hierarchy buried here, but also the names of popes and bishops buried in several other regions of the Cemetery of St. Callixtus. You can still see the rectangular hollow made for that tablet.

De Rossi was able to reconstruct the entire list of those names, starting from the citation in the *Liber Pontificalis* and with the help of the Martyrology of St. Jerome and the Tours Collection. His work here is a masterpiece of scholarly investigation in which very little is mere hypothesis.

In this apparent chronological confusion there is, however, a certain order. In the first column are the names of the martyr popes. In the second, popes who did not suffer martyrdom. In the fourth, foreign bishops. Only the third column is somewhat mixed up, popes and bishops appearing together (ICUR, IV, 9516).

The lunette above this marble catalogue which ran almost the whole width of the wall, contained a mosaic. A few fragments of its *tesserae* remain. Very soon the floor of the crypt and the adjoining Gallery L were covered with *formae* (tombs of devotion).

The walls of the crypt were plastered and embellished with marble, but the inside of the tombs was left as rough tufa. The twelve *loculi* vary in size, both in height and in depth.

The present brick structure of the crypt was done by de Rossi to give greater solidity to the tufa walls. It was also necessary to reconstruct part of the ceiling which had collapsed.

12. TWO POEMS BY ST. DAMASUS

"Hic congesta iacet..."

Before the tomb of Sixtus II, on the lower part of the wall, Pope Damasus placed a poem in Latin hexameters, perhaps the most famous of all his com-

---

"Names of the Bishops, Martyrs and Confessors who were buried in the Cemetery of Callixtus

Sixtus	Dionysius	Stephen	Urban
Cornelius	Felix	Lucius	Mannus
Pontianus	Eutychian	Antherus	Numidian
Fabian	Gaius	Laudiceus	Julian
Eusebius	Miltiades	Polycarp	Optatus

Among these St. Sixtus suffered first
with Agapitus, Felicissimus and XI others".

positions. He commemorates the martyrs and confessors buried in the crypt and in the entire catacomb.

The term "martyr" meant those who had shed their blood in order to remain faithful to Christ, while the term "confessor" referred to all those who, not being put to a violent and cruel death, had witnessed by their exemplary lives that they were good Christians.

In the last two lines of his poem St. Damasus expresses the wish to be buried himself in this holy place together with his predecessors. But he very humbly declares that he is not worthy of this privilege.

The inscription, found by de Rossi in more than a hundred pieces among the debris, was patiently reconstructed by him with the help of documents dating back to the 7th century (the *Sillogae* or collections of verses). It is inscribed in capital letters by the unmistakable hand of the stonecutter Furius Dionysius Filocalus, a devoted friend of Damasus.

Filocalus "created for the purpose a type of lettering distinguished for its high quality from all the others. These inscriptions, harmoniously framed upon large marble slabs, were placed inside the crypts or cemeterial basilicas so as to be clearly visible. Filocalus signed some of his epigraphs, like the one dedicated to the martyr Pope St. Eusebius. Some twenty inscriptions are generally assigned to him, belonging to the decade 370-380" (D. Mazzoleni). The words of the poem are inscribed without spacing. To make it easier reading I transcribe them here with spaces:

fessors sent to us from Greece" probably refers to a group of martyrs: Maria, Neon, Hippolytus, Adria, Paulina, Martha, Valeria, Eusebius and Marcellus. The place of their burial in the "Callixtian complex" has not yet been found (ICUR, IV, 12520).

In the first Christian centuries, when the "brethren" had not yet "separated", contacts between the Church of Rome and the Greek-speaking Church were very frequent.

The great teachers of the faith whom we call the Fathers of the Church, such as SS. Athanasius, Gregory of Nyssa, Basil, Gregory Nazianzen, John

HIC CONGESTA IACET QVAERIS SI TVRBA PIORVM
CORPORA SANCTORVM RETINENT VENERANDA SEPVLCRA
SVBLIMES ANIMAS RAPVIT SIBI REGIA CAELI
HIC COMITES XYSTI PORTANT QVI EX HOSTE TROPAEA
HIC NVMERVS PROCERVM SERVAT QVI ALTARIA $\overline{XPI}$
HIC POSITVS LONGA VIXIT QVI IN PACE SACERDOS
HIC CONFESSORES SANCTI QVOS GRAECIA MISIT
HIC IVVENES PVERIQVE SENES CASTIQVE NEPOTES
QVIS MAGE VIRGINEVM PLACVIT RETINERE PVDOREM
HIC FATEOR DAMASVS VOLVI MEA CONDERE MEMBRA
SED CINERES TIMVI SANCTOS VEXARE PIORVM

"If you are searching for them, here lies united an army of Saints,
these venerable tombs enclose their bodies,
while the Kingdom of Heaven has already welcomed their souls.
Here lie the companions of Sixtus who bear the trophies won from the enemy.
Here lie the brotherhood of popes who guard the altar of Christ.
Here the bishop who lived through a long peace.
Here the holy confessors sent to us from Greece.
Here young men and children, the elderly and their chaste offspring,
who desired to conserve thir virginity.
Here too I, Damasus, confess I would like to be buried
were it not for the fear of disturbing the ashes of these holy persons".[9]

Pope Sixtus' "companions" are four deacons: Januarius, Magnus, Vincent and Stephen, who were martyred with him. The "popes who guard the altar of Christ" are clearly those buried in this catacomb. The "bishop who lived through a long peace" is possibly Fabian or Dionysius or Eutychian. The "holy con-

Chrysostom... had considerable influence on western theological thinking.

Hence the martyrs of one Church were adopted and venerated by the other.

Pope Damasus' reference in his poem is a clear proof of that.

"Tempore quo gladius..."

On the right-hand wall of the Crypt of the Popes two original fragments of a second poem by Damasus, celebrating Pope Sixtus II's martyrdom, can be seen. Here is a translation of this poem:

"At the time when the sword (persecution)
pierced the bowels of the Mother (Church)
I, (now) buried here, taught as pastor (pope)
the word of God (the divine precepts).
When suddenly the soldiers rushed in,
dragged me from the (episcopal) chair.
The faithful offered their necks to the sword.[10]
But as soon as the Pastor saw the ones
who wished to rob him of the palm (of martyrdom)
he was the first to offer himself
and his own head, not tolerating that the (pagan)
frenzy should harm the others.
Christ, who gives recompense,
made manifest the Pastor's merit,
preserving unharmed the flock".

This inscription was placed just in front of Sixtus II's tomb, immediately above the preceding poem. To make room for the two texts Damasus had a second retaining wall built covering the main wall; the one can now be clearly distinguished from the other.

When the martyred Pope's relics were taken away, the sepulchres were simply smashed without regard to their inscriptions. The later pillages completed the havoc beyond repair. Only three bits of the poem *"Hic congesta iacet..."* remained attached to the wall, in the lower right-hand corner.

Pope St. Paschal I (817-824) had the body of Sixtus II translated to the Church of St. Praxedes near St. Mary Major.

13. THREE MORE POPES BURIED IN THE CRYPT

When de Rossi cleared the earth and debris from the Crypt of the Popes, he found no trace of the epitaphs of Popes Stephen, Dionysius and Felix. The sources which document their burial in the cemetery are the *Depositio Episcoporum*, the *Itineraries* and the marble catalogue set up by Sixtus III in the crypt. Since their tombs have not been found elsewhere in the catacombs, it may be supposed that they were buried in the Crypt of the Popes.

St. Stephen I

We know little of Pope Stephen (254-257). The only reliable source which offers some details about his personality and activity are some letters of St. Cyprian, who was not always on good terms with him because of serious theological questions.

He was elected pope on 18th May 254 as successor to St. Lucius, and his pontificate was troubled with religious controversies caused by some bishops, whose orthodoxy was questioned. He died on 12th August 257.

St. Dionysius

Pope Dionysius (259-268) was a Roman. He was one of the college of presbyters who ruled the Church of Rome after Sixtus' martyrdom. He was elected in July 259, during the consulate of Aemilian and Bassus, after a vacancy of about one year.

Dionysius had to deal with questions concerning the faith, often threatened by heresies, and helped charitably the Churches that went through particular difficulties. He died on 27th December 268.

His pontificate coincided with the reign of emperor Gallienus, the son of Valerian, who was tolerant with the Christians. Pope Dionysius is mentioned in Gallienus' edict which restored the Church's possessions and cemeteries. The decree reads: "We order that the so-called 'dormitories' (catacombs) be restored to the Christians". What did Gallienus' change of attitude towards the Christians mean? Political expediency or benevolence towards the new religion?

About Christianity, Publius Egnatius Gallienus (260-268) had entirely opposite feelings to his father's. He at once revoked the edict of persecution, and gave ample liberty to the bishops to practise their ministry. At the request of the ecclesiastical authorities,

he ordered the restoration of both their places of worship and catacombs to the Christian communities.

Most probably Gallienus' tolerance was the fruit of political calculation. He was pro-Hellenic, a neo-Platonist and very far indeed from the Gospel, although his wife Cornelia Solonina seems to have shared the Christian faith. Gallienus' main interest was in obtaining the collaboration of the strong, compact and well-organized Christian minority. Gallienus' edict was nevertheless a milestone (much more than his father's previous edict had been): the recognition of Christianity as a Church. Henceforward the State was to acknowledge the special position of the bishop of Rome (the pope). Other emperors had indirectly done the same. In periods of hostility and persecutions, it was always the bishop of Rome who had to be eliminated, as it happened with Pontianus, Fabian and Sixtus II ...

Emperor Decius (249-251). Musei Capitolini, Rome.

St. Felix I

Though he was Pope for six years (269-274) we know little of Felix. He was a Roman. He governed during a period of peace. Like his predecessor Dionysius, he advanced the organization and diffusion of the Church. He intervened decisively in defence of the true faith, which was still threatened by heretical sects, and in some disputes with the Eastern Church. He died on 30th December 274.

14. THE BISHOPS BURIED IN THE CRYPT OF THE POPES

We do not exactly know the names of the bishops buried in the Crypt of the Popes. The list in Sixtus III's catalogue refers to bishops buried in the whole Cemetery of St. Callixtus, but it does not state precisely where their tombs are to be found.

In the Crypt of the Popes de Rossi found just two fragments of inscriptions which refer to bishops. They are still there.

The first is to be seen under the inscription to St. Antherus: it is a fragment from the lid of a sarcophagus, with a name in Greek, Urban, followed by an engraved Ε (ἐπίσκοπος), meaning "bishop" (ICUR, IV, 10664).

The second is fixed on the right wall of the crypt, beside the fragments of St. Damasus' poem *"Tempore quo gladius"*... ("At the time when the sword"...). Another name in Greek is visible. It belonged to the epitaph of an African bishop, Numidian (ICUR, IV, 10663).

Both these bishops were named in the marble-catalogue above the door of the crypt. Since, as I have said, the piece of the sarcophagus of St. Urban was found among the debris in the Crypt of the Popes, it may well have come from one of the sarcophagi placed in the four niches. The same is true of St. Numidian's mutilated inscription.

---

[1] ICUR, IV, 11196.

[2] See map p. 50.

[3] The "Callixtian complex" belonged to the first ecclesiastical region and was under the authority of the *tituli* of St. Sabina, St. Prisca, St. Balbina, SS. Nereus and Achilleus, and St. Anastasia.

[4] For the *lapsi*, see p. 98.

[5] In this paragraph I rely on the work of Mons. J. Wilpert "La Cripta dei Papi...". Cf. Bibliography.

[6] "Multi sancti, multi martyres, alii quamplurimi, innumerabilis multitudo martyrum".

[7] "Sacratissimi imperatores praeceperunt etiam ne in aliquibus locis conciliabula fiant, nec coemeteria ingrediantur. Si quis itaque hoc tam salubre praeceptum non observaverit, capite plectetur" (cf. Acts St. Cypriani I, 7).

[8] "Xystum in coemeterio animadversum sciatis VII id. Aug. die et cum eo diacones quattuor" (St. Cyprian's letter 80, CSEL III, pars II, 839-840).

[9] ICUR, IV, 9513.

[10] The meaning is that the faithful tried to save the Pope at the cost of their own lives. ICUR, IV, 9514.

Cubiculum of the Sacraments A2: Moses strikes the rock, the fisherman and the multiplication of the bread and fish (1st half of the 3rd century). See p. 79.

VI.
The Area of the Popes and of St. Cecilia

The Crypt of St. Cecilia

1. THE ORIGIN AND DEVELOPMENT OF THE CRYPT

The Crypt of St. Cecilia was originally a *cubiculum* containing several "devotional tombs". Many Christians asked for a place of burial close to the martyrs, in order to benefit from their intercession.

There was also a well here. In the wall opposite the statue of the martyr, a well was dug fourteen meters deep. Water was absolutely indispensable for continuous masonry work. The semicircular depression of the well can still be seen along the wall.

When space was exhausted, after deepening the galleries in the "First Area", in the first half of the 3rd century it was decided to excavate another floor at a lower level. A staircase was dug, beginning from Gallery H, and after 25 steps down an old "pozzolana" pit was discovered.

The diggers quickly took safety measures, realizing that the Crypt of the Popes and of St. Cecilia lay above or beside pre-existing sandstone galleries. They reinforced the galleries and the stairs with solid walls. They also built retaining walls to correspond with those of the underlying sandstone galleries. Perhaps this crypt originally had its own light-shaft. In any case, it was widened in Damasus' time, to allow more comfort to the numerous visitors.

**Crypt of St. Cecilia: Statue of the Martyr
(copy from the original by Stefano Maderno, 1599 ca.).**

2. THE CRYPT OF ST. CECILIA BECOMES A SHRINE

Some time after the corpse of the martyred Cecilia was laid in the catacomb, "devotional tombs" multiplied there. Soon and quite frequently, enlargement work had to be done. It was just at this period that it became necessary to construct the *cryptoporticus* (underground chamber) to accomodate the faithful who crowded in.

Pope Damasus embellished both the Crypt of the Popes and that of St. Cecilia. The passageway between the two crypts was decorated with marble slabs and the vault with mosaics, of which only some faint traces now remain. A marble covering was also on the wall containing the niche where the Martyr was buried.

We can be certain that this Pope, so devoted to the martyrs, would also have had the walls of the crypt painted; but it is now difficult and almost impossible to discern traces of this work, because from the 4th to 9th century the sanctuary was regularly embellished and restored.

Even de Rossi, after his discovery, was compelled to reinforce the walls of the crypt and the *cryptoporticus* with masonry, arches and pilasters, to avoid any possible collapse. The majestic brick arch resting against the wall opposite the statue of St. Cecilia is recent work. It was built by Mons. Wilpert in 1909 following a subsidence in the floor of the crypt.

3. THE TRANSLATION OF THE MARTYR'S BODY TO TRASTEVERE

The Martyr's body lay where her statue is now and it remained there until 821, when Pope St. Paschal I (817-824) had it taken to the basilica dedicated to the Saint, in Trastevere. It was built on the site of her house.

The niche, emptied of the relics of the Martyr, was sealed off with a thin wall on which an inscription in Greek was placed. From the few bits found by de Rossi and put together with his usual skill, it seems that the epigraph referred to the translation of St. Cecilia's relics.

The statue seen now in the niche is a copy of the celebrated work by Maderno (1566-1636), which portrays the body of the Saint as it was found in 1599, when the sarcophagus was opened to identify its remains. Cardinal Paolo Sfondrati (1561-1618) commissioned Stefano Maderno to carve the statue of the Saint in the exact position in which the body lay, as the inscription relates:

"Paul, Cardinal of the title of St. Cecilia. Here I offer you the image of the holy virgin Cecilia which I myself saw lying intact in its sarcophagus, and which I have represented for you in this marble, in the exact position of the body".

The sculptor has given prominence to the cut of the sword on the neck, even though the beheading did not completely detach the head from the body. Moreover, Cecilia holds open three fingers of the right hand and only one of the left. In her agony and death she wished to show in this way her faith in the Trinity and Unity of God: one only God but in three persons: Father, Son and Holy Spirit.

While there is no doubt about the Martyr's existence, unfortunately we really do not know in which persecution she was killed, nor have we any certain details about her life.

4. SAINT CECILIA "PATRONESS OF MUSIC"

Previous to the 15th century, no literary or iconographical sources present St. Cecilia as a musician. In fact, Cimabue and Fra Angelico painted her simply with the palm of martyrdom.

The first representation of St. Cecilia with a musical instrument, the lyre, is found in a panel of 1420, in the Stadel Art Institute in Frankfurt-on-Main. Later, in 1516, Raphael has painted the Saint with several musical instruments in hand or at her feet.

Her relationship with music arose from a mistaken interpretation of a passage in the account of her *Passio*. It reads: *"Cantantibus organis, illa in corde suo soli Domino decantabat dicens: Fiat cor meum et corpus meum immaculatum, ut non confundar"*. That is, "While the musical instruments sounded (at her marriage feast), she in her heart raised a song of praise to her only Lord, saying: Let my heart and body be immaculate, so that I be not confounded".

Very soon, in translating this passage, the words *in corde suo* (in her heart) were left out, and thus the legend arose of St. Cecilia as a musician. Associations of singers sprang up asking her protection, and later on she was taken as "patroness of music".

5. THE FRESCOES

Besides the work of St. Damasus, St. Cecilia's crypt was embellished with mosaics and paintings. These were found along the walls and in the embrasure of the light-shaft. Very little of this imagery has come down to us.

On the embrasure of the light-shaft, after a very recent restoration, we can admire just a cross between two sheep, and a little lower down the martyrs Polycamus, Sebastian and Quirinus.

Polycamus is listed among the martyrs of the Cemetery of St. Callixtus in a 7th century topographical document, transcribed in a 12th century manuscript called the "Malmesbury Itinerary".

Quirinus was bishop of Siseia in Pannonia (Hungary). His body was translated *in catacumbas* in the 5th century. St. Sebastian was the best known martyr of the neighbouring cemetery named after him. He was an officer in the Imperial Guard of emperor Diocletian.

The names in Latin POLICAMVS - SABASTIANVS - CVRINVS are written above their portraits (ICUR, IV, 9526). Although time has badly worn these frescoes, they have been recently restored.

On the left wall, next to Cecilia's burial place, there are some more paintings.

In a small niche, Christ is represented with a halo on which a cross stands out. With his right hand he makes an orator's or teacher's gesture, while his left hand holds the Gospel, decorated with gems. Next to him is the figure of St. Urban (222-250), the martyred Pope mentioned in St. Cecilia's *Passio,* and buried in the neighbouring Catacomb of Praetextatus. The Pope is represented standing with a halo and the *pallium* (the badge of episcopal rank). The name is written vertically on the left of the figure and is preceded by a cross: + VRBAN(us).

Both pictures are in the Byzantine style. The Christ *pantocrator* (omnipotent) is dated between the end of the 8th century and the beginning of the 9th. The figure of St. Urban is in a more decadent style, of a later period.

Crypt of St. Cecilia: The martyrs Policamus, Sebastian and Quirinus (5ᵗʰ century fresco).

Above the niche with Christ *pantocrator* is a figure of St. Cecilia "orante", also in the Byzantine style and recently restored. It was painted over an earlier mosaic, as can be seen from some imprints of *tesserae* at her feet. This fresco and the Christ *pantocrator* are most probably the work of the same artist.

On the fresco of St. Cecilia there are graffiti with several names of priests. The names are regularly set out in four lines and do not appear in the usual confused way. This proves that those signatures had a well-defined purpose. De Rossi undoubtedly gives the right explanation. He says, they are the names of those who carried out the translation of the Martyr's relics. Indeed, one of those signatures is of a notary, (Hildebra)NDO SCRIN(ario). Cf. ICUR, IV, 9525.

The late dating of some frescoes in the catacombs (after the time of translation of the relics) should not surprise us. Some sanctuaries in fact, though deprived of their venerated bodies, were restored anew and visited for some decades.

6. A SENATOR AND A PRAETORIAN PREFECT

Along the walls of the crypt some fragmentary inscriptions are preserved. Three of them are worth remembering.

The memorial tablet in Greek of a senator Fronton and his wife Petilia Lampadia, dating to the end of the 3ʳᵈ century, offers us a splendid testimony of a profession of faith in the Lord.

The inscription is on the slab which sealed their tomb. It was originally set in the floor just in front of St. Cecilia's sepulchre. At each end of the slab two

"I, Septimius Fronton Pretextatus Licinian,
servant of God (Christian) lie here.
I shall never regret having lived an upright life.
I shall serve you even in heaven, O Lord,
and give thanks to your name.
I gave up my soul to God at 33 years and 6 months".
"Petilia (Lampà)dia, an illustrious lady
(senatorial rank) died
on the day... before the Kalends of November
at the age of ...years"[1].

symbolic figures were carved: the dove with an olive branch between its claws and the prophet Jonah resting.

In this crypt de Rossi discovered two more fragments of sarcophagus lids, bearing the names of their proprietors. The first belonged to Octavius Caecilianus, a member of a senatorial family, who died at the age of 44. In the second fragment a (Pompeia) Attica is mentioned, also of senatorial rank, who lived only 17 years, 3 months and 15 days. According to de Rossi "Octavius Caecilianus was the praetorian Prefect of Italy for the year 409. He was very zealous for the unity of the Church against the Donatists and delayed his Baptism until near his death, in about 415. He had the privilege, very rare in those days and almost fallen out of use, of being buried with his wife Pompeia Attica in the crypt next to the Martyr who was his namesake". This Caecilianus would confirm the tie between the Catacombs of St. Callixtus and the *gens Caecilia*, the donors of that estate. The letters V. C. and C. F. on the inscriptions are the initials of the words *vir clarissimus* and *clarissima femina*, honorific titles given to people of the senatorial class (ICUR, IV, 9707, 9655).

7. THE ORIGIN OF A LEGEND

The Catacombs of St. Callixtus contained the bodies of a fair number of martyrs. Some were quite famous: the Popes Pontianus, Fabian, Cornelius, Sixtus II and Eusebius. Young people who had shed their blood for Christ were also worthily represented in these catacombs: Tarcisius, Cecilia, Calocerus and

Parthenius... No wonder then that the faithful preferred to apply for this official cemetery of the Church of Rome for their final resting place.

Speaking of the excavation in the "First Area", I mentioned that the *fossores* gave a sympathetic hearing the requests of Christians to be buried near the tombs of the martyrs; and so they re-opened the tombs in the galleries closest to the Crypts of the Popes and of St. Cecilia, and put the bones of those "wretched" dead in the sandpit under St. Cecilia's crypt. The only fault of those poor fellows was that of having been born a hundred years earlier! Thus, little by little, this spot became a gigantic ossuary. When the "devotional burials" in these sanctuaries came to an end in the first half of the 5th century, the ossuary was walled up. The people of the time knew well who these heaped-up bones belonged to, but later on legends began to spring up.

As Mons. J. Wilpert explains, "Damasus' poem *'Hic congesta iacet...'* ('Here lies united...') had perhaps a wide influence. In the first line the poet Pope speaks of an 'army' of people buried in this holy place ('Here lies united an army of Saints'). In the two following lines he specifies that the expression 'army of Saints' refers to all the martyrs buried in the Cemetery of St. Callixtus ('These venerable tombs enclose their bodies, while the Kingdom of Heaven has already welcomed their souls').

However, the authors of the guidebooks for pilgrims, the *Itineraries*, written three centuries later, took a different view. They saw in those lines an allusion to a 'mass burial of martyrs'. There was a search for that

ossuary and it was easily identified with the one under the Crypt of St. Cecilia. At first this identification was qualified with a 'perhaps', but very soon that possibility was turned into a probability, and then it became a certainty.

In the end, they could even tell you the exact number of martyrs buried in that ossuary. The author of the *Notitia Ecclesiarum...* after naming the sepulchre of St. Cecilia, quickly adds 'eighty martyrs lie under there'. The *deorsum* (under there) refers undoubtedly to the ossuary we are discussing. A more accurate number would be 'eight hundred martyrs', as is given in another guidebook, *De locis sanctis Martyrum...*, dealing with the Cemetery of St. Callixtus, but its author does not commit himself in specifying where exactly they had been buried.

Also the author of *Notitia Ecclesiarum...* was content enough with a general indication, because in the 7th century the ossuary was no longer accessible".

In any case, even from a legend a fact can be drawn: the considerable size of this ossuary proves once again the profound veneration the Christians of the first centuries had for their Pastors, who had died as martyrs (the popes), as well as for St. Cecilia.

---

[1] ICUR, IV, 10685.

Springtime at the Catacombs of St. Callixtus.

VII.
The Area of the Popes and of St. Cecilia

The Cubicula of the Sacraments

Leaving the Crypt of St. Cecilia and going a little way along Gallery I to the left, Gallery B is reached, which is one of the original nuclei of the "First Area" (see map on p. 50). Beyond a gate on the left, traces of a very ancient stairway can be seen. As Fr. Fasola has shown in recent excavations, this stairway was used by the pilgrims of old to return to the open-air after their visit to the two most famous shrines of the catacomb: the Crypts of the Popes and of St. Cecilia.

The walls in this area have been restored, but going a little further on, an original part of recent excavations is reached. After some steps down a small staircase, which indicates a deepening of Gallery B, Gallery D opens on the right. This is without doubt the most spectacular and majestic of the whole catacomb. There has hardly been any restoration here. It is enough to imagine all the *loculi* sealed with marble slabs or tiles in order to envision the gallery as it was seen by the Christians in the 3rd and 4th centuries (see p. 47).

At the end of Gallery B we reach Gallery C. It is interesting to note the connection between these two galleries: walls and *loculi* have been dug out in a curved

Marble slab of Augurinus (3rd century).

form. Some way along Gallery C, two short galleries on the left (Q3 and Q2) lead to the Crypts of St. Gaius and St. Eusebius, but this is another area of the catacomb (see map on p. 50). In a passage near these crypts is the beautiful little epitaph of Augurinus, with the dove holding an olive branch in its beak (ICUR, IV, 9658).

Before entering Gallery A, above the narrow passage of Q3, a slab containing some symbols (the Good Shepherd, the fish, the anchor, the monogram of Christ...) has been fixed.

1. SOME CHARACTERISTICS OF GALLERY A

"The pagans — J. Janssens writes — surrounded their tombs especially with good wishes and farewell greetings. The Christians were no less attentive in caring for their own tombs... but their faith differed from the pagan mentality; through prayer, they were always united to their loved ones who had departed.

Their marble slabs contain many prayers and good wishes, among which many refer to the beatitude yearned for, or by, the deceased. They not only confirm that Christian burials took place in an atmosphere of prayer, but are also full of intimations on the Christian concept of beatitude. The Christians, when speaking of their dead, describe them in the light of faith as those who live in Christ".

The marble slabs

Two of them are particularly meaningful for the profession of faith in Jesus Christ and in the Holy Spirit.

AVGVRINE IN
DO M · ET ☧

"O Augurinus, may you live in my God and in Jesus Christ" (ICUR, IV, 9659).[1]

CAR(tilio) KYRIACO
FIL(io) DVLCISSIMO
VIBAS (i)N SPIRITO SA(ncto)

"To Cartilius Cyriacus, most sweet son, that you may live in the Holy Spirit" (ICUR, IV, 9716).[2]

Acclamations in the Roman tradition always expressed, singly or together, the idea of good wishes addressed to the person of the emperor or to some other illustrious personage. In the contemplative atmosphere of a cemetery, this tradition of acclamation was a voice raised by the living to the dead, in the hope that the departed would live in the peace of the Lord.

A third inscription in these marble slabs deals with the *Caecilii*, a further proof of the tie between this area and the illustrious family of the martyr Cecilia.

SERGIVS ALEXANDER
CAECILIE FAVSTAE
COIVGI SVE BENE
MERIENTI FECIT

"Sergius Alexander made (the tomb) for his wife Cecilia Fausta of happy memory". Cecilia is of course a surname which recalls that well-known Roman family, the *gens* that Fausta came from (ICUR, IV, 9706).

The illuminated loculus

This is a tomb designed for the burial of two persons, probably a married couple. It now contains the remains of small amphorae. This type of *loculus* is often found in the catacombs.

The "tomb of the carpenter"

The Cemetery of St. Callixtus has a quite limited number of sealed tombs. Some are found in this gallery. The first, just opposite the illuminated *loculus*, dates back to the early 3nd century. There is no name on the marble slab, but a carpenter's tool (a kind of saw) appears inscribed, as well as a small flask, the kind made from animal skins. This water skin, part of the carpenter's daily life, was perhaps an allusion to the *refrigerium*. They wished the deceased to find himself in divine peace, where he could quench his thirst.

As D. Mazzoleni writes, "from the very beginning, work was held in great esteem by Christian society, as is testified by many passages from the Fathers of the Church, beginning with St. Paul himself.

The ancient communities, ready to help those who were physically incapable of work, regarded work as a social and moral duty, a means of subsistence for oneself and one's family, but also as a necessary prerequisite if the practice of other forms of charity were to be made possible.

These ideas were destined to be expressed in palaeochristian art. In fact a number of carvings and paintings show the faithful working at their particular trades.

Representations of trades and their related tools appear on the marble slabs, often in a naïve and crude form, but surely with great immediacy...

In general the percentage of those who indicate their trade is relatively small, at least in proportion to archaeological evidence. The existing repertory appears very composite, and certain occupations have not appeared...

It is important to stress that, from the examination of the Christian inscriptions referring to trades or

Scales inscribed
upon the marble slab
of a merchant.

78

professions, no standard formula emerges, which would indicate a specific Christian thought about work, at least nothing new compared with that of the pagans.

The fact remains that the sparse indications offered in the inscriptions give us some idea of the different components of early Christian society, in which members of the different social classes were buried together in the cemeteries of the primitive Church, united in one faith without any evident social distinction".

Immediately after the "tomb of the carpenter", the *Cubicula* of the Sacraments are to be seen, for which Gallery A is deservedly renowned.

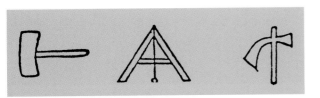

2. THE CUBICULA OF THE SACRAMENTS

The reunited family awaiting the resurrection

"It is well known that in the culture of ancient Rome the family was held in great honour. This tradition, along with the custom of constructing family tombs, has survived among the Christians. The fact that the latter made use of the communal cemeteries made such private constructions less necessary. Nonetheless, the Christians also wanted to be buried in the same tomb with those who had shared the happiness of a family life and from whom death had now separated them" (J. Janssens).

We may be surprised at seeing such family tombs in communal cemeteries like the catacombs, as if they stressed social differences and distinctions between rich and poor. Some explanation may help.

We know from history that the Christians made converts among the poor, as well as among the Roman patricians and the wealthier classes. Christ's message on the use of riches is explicit: "Give what is in your cups and plates to the poor" (*Luke* 11, 41).

This Gospel teaching had been truly put into pratice by the early Christians. The catacombs in fact originated from the generosity of some well-off Christians who provided land for the burial of their more destitute brethren. Thus, having fulfilled the precept of Christian charity (giving what was necessary to everybody), those who could afford it were free to build a family tomb for themselves. It goes without saying that in many of those family tombs decent burial was also provided for many slaves freed by their Christian masters.

And the Church too gave free burial to the poorer faithful. As J. Janssens writes, "the desire to share the same tomb mainly has its origin in the human sentiment that having lived together, people wanted to be still united in death".

The expression "*Cubicula* of the Sacraments" refers to five small chambers or family tombs (Q6 to Q2), particularly noteworthy for their important frescoes.

The reasons for some paintings

The frescoes in these *cubicula* date from the beginning of the 3rd century and represent symbolically the sacraments of Christian initiation: Baptism and the Eucharist.

At this point, we may ask why scenes of Baptism and Eucharist are so frequently repeated on tombs. What did the early Christians wish to confide and tell us by those images?

A partial answer has been already given when talking about the fundamental concept which is present in all early Christian art: the central idea of salvation through Christ, and continued in the Church with the sacraments.

With these drawings the Christians of the first centuries wished to recall their catechumenate and leave a message to their contemporaries. They had become Christians through Baptism and had persevered in their Christian life with frequent Eucharistic communion. They also wanted to remind their dear ones, and whoever visited their tombs, that one day they would be united again if they shared the same means of salvation.

The sacraments of Christian initiation

Along with the Good Shepherd and the "Orante" (see p. 37), representations of Baptism and of the Eucharist (the two main sacraments for attaining

79

Cubiculum of the Sacraments A3:
The fisherman and Jesus baptized by St. John the Baptist in the river Jordan
(1st half of the 3rd century).

Cubiculum of the Sacraments A6:
Multiplication of the bread and fish, prefigurations of the Eucharist
(1st half of the 3rd century).

Cubiculum of the Sacraments A3. From left to right: the Baptism of Christ, the paralytic man, a digger, imposition of hands on the bread, the multiplication of the bread and fish, the sacrifice of Abraham ... In the upper part of the wall: the prophet Jonah (1st half of the 3rd century).

salvation) are the most frequently used in early Christian art. The *Cubicula* of the Sacraments are a clear proof of this.

a) *Baptism*

1. Moses and Jesus

As the Fathers of the Church taught in their writings, these means of salvation were prefigured in the Old Testament. This appears in the miracle of Moses striking the rock, enabling the Jewish people to quench their thirst in the desert (*Exodus* 17, 1-7). This biblical episode is to be seen on the entrance walls in *cubicula* A6 and A3 and on the left wall in A2. The Baptism of Jesus is also a prefiguration of Christian Baptism. The scene of John baptizing Jesus in the Jordan is depicted on the left wall in *cubiculum* A3.[3]

In the meeting with the Samaritan woman at the well of Sichem, Jesus spoke of a mysterious water: whoever drinks it will never thirst again (*John* 4, 1-26). This water is a symbol of the grace that the Christian will obtain through Baptism (entrance wall, *cubiculum* A3). The oldest representation of a true Christian Baptism is found on the back wall in *cubiculum* A2: the person who is baptising places his right hand on the head of the candidate who is immersed in the water.

2. The fisherman and the paralytic

To grasp the meaning of the fisherman episode, we ought to read a passage by Tertullian, an apologist of the late 2nd and early 3rd centuries. He calls Christians "little fishes" caught by the great Fish, Christ. He states that Christians were born in the water through Baptism, and can only be saved by remaining in the water, that is, in the grace offered by Baptism.[4] The fisherman is represented on the left wall of both *cubicula* A3 and A2.

As for the episode of the paralytic in the pool of Bethzatha (*John* 5, 1-16), we know from the Gospel that, from time to time, the angel of the Lord came down and stirred the water in the pool, and the first invalid to enter the water after that was healed. The

**Cubiculum
of the Sacraments A6:
Jonah thrown into the sea
(1st half of the 3rd century).**

82

miracle of the paralytic very soon became for the early Christians one of their favourite symbols of Baptism. In *cubiculum* A5 we see the healed paralytic going off happily with his stretcher on his back.

b) *The Eucharist*

1. The multiplication of the loaves

The Eucharist is prefigured in the miracle of the manna, worked by God to feed the Hebrews journeying in the desert (*Exodus* 16, 1-36), and also in that mysterious bread which nourished Elijah and gave him strength to walk for 40 days (*I Kings* 19, 1-8). As seen in the *cubicula*, for Christians the first preference for symbols of the Eucharist goes to the miracle of the multiplication of the loaves and fishes (*John* 6, 1-15).

Through this miracle, Jesus promised a very particular and different bread: his body (*John* 6, 22-59).

The scene of the multiplication of the loaves is repeated always in the same way: seven persons sit round a table. The number seven is symbolic and indicates that all are called by God to be saved. Two or three dishes with loaves and fishes are placed on the table, and at the sides of the table are baskets of bread which may contain seven to twelve loaves.

2. The Mass

Cubiculum A3 needs special mentioning. On the back wall to the left, a youthful figure places his hands on a loaf and a fish. A veiled "Orante" is beside him. Thanks to the "Orante" (the soul in blessed peace), the scene becomes a clear allusion to the Eucharist. By the mystery of transubstantiation the consecrated bread becomes ΙΧΘΥΣ, i.e. Jesus Christ, the Son of God, the Saviour. Whoever eats this consecrated bread (in other words, whoever receives Holy Communion) becomes an "Orante", a saved soul in peace, and will see God.

If we also bear in mind the other two paintings close by, the seven at table and the sacrifice of Abraham, we have a symbolic portrayal of the Holy Mass as sacrifice and sacrament: the consecration in the laying-on of hands, communion in the group of the seven. The sacrifice of the cross, which is mystically (in a mysterious but real way) perpetuated in the Mass, is called to mind by the sacrifice of Abraham, a prefiguration of that of Christ (*Genesis* 22, 1-19).

The Biblical Jonah

Jonah, the prophet so loved by the early Christians

The prophet Jonah, a biblical figure very dear to the early Christians, appears in all these *cubicula*. Jonah had preached repentance and conversion to the inhabitants of Nineveh, a city of the Assyrian empire. They believed in him and therefore had been saved by the mercy of God. Jonah symbolizes the call to salvation of everyone whether Jews or pagans. Indeed, since the faithful buried in these *cubicula* were originally all pagans, the prophet came to be the image of God's universal mercy.

Jonah is also a symbol of resurrection. Jesus himself quotes Jonah as a figure of this reality: "In the same way that Jonah spent three days and nights in the big fish, so will the Son of Man spend three days and nights in the depths of the earth" (*Matthew* 12, 40).

Jonah at grips with a strange sea monster

Jonah, no doubt, was much loved by the early Christians. His fascinating and eventful story is told in the Bible *(The book of Jonah)*.

God ordered the prophet to go to Niniveh and preach repentance. But Jonah is afraid that he will be killed and prefers to escape in a ship. The Lord, displeased with this disobedience, allows a storm to threaten the boat with shipwreck. Jonah's companions, superstitiously, draw lots to discover who is to blame for their predicament. Jonah is unmasked and at once thrown into the sea.

But God has pity on the rebel. The prophet, swallowed by a strange creature, more like a monster than a whale,[5] is cast ashore after three days.

In the *Cubicula* of the Sacraments, the story of Jonah is shown either in a single scene or in groups of them, called "cycles".

One of these "cycles" is on the left wall of *cubiculum* A6: Jonah thrown into the sea, the prophet swallowed by the cetacean (also called *pistrix*), and finally Jonah left on the seashore. Other "cycles" appear in the highest part of walls, or "lunettes", in *cubicula* A3 and A2. On the right wall of *cubiculum* A5, the prophet is seen resting under a vine.

**Cubiculum of the Sacraments A3:
Jesus and the Samaritan woman
(1st half of the 3rd century). See p. 79.**

The area called St. Miltiades: An "Orante".

On the ceilings of A4 and A2 the Good Shepherd is represented, and on the entrance wall of A6, Lazarus coming alive from the tomb, symbol of the resurrection of the Christians.

In each corner of the back wall in *cubiculum* A3, the figure of *a fossor*, with his spade on his shoulder, is seen. The *fossores* were the humble diggers and patient creators of all that intricate network of underground galleries.

3. CUBICULUM A1

No ancient decorations in *cubiculum* Al have been preserved. In the late 4th century, this small room was turned into a passageway, to allow the pilgrims, after visiting the tombs of the Martyrs in the "First Area", to reach the Crypts of Lucina (see map on p. 155). The *cubiculum* is at a higher level, because it was excavated before Gallery A was deepened, and before the other *cubicula* A2, A3, A4, A5, as well as the Crypt of the Popes, were created. At a later date, after further digging, *cubiculum* A6 was made.

4. THE "MARTYRS' STAIRCASE"

It is at the beginning of Gallery A. It is one of the two stairs from which the first nucleus of the Cemetery of St. Callixtus was developed. It was excavated about the middle of the 2nd century and still preserves steps of that period.

It was called the "Martyrs' Staircase" because the popes buried in the nearby crypt passed that way. It is also thought that young Tarcisius used it when he came to pray at the tombs of the martyr popes, or to fetch the Eucharist and carry it to the Christians in prison or in their homes during persecution.

---

[1] This monogram is composed of interlaced initials of, the words Jesus Christ: Ἰησοῦς Χριστός = I. X. = ☧.

[2] A certain number of paleochristian inscriptions are not free of errors. This is because the stone cutter was unskilled or poorly instructed. Sometimes they wrote as they spoke, in a popular and ungrammatical Latin.

[3] The Baptism of Christ is distinguished from any other baptismal scene by the presence of the dove, which represents the Holy Spirit.

[4] "Nos pisciculi, secundum ἰχθύν nostrum Jesum Christum in aqua nascimur nec aliter quam in aqua permanendo salvi sumus" (Tert., De Baptismo I. CSEL XX, 201).

[5] "Leviathan the fleeing serpent, Leviathan the twisting serpent" of which the Bible speaks. Cf. *Isaiah* 27, 1; *Psalm* 104, 26.

VIII.
The Area called
St. Miltiades

From the Area of the Popes and of St. Cecilia Gallery P1 leads to another area of the catacombs, that of St. Miltiades. It was excavated in the second half of the 3rd century as part of that which was to take the name of SS. Gaius and Eusebius. This area has no staircase of its own. It consists of three levels, but only the second one is of notable size.

Some peculiarities are immediately noticeable in this area: the presence of many *cubicula* (they are not many in the "First Area", except for those of the Sacraments), and there are a lot of *arcosolia*, both inside the *cubicula* and along the walls of the galleries.

Gallery P1 is rather wide. It was constantly used for the visits to the martyrs' tombs, because it was the route that the ancient pilgrims had to take from the Crypts of the Popes and of St. Cecilia in order to reach to the tomb of the martyred Pope St. Cornelius, in the area of the Crypts of Lucina.

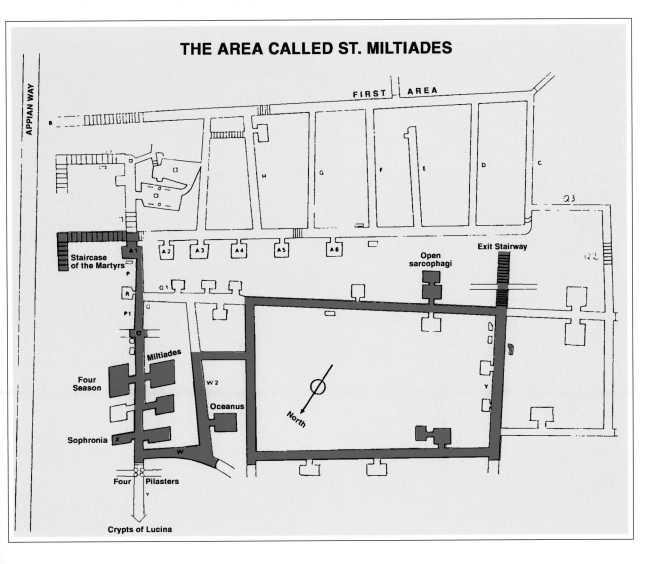

THE AREA CALLED ST. MILTIADES

Perhaps in one of these *cubicula* a venerated tomb was located, but no document has come to light so far to prove it, nor is it enough to point to the presence of *formae* in the floor of the main gallery.

Some *cubicula*, as can be seen, were carefully decorated: walls covered with plaster or marble, painted *arcosolia* and mosaics on their arches... There are also some pictures.

In the second *cubiculum* on the left there is still a little round table which carried oil lamps.

The mythological phoenix, symbol of the resurrection of the body.

1. SMALL OIL LAMPS AND SYMBOLS

After leaving the Martyrs' Staircase, immediately on the right, in a *loculus* of former *cubiculum* A1, some lamps and small terracotta and glass vessels for perfumes have been placed.

2. THE EPITAPHS

The inscriptions located in this area are nearly all found in the first part of Gallery P1.

Priest Julian

Past the above mentioned symbols, on the left begins Gallery Q1, which is 160 metres long. It is a *decumanus*, or main gallery, from which the other side-galleries, called *cárdines*, branch out. In the corner are two inscriptions concerning priests. On one, IVLIA-NVS · PRESBYTER (Julian, priest) is written. The other, though mutilated and without a name, reads: PRESBYTER · IN PACE (priest in the peace of the Lord). Cf. ICUR, IV, 9944, 10354.

The phoenix

Immediately after a crossing[1] with a wide light-shaft, high up on the right is an impressive carving: a phoenix with rays and an aureole surrounding its head (ICUR, IV, 10785).

Irene

Above the *arcosolium* on the right, which still preserves traces of its ancient decoration, there is the beautiful little marble slab of Irene. The Christians of the first centuries greatly loved symbolism. This inscription is full of it, thanks to the name of the dead girl, Irene which means "peace".

Irene is represented as an "Orante" in the peace of heaven. Beside her is the preeminent symbol of peace, the dove. And if this were not enough, the dove holds an olive branch in its beak, the symbol of peace which Irene enjoys in heaven (ICUR, IV, 10598).

"Aquilina sleeps in peace"

In the last *cubiculum* on the left, is an inscription so meaningful that it needs no explanation: *"Aquilina dormit in pace"* (Aquilina sleeps in peace). Death for a Christian is only a state of sleep, a waiting for the final resurrection. Alongside is carved the dove with the usual olive branch in its beak. A clear allusion to the soul of Aquilina who now lives in the peace of the Lord (ICUR, IV, 9642).

3. THE CRYPT OF THE "REFRIGERIUM"

In the old *Itineraries* Pope St. Miltiades (311-314) is mentioned as being buried in the Cemetery of St. Callixtus, in an area near the Crypt of the Popes. Unfortunately his tomb has not yet been identified. The attribution of the first crypt to the left in Gallery P as St. Miltiades' burial place is only de Rossi's hypothesis. At the present state of research, it remains still unproven.

The room is spacious and lower than the gallery from which it is approached. It is 4.18 metres long, not counting the depth of the niche, and 4.20 metres wide, practically a square room.

Originally it was used for liturgical assemblies and for rites of *refrigerium* (the usual family annual commemoration). Indeed a ledge was excavated in the tufa along the walls to serve as a seat. Near the door there

are traces of two small chairs placed slightly higher, intended for those who presided at such public or family gatherings.

At first, according to de Rossi's theory, the crypt had no tomb. Then two *arcosolia* were opened in the side walls and, later still, in the end wall a large opening or niche was excavated, with a depressed arch, to accomodate a monumental sarcophagus.

This burial chamber was built with a barrel vault and painted in its entirety. Undoubtedly it must have been beautiful and inviting. This is confirmed by the rich decorations revealed by a recent restoration. It is in an elegant and classical style, not bound to biblical themes, surely done by a real artist. Its frescoes date back to the 3rd century.

Part of the plaster has fallen down, but it is still possible to admire the painting of a personage placed in a circle with a *virga* (rod) in his hand. Moreover what remains of the pictorial composition is animated by birds, garlands of leaves, stylized flowers, linear motifs and some ornamental figurines typical of classical art (a putto, a girl dancing, a sea monster...), as can be seen on the upper part of the light-shaft's opening.

This light-shaft, now closed, is in the roof of the gallery, just in front of the entrance door. The room was decorated up to the vault with layers of marble, of which remain the imprints and a few fragments.

In the floor, on the right, is the epitaph of Paul, an "exorcist", buried with his wife or daughter Martyria (*"Paul, exorcist... Burial of Martyria, the 6th day before..."*. ICUR, IV, 10026). The exorcist's task was to lay hands on catechumens and the sick and the possessed, to free them from evil spirits.

Inside the crypt, de Rossi found the lid of a huge sarcophagus, the largest ever discovered in the Roman catacombs. It well suited the magnificence of this burial chamber.

We do not know whether this lid was reused by the Christians, or whether it fell from above because of a subsidence. But we should not be far wrong in ascribing it to the owner of the crypt. At the moment, this lid is under the niche where the monumental sarcophagus originally stood. Due to its cuspidate shape, similar to an enormous roofing tile, the excavators (the modern *fossores*) called this room the "cripta del coppo".

Epitaph of Irene with the dove (3rd century).

At each end of the lid, in the *acrotéria*, one bucolic scene is carved: on the right, a shepherd resting with his faithful dog; on the left, another shepherd playing a *sýrinx* (a reed pipe).

4. POPE SAINT MILTIADES

St. Miltiades' burial place has not yet been identified, but the oldest documents agree on his being buried in the Cemetery of St. Callixtus. Who was this Pope?

He succeeded St. Eusebius and was elected on 2nd July 311, *sede vacante* (after a period of vacancy). He came from Africa. During his pontificate, emperor Maxentius returned to the Church its possessions, which had been confiscated under Diocletian's persecution.

A zealous pastor concerned with the spiritual welfare of his flock, Pope Miltiades was a vigilant defender of the faith threatened by the schism of the Donatists, who denied the validity of Baptism administered by heretics.

He died on 10th January 314, assured that Christians were, at last, free to profess their faith in peace. In fact, the two emperors of the time, Constantine and Licinius, with the Edict of Milan of the previous year, had reached an agreement and established that Christianity was no longer to be considered an "illegal religion" in the Roman empire.

St. Miltiades was the last pope to be buried in a crypt in the Cemetery of St. Callixtus. From then on, with the freedom of worship sanctioned by State authority, the "Church of the Catacombs" came to the surface: oratories, mausoleums and basilicas sprang up everywhere, particularly near the old cemeteries. SS. Silvester, Mark, Julius, Liberius and Damasus, who all succeeded St. Miltiades, were the first popes to be buried in those new buildings above ground.

5. THE CUBICULUM OF THE FOUR SEASONS

The little room opposite St. Miltiades' Crypt is called the "*Cubiculum* of the Four Seasons", because personifications of them are painted in its ceiling. Along the walls there are also floral decorations birds in flight, dolphins...

As L. de Bruyne points out, "the art of the catacombs was able to absorb, in a purified form, some artistic themes which for the Christian world had become expressions of hope in a happier life beyond this world. It adopted the innocent poetry of the ancient myth of Orpheus, who sings and plays the lyre among the animals and skilfully transformed it into a symbol of Christ. Or it made use of the myth of Cupid who gathers flowers for Psyche (the soul) in the Elysian Fields.

And why should the Christian art of the catacombs have had to reject the symbolism of the continuity of life, of perpetual renewal expressed in the cosmic figurations of the four seasons, with their attributes of roses, ears of corn, grapes and olives, from which they could create a rich flowering of elements at once decorative and symbolic?".

The dome of St. Peter's Basilica seen from the Callixtian grounds.

6. SORROW MADE MORE BEARABLE BY FAITH: SOPHRONIA

The "*Cubiculum* of Sophronia" is at the end of Gallery P1 on the right, just before a gate. It is so called because the name of that woman appears in some graffiti: two of them on the left of the back wall in the *cubiculum,* and two more in a wall close to the Crypt of the Popes.

Probably this is the story: a Christian, perhaps called Felicissimus, deeply saddened by the loss of his beloved wife, went down one day into the catacombs in search of comfort. At the bottom of the stairs, he wrote a prayer on the wall: "O Sophronia, may you live". A little later, in a small gallery near by, he repeated the name, sure that the dead woman continued to live in God: "Sophronia (lives) in the Lord".

Praying at the tombs of the Martyrs, Felicissimus' great sorrow lost all its bitterness, and faith enlightened him on the fate of his sweet Sophronia. Reaching the *cubiculum,* he felt the need to write: "O sweet Sophronia, you will live forever in God". And as if that were not enough, tenderness overflowed from his heart with great serenity: "Yes, Sophronia, you will always live!" (ICUR, IV, 10195; see also ICUR, IV, 10194).

7. THE MYTHICAL OCEANUS IN THE CATACOMB

Leaving Gallery P1 and turning to the left through the short Gallery W, Gallery W2 is reached (see map on p. 85). Almost at the beginning of it on the right, the "*Cubiculum* of Oceanus" is to be seen. It is so called after the mythical personification of the sea painted on the vault.

It is modest in size, decorated with strongly marked red bands. Birds, peacocks, genii, floral decorations and a painted bust of a dead woman appear on the walls and on the vault.

In D. Mazzoleni's remarks, "Christian art did not spring up suddenly from nothing, disowning the past and ignoring the pagan representation of its time. If the originality of its ideas is beyond discussion, its forms of expression do not lack contact with the world in which it lived... We may also include in this group of images the bearded head of Oceanus still with some pagan significance". The *cubiculum* was illuminated from a light-shaft, now walled up, which was situated in P1 and accessible through an opening in the roof.

8. THE SARCOPHAGUS OF THE CHILD

The "Sarcophagus of the Child" is so called because of its size. It belongs to the first mid-4th century. After several vicissitudes it is now placed, without its lid, in the Eastern *Trichora*.

This sarcophagus may be regarded as a concise illustrated catechism. Indeed the entire front is sculptured with biblical episodes: Noah in the ark with the dove above him, a prophet holding the scroll of the divine law, Daniel in the lion's den, a child praying between two saints, the miracle of Cana and the raising of Lazarus[2]... Kneeling at the feet of Jesus is Mary the sister of Lazarus (*John* 11, 32). At the centre of the lid two little genii are holding the tablet *(tabula)*. At each end is sculpted an ornamental face.

The symbolism of the figures

The scenes on this sarcophagus describe real events and reveal a profound symbolism, which is also explained by the catechesis of the Fathers of the Church.

Noah in the ark recalls the Flood and the following destruction of sinful mankind. The Flood therefore becomes a symbol of Baptism which destroys evil and sin in the heart of man (*Genesis* 8, 1-19). Daniel in the lion's den is shown as "Orante". He is imagined, therefore, as free of all danger and in blessed peace. The prophet Habakkuk offers him a loaf with the monogram of Christ impressed on it. Hence the reference is not so much to the material bread which satisfied Daniel's hunger in that tragic circumstance, but rather to the Eucharist (*Daniel* 14, 30-42).

The child too, at the centre, is as an "Orante" accompanied by two saints. Then follow the scenes of the miracle of Cana (*John* 2, 1-11) and of the raising of Lazarus (*John* 11, 1-44).

The succession of the scenes is not fortuitous, and the message is at once evident. A Christian is born to divine life through Baptism (Noah). This divine life is nourished by the bread (Habakkuk) and the wine (Cana) consecrated in the Mass, that is, with Holy Communion. The Eucharist is offered as a pledge of final resurrection (Lazarus).

The "Sarcophagus of the Child" with biblical scenes (1st half of the 4th century).

In this way a Christian (the child) will reach and live in Paradise ("Orante"). We find the following words of Jesus echoed here: "Whoever eats my flesh and drinks my blood has eternal life, and I will raise him to life on the last day" (*John* 6, 54).

The central figure unfinished

The face of the child in this sarcophagus is sculpted roughly. It is known that in the 4th century, Christian sarcophagi were produced in workshops by craftsmen, who used to leave the shape of one face only partially carved. At the moment of sale, the sculptor had to trace the likeness of the dead person on that unfinished face. Perhaps this was not done here because the buyer was in a hurry.

Furthermore, at the centre of the lid, two little genii hold a tablet where the name of the deceased and the date of his burial should have been carved. Unfortunately, this too was omitted.

9. THE INCREDIBLE WALK OF THREE FRIENDS

Near the exit stairs, on the left, there are two *arcosolia*. The first has a double niche. It is painted with a strong reddish tint. Of the various scenes represented, the only recognizable one is that of the three young men thrown into the fiery furnace by King Nebuchadnezzar of Babylon.

A fourth figure also appears, the angel who allowed those young friends to walk through the flames unharmed (*Daniel* 3, 8-30). The punishment was decreed by the king because the three youths, believing in God, refused to adore the statues of the monarch.

An ancient pilgrim, visiting the Roman catacombs, came frequently across images from the Old Testament decorating *cubicula* and *arcosolia* (Noah in the ark, the sacrifice of Abraham, Daniel in the lions' den, the three youths in the fiery furnace of Babylon, the story of prophet Jonah, Susannah accused by the elders...).

These are all figures or symbols of God's divine intervention, delivering people from some grave danger. Christians also can benefit from God's help if they imitate the faith of those just ones, who are often portrayed as "Oranti", because they already enjoy eternal peace.

In the centre of the second *arcosolium* there is an image of the Good Shepherd. In the arch, an "Orante", and along the walls, pastoral scenes, with ducks and a he-goat.

The composition shows that "the Church allowed the places of final rest to contain the same art that adorned the houses of her children during their earthly life. Everything which could make them forget the sadness of separation and the coldness of death was reproduced in the *cubiculum*: the cheerful walls of stucco, the play of friezes in lively colours, flowers, garlands, birds, all reminders of countryside life... Everything that was enchanting for mankind during this life was concentrated within the tomb, so that relations and friends who came to pray for their brethren should still feel the pleasant air of home" (L. de Bruyne).

10. "REMEMBER, THAT THOU ART DUST"

The "*Cubiculum* of the Sarcophagi" is in Gallery Q1, a few metres from the exit stairway. It was de Rossi who found here the two sarcophagi, buried together with that of the "Child" in the floor of the double *cubiculum*.

In the 4th century, during the reign of Constantine, conversions to Christianity steadily increased. Little by little the Christian community in Rome called upon expert sculptors capable of preparing a series of sarcophagi with all the repertory of figures and scenes drawn from the Bible.

The sarcophagus on the left had a lid consisting of a heavy slab of re-used marble; now it is propped against the wall. The roughly carved name of Alexandra can be read. In all probability the name has nothing to do with the dead person, whose remains are hardly recognizable inside the sarcophagus. On the outer side of the sarcophagus, at the centre, is the image of a dead woman, her head covered with a veil. In her left hand she holds the scroll of the Gospels, the true doctrine which has illuminated her life on earth. The Good Shepherd is represented at both ends for symmetry.

The other sarcophagus on the right contains a dead man wrapped in a shroud and tightly bound in bandages. Christians did not mummify their dead. The outer side of the sarcophagus has no sculpture but a simple strigil pattern (an S-shaped design), resembling waves.

11. THE EXIT STAIRWAY

At this point, the normal tourist route to the Catacombs of St. Callixtus comes to an end. The exit staircase was built in the second half of the 3rd century to open up both the Areas of St. Miltiades and that of SS. Gaius and Eusebius.

The staircase was built with salvaged materials. The lower part is original, and the stucco on the walls is also ancient. About half way up, there is a landing which is modern (XVII cent. ca.); but prior to de Rossi, it adjoined the two galleries on the first floor.

This junction modified the upper part of the staircase. Cutting out a step involved lowering all the others, as can easily be seen along the walls. The last flight of the stairs, which leads to the surface, was completely rebuilt in modern times.

At the time when the catacomb had become the shrine of the martyrs, this staircase was used to facilitate visits to the tombs of Popes Gaius and Eusebius and of the martyrs Calocerus and Parthenius.

In fact, at the bottom of the stairs Gallery Y and the first part of Gallery Q1 were quite obviously walled up, thus making an obligatory and safe route for pilgrims.

Near the exit door some "terracotta" bricks bearing the imperial seal are shown. Brickworks were mostly imperial property. Their marks confirm this: "*Ex praediis D.N. Imp...*", i.e., a tile which comes "from the factory of our lord the emperor...".

It is interesting that the temperature in the catacombs is always constant, at 15° C. The difference of temperature within compared to the external one is particularly felt in summertime.

---

[1] The left hand gallery has a stair which goes down to the third floor.

[2] This last scene shows Jesus holding in his left hand the scroll of the Gospel, the Word of salvation, and in his right hand a staff, a sign of his divine power.

IX.
The Area of SS. Gaius and Eusebius

The Historic Crypts

1. THE CEMETERY COMPLEX OF ST. GAIUS

This is the area which was excavated independently from the "First Area" and has its own staircase (Z on the map, which is the present exit staircase). It originated towards the end of the 3rd century, around 280. In the late 4th century a first floor was also excavated, but its extent was limited.

In Pope Damasus' time, Galleries Q2 and Q3 linked this area with that of the Popes and of St. Cecilia; thus the Cemetery of St. Callixtus was enlarged.

In the first part of Gallery Q1 (about 19 metres) and at a depth of 11.35 metres, a cemetery complex was developed, made up of several *cubicula* with particular characteristics. These burial chambers differ from the norm in a number of ways. A clear indication that we are in a privileged area is the presence of venerable tombs.

The St. Gaius complex has a history of five centuries. In its first phase it developed like any other underground cemetery. After the middle of the 4th century, with Pope Damasus' renovations, the area was profoundly altered: the complex became a real monumental shrine.

The first indication of this is to be seen in Gallery Q1 starting from the staircase, where the tufa walls of all galleries have been reinforced with brick walls and covered with white stucco. The little loopholes on the right wall allow us to see the *arcosolia*, which the restructuring had covered up.

A third period, from the 6th century onwards, saw the barbarian invasions of the Goths and Lombards. These brought serious damage to the catacombs.

Much restoration work was done until the beginning of the 9th century, when the cemetery complex was finally given up.

2. THE CRYPT OF POPE ST. GAIUS

The Crypt of St. Gaius has a special place in this cemetery complex because of its exceptional proportions.[1] It can hold more than sixty persons! It was never deepened or reconstructed. From the beginning, it was designed on this scale to provide for the community assemblies. By means of the ample light-shaft in Gallery Q1, the crypt was well lit and sufficiently ventilated.

The decorations are sober: the walls were covered with a single layer of white stucco. It is no surprise that during Damasus' pontificate this crypt was not embellished with marble like its neighbour, the Crypt of St. Eusebius. The absence of a poem by Damasus was perhaps one of the reasons why that was not done. Anyway, the poet-Pope could not have taken care of all tombs of the martyrs and of his predecessors. No doubt he made his selections for pastoral reasons. This alone can explain certain preferences in the writings of his epigrams.

When de Rossi discovered this crypt in 1856, it was entirely obstructed with debris and the roof had largely fallen in. The illustrious archaeologist was able to identify it when he found nine fragments of the Greek funerary inscription of St. Gaius at the foot of the stairs and beneath the light-shaft.

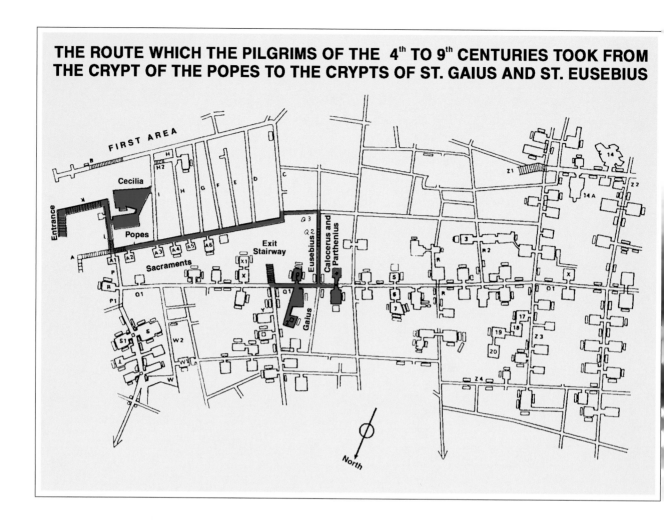

There are also numerous graffiti by priests and pilgrims on the walls of this crypt.

3. THE TOMB OF ST. GAIUS

While there are very many *loculi* on the side walls of the crypt, on the end wall there are only three. The *loculus* in the middle stands out because of its size. It is the most important in the whole crypt.

It is neatly cut in the tufa and at a remarkable distance from the other two. Perhaps it was originally covered in marble and its outer edge decorated with a line of red paint.

The tomb would suggest a bishop rather than a martyr. In fact, we know that when those witnesses of the Faith were buried, they were usually put in common tombs.

But why, it may be asked, was St. Gaius not buried in the Crypt of the Popes? An easy answer is not available. It may be that at the time of his death the spaces were all filled.

St. Gaius' tomb quickly became important for the faithful of Rome. Indeed an inscription, dating back to the first half of the 4th century (now in the Liberian Area), states that the area of the catacomb near his tomb was named after him: "Jovina ... bought an *arcosolium* in Callixtus near St. Gaius" (ICUR, IV, 9924).

4. THE SEPULCHRAL INSCRIPTION

Once de Rossi had pieced together the nine fragments which he had found, he was able to reconstruct the Greek sepulchral inscription of Pope St. Gaius.

Γ(αϊο)Υ ΕΠΙ(σκόπου)
ΚΑΤ(άθεσις)
ΠΡ(ὸ ί) ΚΑΛ(ανδῶν) ΜΑΙΩ(ν)
"Burial of Gaius, bishop. April 22" [2].

Biographical information on this Pope is also scarce, perhaps because of the destruction of the Church's archives under Diocletian. Hagiographical traditions[3] about St. Gaius abound, but they are not historically reliable.

He came from Dalmatia, was elected pope on 17th December 283, and died on 22nd April 296. The entire pontificate of Gaius was within Diocletian's reign during the period when this emperor had not yet begun persecuting the Christians.

5. THE AFRICAN BISHOP SAINT OPTATUS

Dealing with the Crypt of St. Gaius, I emphasized the simplicity of its decorations. If we look carefully at the lower part on the left wall, however, it is possible to make out the small and singular *arcosolium*. It is greatly damaged, with its walls knocked down, and partly hidden by one of the three pillars of the crypt.

This *arcosolium* has peculiar characteristics: its reduced size makes it more suitable for placing relics rather than for an entire dead body. Its location also seems very awkward, since it is partly below the floor of the crypt. It still has traces of mosaic decoration.

All these features suggest that it was the tomb of an important person, created at a late period in a space still available in the crypt, and close to a venerated tomb.

During his excavations, de Rossi found, in the Crypt of St. Gaius, in that of St. Eusebius and in the nearby area, some fragments[4] of an epitaph which names a bishop of Vescere (in Numidia). De Rossi thinks that this inscription belonged to the tomb of St. Optatus, who in fact had been bishop of Vescere in Numidia (now Biskra in Algeria).

The name of St. Optatus appears in the marble catalogue placed by Sixtus III in the Crypt of the Popes and in the catalogue of relics transferred to the church of St. Praxedes. He is also named in an itinerary *(Notitia portarum...)* which locates his tomb in the Cemetery of St. Callixtus. Moreover, as we shall see, his picture is among those found in the Crypt of St. Cornelius.

On the walls of the Crypt of St. Gaius, though the name of St. Optatus is not expressly cited, the graffiti indicate the names of three African bishops, among them a Maius (ICUR, IV, 9540). These are all important clues which would lead us to think that this little *arcosolium* is the tomb of St. Optatus.

But this hypothesis, though attractive, encounters some difficulty. From a close analysis of the *formae* in the floor, Prof. Reekmans concludes that this small decorated *arcosolium* in the Crypt of St. Gaius is probably part of the "monumentalizing" work done in the second half of the 4th century. So he doubts if it could have been the tomb of bishop Optatus.

St. Optatus died in Africa around 428 A.D. His relics were brought to Rome around 440 by the African bishops who were driven from their sees by the Vandal persecution of Genseric (428-477). Optatus was finally buried in the Cemetery of St. Callixtus, but some uncertainty still remains about the exact place where his tomb was located.

... EPISCOPVS VES(ce)RITANV(s)
REC(essit) NVMIDIAE Ɍ (= recessit) PR(idie) ID(ibus)...
"Bishop of Vescere. Died in Numidia.
He left this world on the day before the ides of ..." [5].

6. ICONIUS,
AN EXPERT DECORATOR

During the period of the cult of the martyrs, the floor of the crypt and of the nearby gallery was filled with *formae*. One of these deserves mentioning. It is just in front of the tomb of Pope St. Gaius. It is sealed with a marble slab with an epitaph in Greek: "The burial of Maxima, unforgettable and God fearing, five days before the Ides of December" (December 9th). Cf. ICUR, IV, 10652.

These tombs set in the floor confirm the veneration of the early Christians for Pope St. Gaius. These faithful thought themselves fortunate not only to have a tomb next to their Pastor but also to enjoy his intercession.

During the barbarian invasions the Crypt of St. Gaius suffered the same fate as did all the others. When the scourge had passed, the crypt was restored in the 6th century and reinforced with three heavy pillars square in section.

In the corner, on the right of the front wall, there is a passage which leads to a *retrosanto* (a burial chamber behind the shrine) belonging originally to a family. The *cubiculum*, rather narrow, was excavated in the late 4th century and was illuminated by a broad light-shaft. It houses three *arcosolia* of exceptional size, which contain sarcophagi.

The walls of the *cubiculum*, like those of the Crypt of St. Eusebius, were covered with polychrome marble of which considerable traces survive.

On the preceding page:
The Crypt of Pope St. Gaius (late 3rd century).

The floor was in *opus sectile*, i.e. faced in marble so as to represent various geometrical forms. The name of the decorator of this burial chamber is known. In fact, on the wall of the little entrance passage the artist has painted his portrait with Christ's monogram and has also added this graffito: "Iconius fashioned and white-washed this place in ten days" (ICUR, IV, 9542).

7. THE EXCITEMENT OF A DISCOVERY

"I feel great joy — wrote de Rossi in his *Roma Sotterranea Cristiana* — in telling the story of one of the most splendid discoveries that has crowned my research work in the Cemetery of Callixtus...

In 1852, in an area between the tomb of Cornelius and the Crypt of the Popes, at that time still un-explored, I saw a piece of a large epigraph which roughly imitated Damasus' lettering. On the much mutilated slab I could read a few letters, among them EVS... At once memory suggested to me the whole verse: '*Eusebius docuit miseros sua crimina flere*'[6]. The line, an hexameter, belonged to a poem by Damasus which has come down to us in some collections. The reader can imagine the emotion that such a find created in my mind...

But another four years were to pass before I could begin the excavations which enabled me to discover the Crypt of St. Eusebius. At last, in 1856 the work began, and at once it proved extremely difficult because of the enormous mound of rubble which had fallen from above...

I explored among the stones of this ruined masonry and came to the foot of a sloping vault, an evident sign of a buried staircase. Under the vault, not only did I find the steps which led to the open air but observed that the entrances to the galleries, except for one, had been walled up and closed to visitors. Thus I found that, during the centuries of religious peace, the staircase had served to take pilgrims directly to the Crypt of St. Eusebius and to the other venerated crypts nearby.

In the first days of May, my digging reached what I so much longed to see, the sacred floor of the Crypt of St. Eusebius. As soon as the first rubble accumulated at the door was removed, I saw there many marble pieces of the rough copy of Damasus' poem, the first fragment of which I had found on the ground above, four years earlier..." (R.S.C., II, 191-193).

8. EUSEBIUS "SWEET CHRIST ON EARTH"[7]

A sentence from the prophet Ezekiel tells us about God's attitude to the sinner: "I do not enjoy seeing a sinner die. I would rather see him stop sinning and live" (33, 11).[8]

If this should be the attitude of every good Christian towards his erring brother, what must be said of those who have been chosen as God's ministers and must represent him on earth?

Pope Eusebius understood this truth and wished to be the faithful interpreter and dispenser of divine mercy. He was the hand of God stretched out to raise the fallen, to exhort them to goodness and encourage them to return to the right path.

We do not know the exact date of his pontificate, of his death in exile, and when his body was brought to Rome. The *Liber Pontificalis* in the 'Liberian' edition says that he was a Greek and the son of a doctor. This source ascribes to him a very short pontificate, dating from April 18th to August 17th without specifying the year, which may be 309 or 310. The *Depositio Episcoporum*, the ancient liturgical calendar of the Church of Rome, states that Eusebius was buried in the Cemetery of St. Callixtus on September 26th, but again without giving the year.

If his biographical dates are uncertain, there is reliable information about his pastoral ministry in Rome. The most serious and controversial question he had to deal with was that of the *lapsi*.[9] We shall see that the epigraph placed in his crypt refers to it. The situation worsened to the point of disturbing public order. Emperor Maxentius, anxious for peace and tranquillity in anticipation of his clash with Constantine, banished the religious leaders of both op-posing positions. Eusebius was forced into exile at Syracuse in Sicily. He bore that punishment, with all its hardship and sufferings, with great courage, and there he died. Although he was not executed, the Church quickly considered him a martyr. When calm was restored in Rome, Eusebius' body was translated by his successor, St. Miltiades, and buried in the Catacombs of St. Callixtus. To understand the drama of the *lapsi*, which caused the Church so much suffering during the persecutions, we must look at it in its historical context.

Who were the Lapsi?

From the time of St. Cornelius' pontificate (251-253), the Church had to confront the serious problem of the *lapsi*, that is, those Christians who in order to avoid martyrdom or other forms of persecution, such as torture, confiscation of goods, or exile, had renounced their faith, and signed the certificate which confirmed that they had obeyed the imperial decree requiring the sacrificing to idols. This certificate was called *libellus*, and this is why the *lapsi* were also called *libellatici*. From the time of Decius (249-251) the imperial authority required this certificate as a guarantee that the sacrifice had been done. Often, however, thanks to bureaucratic complicity it was enough just to sign the certificate *(libellus)*. Sometimes one could simply purchase a signed *libellus*, thus avoiding the sacrificial act of idolatry. Many, unfortunately, had availed themselves of this escape route and were considered apostates.

Once the persecutions ended, the greater part of those apostates asked to be readmitted to the Church community. These requests were opposed by rigorists who were against granting pardon, while the laxists, on the other hand, favoured the readmittance without any penance of the *lapsi*.

Both the laxists and the rigorists were in complete contrast to the Church's teaching, which favoured pardon and readmission after an adequate period of heavy penance (two or three years).

Emperor Diocletian

Caius Aurelius Valerius Diocletianus Augustus (284-305) was one of the most outstanding personalities of the Roman empire. His origins were very humble, his father was a slave. Enlisted in the army, he rose through the ranks to become commander-in-chief of his legions. Prudence and a sharp practical sense persuaded him that the State had nothing to gain by persecuting the compact Christian community, though he himself was deeply attached to traditional paganism.

For years he hesitated between the intransigence of his principles and the tolerance suggested by political strategy. In 303, however, at the instigation of his *Caesar*

The Crypt of the martyr Pope St. Eusebius (4th century).

or vice-emperor, Galerius, he unleashed the last great persecution. Two years later, he abdicated and retired to his beloved *Salona* (the modern Split) in Dalmatia. In the West, the persecution was comparatively brief, while in the East, under Galerius and his *Caesar* Maximin Daia, it went on for nearly a decade causing many victims. Christians were ordered to renounce their faith; when they refused, they were put to death. Moreover, their personal goods were confiscated, as well as their sacred furnishings, vessels, vestments, liturgical books and writings. This explains the lack of reliable chronological data about the popes and the scarcity of authentic *Acta* of the martyrs in the different Churches. Christians who gave up the sacred books were called *traditores* (*trádere* is Latin for "to hand over"). There were many defections and the number of *lapsi* increased.

The Church came out of this tragedy sorely tried but not defeated. St. Ambrose later wrote: "Among the many trials of this world the Church stands unmoved, built on the apostolic rock, and on that foundation she stands unshaken by the fury of the storm. She is beaten by the waves but not shattered and, though often the elements of this world, battering her, make a great clamour, she still has a most secure haven of salvation in which to welcome the weary" (Letter 2, 1. PL XVI, 879).

9. THE CRYPT
OF ST. EUSEBIUS

This crypt is opposite that of St. Gaius. It is rectangular and not very spacious. It quickly draws attention because of the monumental aspect given to it by the presence of three *arcosolia*. A modern light-shaft now opens where the roof had partly collapsed. The original light-shaft was located in the ceiling of Gallery Q1, also shared by the Crypt of St. Gaius.

The crypt originated out of a family *cubiculum*. Its decoration was very simple: the walls were covered with white stucco. Above the lunette of the central *arcosolium* a Good Shepherd between two trees was painted. Traces of this painting are still visible. In the second half of the 4th century, the *cubiculum* was radically transformed. The three *arcosolia* were widened to make room for sarcophagi. In the central one a smaller *arcosolium* was added, and the same was done to the *arcosolium* of the left wall. All three *arcosolia* had their arches embellished with mosaics.

The walls of the crypt were decorated with marble *(opus sectile)* forming various geometrical patterns. The ceiling was painted to look coffered, using blue and Pompeian red and with some figurines inside the painted coffers, birds resting on branches and stylised floral motives.

The floor was filled with *formae* grave and covered with polychrome marble. To the Christians of the late 4th century, the crypt must have looked like an art-treasure no less impressive than the nearby *retrosanto* of the Crypt of St. Gaius.

10. THE TOMB
OF THE MARTYR POPE

After his translation from Sicily, St. Eusebius was laid to rest in the *arcosolium* located in the right wall of the crypt. It was decorated like the other two *arcosolia*, even though it presents special characteristics of its own.

It takes up more than half the wall. It held only one tomb and above the arch was placed a *tabula ansata*, a rectangular slab of marble with thickened edges. This large slab was not intended for an epitaph but for a commemorative inscription or eulogy. Its purpose obviously was to draw the pilgrims' attention to the tomb below, because the person, who had been buried there half a century earlier, had a special importance for the Christians of the second half of the 4th century.

The inside of the tomb was lined with marble (white and antique red). The arch, as already stated, was decorated with mosaic. The imprints of the *tesserae* are still visible.

All this work was completed during the pontificate of Pope Damasus, who was specially devoted to the martyrs.

11. DAMASUS'
POETIC INSCRIPTION

Anyone entering the Crypt of St. Eusebius today is surprised to see a monumental marble slab engraved on both sides. The slab rests on two sturdy little columns, set up by de Rossi in the floor of this burial chamber.

At the same time, we find a second, modern slab with the same inscription of Damasus inside the *arcosolium* where St. Eusebius was buried. How is all this explained?

Crypt of St. Eusebius: Copy of the Damasian inscription in honour of Pope St. Eusebius (late 6th century).

We know that de Rossi discovered several fragments of a poem by Damasus at the entrance of the crypt. This was, as we have stated, a rough copy dating back to the end of the 6th century. The inscription is not free of errors, caused by a faulty knowledge of classical Latin.

After the destruction done by the Goths in the catacombs, the tombs of the martyrs needed restoring. In order to engrave St. Damasus' epigram anew, the Christians utilized a monumental slab which already bore an inscription in honour of emperor Caracalla (211-217).

As a curiosity, we are to cite this eulogy written by a senator Asinius to his sovereign. The inscription shows how the most abject servility and unbridled adulation go hand in hand. Honorific titles are wasted like medals on the uniform of a modern dictator...

"To the great and unconquered (unconquerable) emperor, Caesar Marcus Aurelius Antoninus, Pius, Felix, Augustus, Particus Maximus, Britannicus Maximus, Germanicus Maximus,[10] *Pontifex Maximus,*[11] *in the seventeenth year of his potestas tribunicia,*[12] *(acclaimed) emperor for the third time, consul for the fourth time, Father of the fatherland, proconsul, Marcus Asinius Sabinianus, a most illustrious man (i.e. of senatorial rank) (dedicated this inscription) for the outstanding favour and benefits granted him by the emperor".* This inscription is dated 214 (CIL VI, 1067).

Given the large size of this slab, and that it was designed to be read, no doubt it was propped in front of the parapet of the *arcosolium* of St. Eusebius. The inscription to Caracalla was of course hidden, as it was on the side propped up against the wall.

But tireless de Rossi was luckier than he could have imagined. Sieving the earth a handful at a time, he managed to find thirteen fragments of the original Damasian poem.[13]

The honorific inscription by Damasus may now be easily read on the marble slab inside the *arcosolium* which once contained the martyred Pope's remains. This modern slab contains the original fragments inserted in their proper place. The poetic inscription was cut on the marble in splendid lettering by Furius Dionysius Filocalus, who added his signature and dedication vertically down the sides: "Furius Dionysius Filocalus, devoted friend of Pope Damasus, engraved".[14]

101

Here is the text of the poem:

> ## "BISHOP DAMASVS COMPOSED (THIS POEM)
>
> *Heraclius did not admit that the lapsi*
> *could do penance for their sins.*
> *But Eusebius taught that these unhappy ones*
> *should weep for their faults (do penance).*
> *The people, as their passion grew,*
> *became divided into two parties.*
> *Tumults, carnage, strife, discord, lawsuits followed.*
> *Suddenly both (Eusebius and Heraclius)*
> *were exiled by the cruel tyrant.*
> *The Pope bore his exile serenely*
> *awaiting divine judgement*
> *because he had kept faith*
> *with the pledges of his ministry of peace.*
> *He left the world and earthly life on Sicilian shores.*
>
> ## IN HONOVR OF EVSEBIVS, BISHOP AND MARTYR"[14]

Heraclius was one of the clergy who did not accept Pope Eusebius' teaching on some doctrinal questions. The "cruel tyrant" was emperor Maxentius (306-312).

The usurper Maxentius

Marcus Aurelius Valerius Maxentius, "unconquered prince", was the son of Maximian called "the Herculean" and Constantine's brother-in-law. He was proclaimed emperor by the praetorian Guard in Rome on 28th October 306. His nomination, however, was never recognized by the retired Diocletian or by the reigning tetrarchs: Licinius and Constantine, Galerius and Maximin Daia.

This emperor, though attached to traditional paganism, was not a persecutor. Political strategy led him to restore the liberty of worship to the Christians when he rose to power, and in 311 he gave back to the Church its possessions confiscated by Diocletian, including the catacombs. He died on 28th October 312, drowned in the Tiber during his battle with Constantine at the Milvian Bridge.

History presents him as a cruel, rapacious and dissolute sovereign... The loser's lot, as usual! But though he cannot be acknowledged for outstanding qualities as a man and as a ruler, nevertheless his imposing public works (the Basilica in the Forum and the Circus on the Appian Way...), the care he had for the great roads of Italy and his affection for his son Romulus who died prematurely, suggest something better than his reputation allows.

12. THE MARTYRS CALOCERUS AND PARTHENIUS

Leaving the Crypt of St. Eusebius, beyond two intersecting galleries,[15] the Crypt of SS. Calocerus and Parthenius is on the left. Our attention is at once attracted by two graffiti next to the entrance and the extensive restoration work done in ancient times.

The crypt

The burial chamber originated as a family *cubiculum* towards the end of the 3rd century. The left wall and the one beside the door were reinforced in late antiquity

(6th and 7th centuries) with massive blocks of "peperino" (from Lat. *piper*, pepper, a kind of volcanic rock) to prevent the collapse of friable tufa. The other two walls and a good part of the ceiling were restored by de Rossi in 1859.

As things are now, it is hard to determine the primitive decoration of the crypt. It was not monumentalized in Damasus' time, as was the Crypt of Eusebius. Analytical examination of the walls by Prof. L. Reekmans has shown that during the time of Damasus only the outer wall and the entrance door with its arch were renovated.

We have referred to a radical intervention at a later period. If it was just because the vault threatened to collapse, was it not enough to fill the crypt with earth and make it inaccessible once and for all? The Christians of the time must have had good reasons for keeping it open and undertaking those costly renovation works.

Only the presence of martyrs' tombs could have justified all those interventions. Since their tombs lay on the pilgrims' route from the Crypt of the Popes to those of St. Gaius and St. Eusebius, these martyrs were fortunate enough not to fall into oblivion as did so many others.

The floor of the crypt is full of devotional tombs *(formae)*, as normally are the burial places of the martyrs.

The venerated tombs

The Itinerary *De locis sanctis Martyrum*, while dealing with Eusebius, Calocerus and Parthenius states that their tombs were near each other but separate *(per se singuli iacent)*.

The martyrs Calocerus and Parthenius were therefore buried in two *loculi* in the right wall of this crypt. As places of rest awaiting resurrection they originally had two simple and humble tombs.

At the side of their tombs, in the reinforcing pillar of "peperino", there is a small rectangular niche for oil lamps. We notice that this small niche was not eliminated at the time of renovation, when family

The Crypt of the martyrs Calocerus and Parthenius.

The crypt called St. Miltiades. (See p. 87).

reunions for the rites of *refrigerium* in honour of the dead were no longer practised. And relations had now died out. If, then, the small niche was still needed in the 6th and 7th centuries, it means that at this period the crypt was still considered a true martyrs' sanctuary.

Unfortunately, neither de Rossi's excavations nor Reekmans' have yielded inscriptions or pieces of marble which shed light on the successive transformations of the primitive *cubiculum*. So we know nothing of how the two martyrs' tombs were decorated.

Some information about these two martyrs is to be found in the *Acta* of their sufferings. But those writings, compiled much later in admiration for the holy martyrs, must be read with some caution. It can, however, be mantained that what they say about topography is reliable, since the places that they describe were well known to their readers. Among other things, the legendary *Passio* of SS. Calocerus and Parthenius states that their crypt was embellished with porphyry columns, thus creating a kind of ciborium before their tombs.

The graffiti

It was actually the graffiti which enabled de Rossi to identify the Crypt of SS. Calocerus and Parthenius. Next to the entrance door, on the left wall, there are two graffiti written in Latin by two different hands.

The upper one, in italics (written in free hand) records the date of an anniversary. Prof. Ferrua offers the following reading:

"Tertio ibid (= idib = idibus) se(p)t(embribus) $\overline{VA}$"... i.e. September 11th. A name follows, perhaps that of the deceased or of a pilgrim who had come to attend the *refrigerium* of the martyrs on the *dies natalis*.[16] The second graffito, some distance below the first, gives in small capital letters only the names of the two martyrs:

PARTEN(i) MARTIRI
CALO(c)ERI MARTIRI

That is: *"Sepulchre of martyr St. Parthenius, Sepulchre of martyr St. Calocerus".*[17]

Taking into account the fact that the two expressions are identical, with the same arrangement of the words and the same size of the letters, it must be concluded that the two names and titles are the work of the same hand. Furthermore, both the names and the title of "martyr" are in the possessive genitive, but wrongly written. The correct expression would be: *"Parthenii Martyris, Caloceri Martyris".* The origins and occupations of SS. Calocerus and Parthenius are unknown. The information given by their *Passio* is late and unreliable. Perhaps these two martyrs were victims of Diocletian's persecution in 304.

An unusual "retrosanto"

The *cubiculum* excavated opposite to that of Calocerus and Parthenius is of really considerable proportions. It measures 4.73 by 2.94 metres and is 3.32 metres high. These are exceptional dimensions for an average *cubiculum*. The walls were covered with white stucco. They contained many *loculi* and two *arcosolia*. The latter were decorated with marble and their vaults with mosaic. The floor and the nearby Gallery Q1 were filled with *formae* dating from the 4th century. Since this area was excavated at the end of the 3rd century, these features of the *cubiculum* suggest something quite extraordinary.

We have mentioned that the Crypt of SS. Calocerus and Parthenius underwent important renovation works in late antiquity. This reduced its size notably, which means that it was not big enough for meetings.

Here then was the possibility of utilizing the nearby *cubiculum* to supply the needed space. Its considerable size offers a plausible explanation if we consider it as an exceptional *retrosanto*, and as a place for worship next to the venerated tombs. Moreover, the wide light-shaft near the gallery provided sufficient light and air for those prayer meetings (see p. 13).

The early Christians certainly did not lack imagination for solving logistical problems even in such unusual surroundings.

---

[1] The crypt is 5.56 metres long, from 3.50 to 4.40 metres wide and 4.70 metres high.

[2] ICUR, IV, 10584.

[3] About the life of a saint.

[4] The inscription of St. Optatus is now fixed to the wall of Staircase A (the Martyrs' Staircase).

[5] ICUR, IV, 9517.

[6] Eusebius taught these unhappy ones to weep for their sins.

[7] The well-known expression of St. Catherine of Siena (1347-1380) aptly suited to this Pope, because Eusebius could be good and merciful to sinners like his master Jesus Christ.

[8] Cf. *Luke* 15, 1-7; 8-10; 11-32.

[9] From the Latin *lapsus*, fallen.

[10] He was the greatest of the conquerors of the Parthians (the population of what is now Iran), of the Britons, of the Germans.

[11] The highest priestly office of the Roman state religion.

[12] That which gave him right of veto over the laws of the Senate and allowed him to summon the Senate itself.

[13] The first fragment was found on 16th December 1856 among the debris on the stair. All the others were found one by one in the most unlikely places: in the galleries near the Crypt of St. Eusebius, among the rubble below the light-shaft of the Crypt of St. Cecilia, in the vineyard near the skylight of the Crypt of the Popes (Nov. 1861). The last piece has a really extraordinary story. De Rossi writes: "I found it in the cellar of the Campana Gardens, near the Lateran, among a heap of old marbles collected here and there in the suburbs for sale".

The pieces thus recovered may at first sight seem insignificant, but as the great archaeologist said: "It is to the careful study of such neglected trifles that I owe the finest fruits of my researches in the Roman catacombs".

[14] ICUR, IV, 9515.

[15] The gallery opening to the right was walled up in antiquity to make the pilgrims' route easier. There are still abundant traces of this operation.

[16] Other scholars (De Rossi, Reekmans) prefer the following reading: *Tertio idus fefru(arias = februarias)*, i.e. 11 February.

[17] ICUR, IV, 9543.

X.
The Area of SS. Gaius and Eusebius

Some interesting cubicula

1. "SWEET" LITTLE SEVERA WILL ONE DAY RISE AGAIN!

Besides the historic crypts, in the Area of SS. Gaius and Eusebius there are some more interesting *cubicula* worth consideration. They were visited by thousands of pilgrims during the first centuries and were also known to such explorers of the past as Bosio, Boldetti, Marangoni and Bottari...

Following the route along Gallery Q1, there is on the right a double *cubiculum*, which in ancient times was illuminated by a wide light-shaft. In the inner *cubiculum* a marble *transenna* is preserved. It closed one of the *arcosolia*.

On the panel is a long inscription in verse from the time of Diocletian, very important for its historic and doctrinal content. Which is:

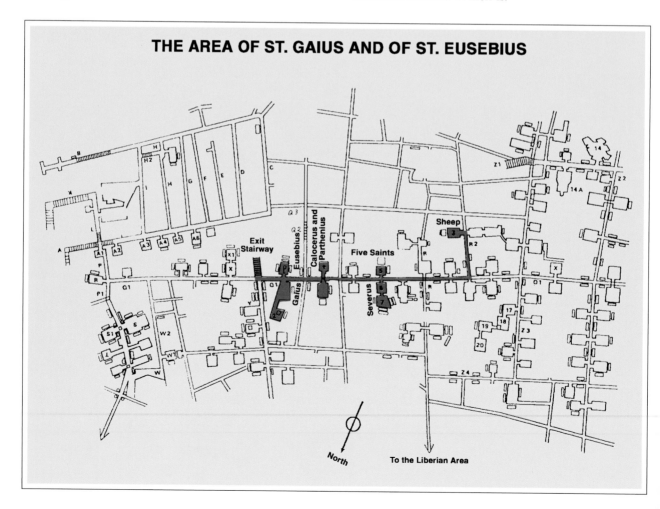

THE AREA OF ST. GAIUS AND OF ST. EUSEBIUS

North

To the Liberian Area

The Cemetery of St. Callixtus depended on the pope

From the inscription we learn that the double *cubiculum* belonged to deacon Severus, who was authorized to excavate it by Pope Marcellinus (296-304): IVSSV PP (= *PaPae*) SVI MARCELLINI. We may conclude that the Cemetery of St. Callixtus was under the authority of the pope, that is, of the Church of Rome.

The deacon calls the *cubiculum*, built for himself and his family, the "house of peace". In an *arcosolium*, his daughter Severa, just nine years old, was buried. At the time the clergy could still have a family. Indeed, during the first three centuries of Christianity, there was no particular ecclesiastical legislation on the matter. Celibacy (renouncing marriage) spread initially from personal choice, then it became compulsory, particularly in the West, from the 4th century onwards.

The bishop of Rome is called "pope"

Deacon Severus' inscription is one of the most important and enlightening in early Christian subterranean Rome.

It is important from a dogmatic point of view, insofar as it expresses the faith of the Christian community in the resurrection of the body. It is also important historically, because it is the first epigraph in which the bishop of Rome is given the title of "pope" (father). This word originated in an Egyptian milieu at a late period. Here is part of that inscription:

for himself and his own, to keep for a long time those beloved members sleeping and waiting for God their creator and judge...".

Marcellinus was pope in a dramatic period of Church history, afflicted by the dreadful persecution of Diocletian and Galerius. The inscription belongs either to the end of the 3rd century or the beginning of the 4th, but not later than 304, the year of Marcellinus' death.

Before that time the term "pope", in Greek πάπας, was used sporadically, in the sense of father, an affectionate form of address to bishops and priests. As a synonym for the bishop of Rome, the term appears for the first time in this particular inscription.

In the *transenna* the word is not carved fully but as the abbreviation PP. It may be noted that this is still used by the popes: Joannes Paulus PP II = Pope John Paul II.

The exclusive use of the term "pope" for the bishop of Rome

As we shall see, the abbreviation PP (PaPa) is also found in the frescoes, dating from the beginning of the 7th century, in the Crypt of St. Cornelius. Evidently at that period the title of pope had become exclusive to the bishop of Rome.

Before that the pope was referred to by the title EPISCOPVS, from the Greek ἐπίσκοπος (bishop, inspector). This is indicated in the sepulchral inscriptions that we have already seen of Pontianus, Antherus, Fabian and Eutychian, buried in the Crypt

CVBICVLVM DVPLEX CVM ARCISOLIIS ET LVMINARE
IVSSV PP SVI MARCELLINI DIACONVS ISTE
SEVERVS FECIT MANSIONEM IN PACE QVIETAM
SIBI SVISQVE MEMOR QVO MEMBRA DVLCIA SOMNO
PER LONCVM TEMPVS FACTORI ET IVDICI SERVET...

Here is a translation-interpretation of it:

"This deacon Severus, authorized by his Pope Marcellinus, made a double cubiculum (formed of two adjoining rooms) with arcosolia and a light-shaft, a quiet and peaceful resting place

of the Popes between 235 and 283. The name of the pope is followed by the abbreviation ΕΠΙ or ΕΠΙΣΚ (ἐπίσκοπος). On the slab of Cornelius it is written in Latin: CORNELIVS EP(iscopus).

This custom continued during the entire 4th century and beyond. Sixtus III (432-440) renovated the basilica of St. Mary Major after the Council of Ephesus (431), and he still chose this dedication: XYSTVS EPISCOPVS PLEBI DEI, "Sixtus Bishop to the People of God".

comparable, and, as the Greeks used to say, unforgettable" (J. Janssens).

In his inscription, Severus so goes on, referring to his daughter: *"Severa, sweet to her parents and to her servants, gave up her innocent soul on the 25th January. It pleased God to grant her marvellous wisdom and beauty from birth".*

The affection of Severus, a father, for his daughter

"Inscriptions truly testify to the affection and admiration that parents had for their children. They expressed these feelings either in verse or in simple words. Their love was such that every child was for them: sweet, dear, devoted, tender, affectionate, in-

Faith in the resurrection of the body

As I have pointed out before, the inscription of Severus is also important from a dogmatic point of view, that is, from the viewpoint of faith: the father states that one day the body of his "sweet" Severa will rise again.

... HIC EST SEPVLTVM DONEC RESVRGAT AB IPSO
QVIQVE ANIMAM RAPVIT SPIRITV SANCTO SVO
CASTAM PVDICAM ET INVIOLABILE SEMPER
QVAMQVE ITERVM DOMS SPIRITALI GLORIA REDDET...

Deacon Severus says, in fact, that *"the body* (of sweet Severa) *is buried here* (in the cubiculum) *until she shall rise again. And the Lord who has taken* (from Severa) *her chaste, pure and forever inviolable soul with her saintly spirit, will give it back adorned with spiritual glory. She lived nine years, eleven months and fifteen days. Thus she passed from this* (earthly) *life"* (ICUR, IV, 10183).

2. AN ENCHANTING GARDEN

Opposite the *Cubiculum* of deacon Severus is the *"Cubiculum* of the Five Saints", so named because on the back wall five persons "Oranti" in a garden are painted. The scene, graced by the song of birds, and with trees laden with flowers and fruit, is a clear image of Paradise, the blessed land reached by the fortunate souls. Two peacocks are painted below the figures and at the sides of the *arcosolium*. On the lower part of the wall appear three vases containing water from which many birds are drinking.

The artist has chosen to paint the persons with distinctive features: pearl necklaces, different hairstyles... The name with the greeting "in peace" is written over each figure: *"Dionisia in pace, Nemesius in pace, Procopius in pace, Eliodora in pace, Zoe in pace, Arcadia in pace"*. The portrait of Arcadia does not appear in the picture, but her name with the phrase *in pace* is seen above the peacock on the left.

The six "Oranti" now live in the peace of heaven as we read in the *Revelation:* "'Now God's home is with mankind! He will live with them, and they shall be his people. God himself will be with them, and he will be their God. He will wipe away all tears from their eyes. There will be no more death, no more grief or crying or pain. The old things have disappeared'. Then the one who sits on the throne said: 'And now I make all things new!'" (21, 3-5).

The whole picture dates back to the pre-Constantinian period, to the beginning of the 4th century (ICUR, IV, 9770).

3. AN INTERESTING CARTOON

A dove holding a *stilus* (a style, a pen) in its small claw and writing something that seems to belong to the world of Walt Disney cartoons. Yet something of the kind happened 1700 years ago. Such a scene is to be seen on a small stone-tablet in the *"Cubiculum* of the Five Saints": a dove that writes the monogram of Christ with a *stilus* in its claw. This is really unique in early Christian iconography and epigraphy. It is the good soul of someone who courageously proclaims: "I belong to Christ! I am a Christian!".

**Cubiculum
of the Five Saints:
Detail of the fresco.**

Cubiculum of the Five Saints (4ᵗʰ century).

4. PETRONIA, A REAL MOTHER TO HER FORMER SLAVES

Some interesting stone tablets are also in Gallery Q1.

One may be transcribed as an example:

> PETRONIAE AVXENTIAE · C(larissimae) · F(eminae) · QV(a)E · VIXIT ANNIS XXX LIBERTI FEC(erunt) (be)NE MERENTI IN PACE ·

"For Petronia Auxentia, most noble woman (of senatorial rank), who lived for thirty years, in loving memory, her freedmen made this sepulchre. In pace". (ICUR, IV, 10085).

The dead woman belonged to the noble family of *Petronii*. The inscription shows that Christians normally freed their slaves and treated their servants in the most human fashion, as stated by St. Justin Martyr in a letter to emperor Antoninus Pius (138-161) and by Tertullian *(Apologeticum).*

Justin wrote that when one becomes a Christian he is quickly called a "brother", whatever his social extraction. Tertullian maintains that whoever becomes a servant to God cannot be a slave of man.

In fact, in Christian epigraphy the word *servus* or *serva* is used above all in expressions such as *"servus Dei, servus Christi, servus Domini"*, servant of God, of Christ, of the Lord.

5. A PLEASANT LANDSCAPE

Proceeding through Gallery Q1 and turning to the left, Gallery R2 is reached, with the pleasant surprise of the so-called *"Cubiculum* of the Sheep". It is a further development of the Area of St. Gaius and St. Eusebius. That this *cubiculum* is important and worth visiting is confirmed by the signature of Antonio Bosio (BOSIVS) beside its entrance.

The *cubiculum* was excavated with a barrel vault and a large niche for a sarcophagus in the back wall. It was decorated with frescoes in the middle of the 4th century, and has been badly damaged by the opening of some

On the preceding page:
Reconstruction of the fresco.

loculi. During their preparation for baptism (catechumenate), Christians memorized the Credo and some Psalms of King David, the prophet. Psalm 23 (22), a marvellous synthesis of Christian initiation, was a favourite one.

The Fathers of the Church, in fact, always interpreted the words of this psalm typologically, as referring to Baptism and the Eucharist. Baptism, Confirmation and the Eucharist, also called "the sacraments of Christian initiation", were administered to catechumens during the great Paschal Vigil (Holy Saturday night).

"The Lord is my Shepherd"

A translation of Psalm 23 into images has been done here in the *"Cubiculum* of the Sheep":

> *"The Lord is my shepherd;*
> *I have everything I need.*
> *He lets me rest in fields of green grass*
> *and leads me to quiet pools of fresh water.*
> *He gives me new strenght.*
> *He guides me in the right paths,*
> *as he as promised.*
> *Even if I go through the deepest darkness,*
> *I will not be afraid, Lord,*
> *for you are with me.*
> *Your shepherd's rod and staff protect me"* (1-4).

At the centre of the *arcosolium* is the image of the Good Shepherd with the lamb on his shoulders. The sheep is a clear symbol of the soul who, saved by Christ, now lives happily in Paradise.

Beside the Good Shepherd, in the middle of a green pasture, are a ram and a few other sheep: one is grazing, the others are resting, sure that the Good Shepherd is looking after them.

Two men, one on each side of the picture, move eagerly to drink at the two springs which gush from the rock. They are two of the blessed, refreshing themselves at the fountains of the living water, Christ.

This moving scene brings to mind the words of *Revelation:* "He who sits on the throne will protect them with his presence. Never again will they hunger or thirst; neither sun nor any scorching heat will burn them, because the Lamb... will be their shepherd, and he will guide them to springs of life-giving water. And God will wipe away every tear from their eyes" (7, 15-17; see also *Isaiah* 49, 9-10).

Cubiculum of the Sheep: Fresco of the Good Shepherd and Moses-St. Peter (4th century).

Reconstruction of the fresco of the Good Shepherd.

Cubiculum of the Sheep: Detail of the multiplication of the bread and fish (4th century).

The Eucharist

Psalm 23 goes on:

"You prepare a banquet for me,
where all my enemies can see me;
you welcome me as an honoured guest
and fill my cup to the brim.
I know that your goodness and love
will be with me all my life;
and your house will be my home
as long as I live" (5-6).

On the left wall of the niche we find a scene uncommon to frescoes, though frequently represented in sculpture: Jesus lays his hands, as a gesture of benediction, on the loaves and fishes presented by two apostles. On the ground are six baskets of loaves, each loaf marked with a cross. The seventh basket is held by an apostle. The fresco was subsequently damaged by the digging of a small niche for oil lamps. In the catechetical preparation for Baptism, Confirmation and the Eucharist, Christians frequently heard the story of the multiplication of the loaves and fishes, presented as a type, or image or symbol, of the Eucharist. In short, a prefiguration.

Jesus himself had taken this miracle as an opportunity for talking about the spiritual bread as nourishment for the soul of man *(John 6, 22-71)*. The visitors of this *cubiculum* realized that the salvation of those deceased came from that spiritual food.

Baptism: Moses and the spring in the desert

Two scenes from the life of Moses, the great legislator and leader of the Hebrews, who freed them from slavery in Egypt, are represented on the right wall of the *arcosolium*.

First we see Moses, a beardless youth, in the act of taking off his shoes, obeying God's command who is symbolized by a hand reaching out from the sky *(Exodus 3, 1-12)*. In the very next scene, Moses, this time bearded, strikes the rock in order to get water from it during a moment of great difficulty, when the Hebrews were crossing the desert. A soldier, sword at his side, takes the water in his hand to quench his thirst *(Exodus 17, 1-7)*.

This soldier, as portrayed by the painter, is not Hebrew but Roman, easily recognizable from his uniform and weapons. Moreover, the features of Moses, who is striking the rock, are very similar to those of the apostle Peter as we normally see them represented in early Christian iconography. Why?

As U. Fasola writes, "the insistence with which the early Church writers compare the miracle in the desert with Christian Baptism, offers a most convincing explanation: the water which springs forth miraculously in the desert to save the thirsty Israelites symbolizes the saving water of Baptism. This is confirmed by the way the artists transformed the ancient Exodus scene into a 'Petrine' subject. Almost always the artists give Moses the facial features of Peter.

Cubiculum of the Sheep: Moses loosening his sandals and Moses-Peter striking the rock (4ᵗʰ century).

We do not know on what grounds they have standardized this in art, but those facial features are at once recognizable, because very often the name itself of the apostle is added to them.

Yet, in the '*Cubiculum* of the Sheep', the painter wanted to differentiate the two figures by placing, alongside the scene of Moses-Peter striking the rock, another scene of Moses, where the prophet is taking off his shoes out of respect for God's presence, symbolized by the hand coming out of the clouds. Here Moses is represented with a countenance and clothing totally different from that of the first scene".

In this respect, the analogy between Moses-Peter seems to me even clearer: as Moses had been the charismatic leader of the Hebrews to make them a free people, so Peter, appointed by Christ to feed his flock (*John* 21, 15-17), was the undisputed guide of the new Christian people.

It is surprising how the early Christians knew the Bible and were able to draw, from the word of God, allusions to the sacraments they had received. In the water pouring out of the rock they saw a prefiguration of Baptism which had made them children of God, and in the miracle of the multiplication of the loaves they discerned a symbol of the Eucharist, the spiritual food offered to them as nourishment during their earthly pilgrimage. In all these biblical figures they also saw a gesture of divine goodness, always ready to intervene in moments of trial and need, just as Psalm 23 had proclaimed.

In the lower part of the niche, on the right, is an image of Paradise, a garden rich with flowers, the eternal home of the just. "Your house will be my home as long as I live".

Inscriptions and signatures

In this *cubiculum*, de Rossi in 1852 found part of an inscription with a consular date, that of Messalla. The remaining part, with the name of the second consul Sabinus, was discovered in 1975, during excavations in the Western Area.

The inscription did not belong to a Christian grave, but to a pagan tomb overground. It had been taken and cut by Christians and reused to seal a child's tomb. Now the two parts are joined again and are found at the beginning of Gallery Z3, near the four adjoining *cubicula* with the same passageway.

Much earlier than Bosio, in 1462, the abbot of St. Hermes in Pisa and seven of his monks visited this *cubiculum*. So did Ranuccio Farnese, the mercenary commander, in 1490. In 1649 Angelo Santini, nicknamed "il Toccafondo", came and copied its images. He was a friend of Bosio and accompanied him on his underground explorations, often leaving his name in the catacombs together with that of the great explorer.

Through a modern passage opposite the *"Cubiculum of the Sheep"*, a new area is reached, located on the western side.

114

XI.
The Western Area

De Rossi labelled this section of the big cemetery as the "Area of St. Soter", after the name of the woman martyr, who was great-aunt of St. Ambrose of Milan (334-397). Ancient documents indicate that the burial area of St. Soter was, in fact, part of the "Callixtian complex", but nothing has been found, so far, to justify de Rossi's hypothesis.

The Western Area originated at the beginning of the 4th century and developed during the period of religious peace. Its Staircase $Z1^1$ occupied a stretch of a pre-existing gallery, and along its walls fragments of pagan sarcophagi from above ground are found, placed there to save them from greedy hands.

The area was used solely for burial, and no tomb displays any particular signs of devotion. The area shows how the Christian cemeteries developed immediately after the end of the persecutions. The zone was quickly connected to the nearby Area of SS. Gaius and Eusebius, thus greatly expanding the Cemetery of St. Callixtus. Its chief feature is that it has a fair number of *cubicula* with elegant architectural refinements: groined and domed vaults, pilasters at the four corners, corbels...

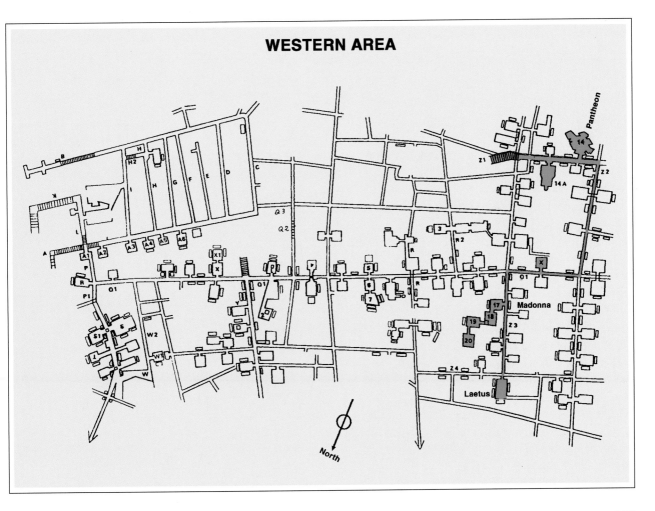

WESTERN AREA

Underground mausoleum nicknamed "Pantheon". Middle of the 4th century.

It must, therefore, be assumed that many of the *fossores* working in the excavations were not simply men with strong muscles, but true and genuine architects.

1. A MASTERPIECE OF UNDERGROUND ACOUSTICS

Very close to Staircase Z1 is a large round *cubiculum* (14) with a particular architectural feature, a dome-vault. Some fifty corpses were buried in it. This "underground mausoleum" evidently belonged to a group of families or to a corporation.

The round vault rests on a circular architrave supported by six small columns. The curvilinear wall opposite the entrance has a niche similar to a small apse. It was probably excavated to take a sarcophagus.

Later on, the wall of that niche was utilized for burials by excavating curved *loculi*. To the right and left of the niche there are two half *cubicula*, which were created by breaking the existing plaster, and the small pilasters were partly cut as well.

A characteristic of the "mausoleum" is the perfection of its acoustics. Here, too some distinguished visitors have left their memory. On the right of the inner wall, next to the entrance, appears Antonio Bosio's signature (ANTONIVS BOSIVS). Very interesting for its architectural refinements is also *Cubiculum* 14A, dug almost opposite the "mausoleum".

2. SEALED LOCULI

Walking through the nearby Gallery Z2, we notice some *loculi* close to the floor, which are still sealed. Some more sealed *loculi* are inside the *cubicula* along the gallery. Halfway along it, on the left, begins another gallery which leads to two more underground mausoleums, very similar to those found at the surface.

Finally, at a crossing, Gallery Q1 is reached, the "main route" of the Western Area in its final section. Going through it in the opposite direction, the first *cubiculum* on the right is worth visiting.

3. "APRIL 26th 1748..."

The custom of writing on walls is certainly not to be recommended. Deplorable in itself in whatever epoch, it has nevertheless served as a historical source of documentation.

We must acknowledge that, when a Christian archaeologist finds inscriptions or graffiti on the walls of a church or on the plastered wall of a catacomb *cubiculum*, he is very happy. Indeed, very often the interpretations of such writings have been a great help in the topographical study of monumental complexes or in finding explanations of things that have happened through the centuries.

In the galleries of the catacombs or inside the *cubicula* we not only find graffiti of pious invocations, prayers of pilgrims or the names of priests who have celebrated Mass at the tomb of a martyr, but also the signatures of explorers and illustrious visitors of the post-Renaissance period.

Sometimes we come across the signatures or writings of workmen who were employed in the catacombs. It is further valuable information which sheds light on what is called "the dark age" of the catacombs.

What we are now visiting may be labelled the *"Cubiculum* of the Orante", because of an "Orante"-woman carved on a sarcophagus almost a metre below the floor. Unfortunately, this hidden burial place has not been spared from being broken, open and rifled.

At the centre of the front side of the sarcophagus, is the image of a woman in the "Orante" position, her head covered with a veil. On either side of her, two saints accompany her to heaven. The room, very large and with only a few tombs, contained four sarcophagi which had been lowered there through the light-shaft.

Near the entrance door, a narrow passage opens to the left. On the wall, again on the left, two inscriptions can be seen, both relevant for the history of the catacombs. One of them reads:

"Tomasso de Angelis
on the day of 16th April 1748 came
to cut open an urn in this
holy place by command".

Tomasso *(sic)* de Angelis should not be thought of as one of those modern barbarians called *corpisantari* (thieves of the bodies of saints). Rather he was an excavator who came to open a tomb "by command", that is, by order of his employer, the authority in charge of the catacombs. The purpose was to find out whether the tomb was that of a martyr or not.

The other inscription is of the illustrious and learned Giovanni Battista de Rossi, who visited this *cubiculum* on three different occasions:

IOANN. BAPT. DEROSSI MDCCCLI (1851),
MDCCCLVI (1856), MDCCCLXIII (1863).

4. THE MOTHER OF JESUS

Until the first half of the 5th century, that is, up to the time of the Council of Ephesus which in 431 proclaimed the divine motherhood of Mary, the Virgin appears many times in iconography, but in scenes which are eminently Christological. In all those images the focus of the composition is Christ, who came to bring salvation to humanity, as is so often reaffirmed in the writings of the Fathers of the Church in the first centuries.

Scholars maintain that the oldest representation of the Madonna in the catacombs is the one in the Cemetery of Priscilla, painted between the end of the 2nd century and the beginning of the 3rd.

Very simple but extremely significant are also the portrayals of the Magi, which date back to the beginning of the 3rd century as well. With few variations, these images are repeated dozens of times especially in paintings, but also in sculptures and other precious objects, such as reliquaries, ivories, pendants and rings.

It has been already pointed out that the main idea of early Christian art is summed up in the figure of Christ the Saviour (the Good Shepherd) and in that of the soul saved by him (the "Orante"). In theological reflection, and secondly in art, the presence of Mary mother of Jesus, true man and redeemer, could not be neglected.

Among the various Christological scenes, besides the Nativity, the Epiphany also involved the Holy Virgin directly. Together with her Son, she had cooperated in the salvation of all men even pagans, represented here by the Magi. It was therefore right that she should be represented in the catacombs.

It was natural too that the early Christians wished to remember this event at the place of their burial, thus showing their gratitude to the Mother of God.

The adoration of the Magi Kings: Mary presents Jesus (4th century).

The Epiphany Scene

Back to Gallery Q1 and turning, after a few metres, to the left into Gallery Z3, there is the unexpected and pleasant surprise of the "Madonna *Arcosolium*", which dates back to the first half of the 4th century. Its frescoes are now badly deteriorated: the Good Shepherd, the miracle of Moses striking water from the rock...

The best preserved scene is that of the Epiphany. The Madonna is seated on a throne with her head veiled, wearing a long tunic. On her knees she bears the child Jesus, dressed in a short tunic. The Magi, who represented the first pagans who received faith, hurry to offer their gifts to the Child. If the figures of the Magi have partly faded away, it is still possible to describe them and compare them with other similar images. They are dressed in oriental clothes, with soft and pointed Phrygian caps which reveal their hair style, with tunics tightly bound by a girdle and trousers closely fitting at the ankles. Short cloaks cover their shoulders and they are shod with high boots.

5. FOUR YOUNG MEN FOUND AN ASSOCIATION

In front of the "Madonna *Arcosolium*" a passage leads into four communicating *cubicula*. A single light-shaft illuminates three of them. The architectonic excavation here is amazing, to the point that it seems to defy the laws of statics.

It was exactly in this place that, thanks to the enthusiasm and high ideals of four young men, an important association came to life: the *Collegium Cultorum Martyrum*, dedicated to the devotion to the Martyrs. Here is its interesting story, as related by one of them.

A providential meeting

"One day in April 1870 two youngsters barely eighteen, Mariano Armellini and myself Orazio Marucchi, were going home after a visit to the Catacomb of St. Agnes. On the Via Nomentana they met Pius IX, who was returning to the City with some

118

dignitaries. The Pope, seeing those young men who were carrying books and maps, asked them where they were coming from. He learnt that they were on their way back from the Catacomb of St. Agnes, where they had been sent by de Rossi.

The Pope then spoke to them with words they never forgot: 'Well done, my sons. You are in good hands. Pray often to the holy Martyrs of the catacombs and study them under the guidance of my dear de Rossi. Tell him also that the Pope wishes you to visit the Catacombs of St. Alexander which are on this same road but a little further out'. Having said this, he blessed them.

The two were moved by the Pope's kindness and that same evening went to see de Rossi, who then lived in Piazza del Gesù. They reported the fatherly words of Pius IX to him. De Rossi was moved too, and took those words as an authoritative recommendation for initiating those youngsters into the study of Christian archaeology and encouraging them in their devotion to the Martyrs".

The small seed grows

"The two friends collected some schoolmates and other young people of the same age, and formed a group of students, all eager to learn.

Following the end of political turmoil (the Breaching of Porta Pia, the almost bloodless takeover of the City by the Italian army, 20th September 1870), those students began in 1872 meeting at the Catacombs of St. Callixtus, where de Rossi very often joined them".

They prayed like the early Christians

"They then chose the four *cubicula* of the Western Area of St. Callixtus as their meeting place for prayer. The structure of the four *cubicula* facilitated the singing of Psalms, because the light-shaft above allowed the voices to be heard from one room to the other. They immediately called that group of four rooms the

119

A Christian sarcophagus (4ᵗʰ century). See p. 92.

'quadruple *cubiculum*', in imitation of the nearby *Cubiculum duplex* of deacon Severus and considered it as their little private church".

A marvellous idea

"During the 1878 Christmas holidays, four of them (Mariano Armellini, Orazio Marucchi, Enrico Stevenson and Adolfo Hytreck) agreed to celebrate the feast of the Epiphany in that 'quadruple *cubiculum*'.

They went to the great catacomb on the Appian Way, and during the trip they talked about the important historic monuments in the Cemetery of St. Callixtus and were sorry that the public at large didn't know anything about them. They hoped for the day when the ancient underground sanctuaries of the Martyrs would be regularly visited by the faithful as they were by the early Christians".

A moving Mass

"They descended into the Catacomb and the young German priest Adolfo Hytreck celebrated Mass in the 'Madonna *Arcosolium*', lit by two ancient lamps which cast their uncertain flickering light on the fresco depicting the Epiphany. After Mass they sang Psalms in the 'quadruple *cubiculum*' where they often met".

The birth of the "Collegium Cultorum Martyrum"

"They then went to the surface where there was a dilapidated farmhouse built in 1700 on the ruins of an ancient Christian oratory, the present Western *Trichora*. In one of the rooms of that rustic building the four young friends breakfasted and resumed the conversation interrupted by the short liturgical service.

They said how moving it was to have celebrated Mass in the catacomb, but that it was not enough to do it only on the feast-day of St. Cecilia. All were in agreement that an association should be set up, whose aim would be the devotion to the Martyrs in the catacombs. They decided to call it the *Collegium Cultorum Martyrum*". This association continues to the present day with the name: *"Academia Cultorum Martyrum"*.

6. THE "PROFANATION" OF THE CATACOMBS

Something must now be said about another group of young people, whose ideas and behaviour were utterly opposed to those of the group above mentioned.

All high-school students, delving into the cultural phenomenon known as Humanism, are familiar with the name of Julius Pomponius Laetus (1428-1497) and of the "Associates of the Roman Academy of Antiquarians".

The "Maestro"

Pomponius Laetus was an admirer of the great Romans to the point of imitating them in daily life. Like Cato, he lived in ostentatious poverty and, following the advice of Varro and Columella, he farmed a little vineyard.

Like Cola di Rienzo (1313-1354) he wandered among the ruins of Rome and mourned the fate of the grandeur of imperial Rome so much that he wept over those ruins. He sought out and read the Latin classics avidly, which he copied in fine handwriting. A jealous guardian of pure Latin, he even refused to learn Greek.

The "Associates of the Roman Academy of Antiquarians"

In Pomponius' house on the Quirinal Hill, friends, disciples and admirers met and took part in discussions about the ancient authors and some philosophical questions put by the master.

Those gatherings marked the beginning of the "Roman Academy of Antiquarians". Its associates, all young humanists with a pagan trend in their ideas and unfortunately also in their style of life, through the cult of pagan antiquity sought a substitute for their lost Christian faith. Infatuated as they were, they came to think of themselves as a pagan priestly college, giving themselves special names and calling their master Pomponius Laetus, *pontifex maximus*, high priest. They had their own religious rites, which ridiculed Christianity.

The visit of these "Antiquarians" to the catacombs

Pomponius Laetus and his associates looked almost everywhere for classical Latin inscriptions. They even searched in some catacombs, and managed to enter the Cemetery of St. Callixtus through openings made by subsidence, but they did not succeed in identifying it. They entered a *cubiculum* of this area, situated at the end of Gallery Z3. The architecture of this *cubiculum* is very unusual.

It is a unique excavation, pleasing to the eye. Near the roof, an architrave runs along the walls, supported on graceful corbels. Both the corbels and the architrave were cut out of the rock, using a particular way of working the tufa. High on the left wall appear the names of Pomponius Laetus and of his associates, together with their rank as scholars and a definition of themselves which, to speack frankly, is disrespectful to the holiness of the place.

1475 XV Kt Feb
Pantagathus, Mammeius, Papirius
Minicinus, Aemilius
unanimes perscrutatores antiquitatis
regnante Pom. Pont. Max.
Minutius
Rom. Pup. Delitie

Here is the translation:

"January 18, 1475
Pantagathus, Mammeius, Papirius,
Minicinus, Aemilius,
unanimous searchers of antiquities,
Pomponius Laetus, reigning as Pontifex Maximus
Minutius
delight of the 'dolls' of Rome".

The abbreviations of the last line *Rom. Pup. Delitie* read: *Romananum Puparum Deliciae*. They were learned persons, of course, but not serious enough, at least in their private lives...

7. WHAT ALL CHRISTIAN MOTHERS LONG FOR

Leaving the *cubiculum* with the signatures of the "Antiquarians" and following on the left a stretch of Gallery Z4, Gallery R is reached, on the left of which is the Liberian Area and on the right the Area of SS. Gaius and Eusebius.[2] Going this way, before reaching Gallery Q1, the *"Arcosolium* of the Oranti" is to be seen on the left. The main figure is a mother among her four sons.

Every mother wishes for the health and happiness of her children. She faces great sacrifices to bear them, bring them up and educate them. She would always like to be with them and see them one day beside her in Paradise.

This mother is happy among her four children, because she knows that from now on nothing can separate her from them.

This is a good wish extended to all mothers...

---

[1] See map on p. 115.
[2] See map on p. 115.

XII.
The Liberian Area

Parents and Children

The Liberian Area is in the northern part of the Cemetery of St. Callixtus and was excavated in the second half of the 4th century. This was its last development.

It originated from a staircase of its own which is now walled up. It was planned systematically, with a broad *decumanus* or main gallery, and developed on three levels, but the first and the third ones are rather limited. In the late 4th century it was joined to the Western Area and to those of SS. Gaius and Eusebius, as well as to that of St. Miltiades.

1. THE NAME

The name was given by de Rossi following the discovery in this area of three sepulchral inscriptions from the time of Pope St. Liberius (352-366), St. Damasus' predecessor.

One of these inscriptions, now in the Museo Pio Cristiano in the Vatican, refers to a certain Euplia, a five-year-old girl, *deposita in pace sub Liberio papa*, "buried in peace under Pope Liberius" (ICUR, IV, 10852).

Recent excavations in this region by Prof. Fasola have confirmed de Rossi's view. Among others, two inscriptions have come to light which mention a presbyter, Simplicius, and a lector, Victor, also buried here during the pontificate of St. Liberius.

2. ITS CHARACTERISTICS

In the Cemetery of St. Callixtus, the Liberian Area is the climax in the perfection of the excavatory art. Its chief feature is the presence of large *cubicula* with either groined or barrel vaults, with columns or sometimes pilasters at the four corners.

Near the *arcosolia*, semi-circular niches are very frequent, as are little round or square tables inside the *cubicula*. In the wider niches, larger lamps were placed, some in metal, while candelabra stood in front of the *arcosolia*. The tables often held vessels, similar to dishes, where oil lamps were laid.

Horizontal marble slabs, which held lamps, often protrude like brackets in front of the *loculi*. All the lamps served both to give light and to honour the tombs of the dead. They were lit especially on the anniversaries of burial. They testify to the affection of surviving relatives and friends, and their care for the tombs. As de Rossi has pointed out, the atmosphere offered by the Liberian Area in the late 4th century must have been a solemn one. The long straight galleries, flanked by an uninterrupted sequence of *arcosolia* and imposing *cubicula*, were illuminated at intervals by skylights. The daylight which came through the light-shafts dimmed the many small flames of the lamps placed before each tomb or above the doors of the *cubicula*.

The candelabra shed their flickering light amongst the *transennae*, the sculptured and perforated marbles, the sepulchral inscriptions, the mosaics and frescoes, while nard filled the air with scent, making the visit there very impressive and most agreeable.

The "Cemetery of Mouths"

The great number of skylights, quite visible above ground in this area as in the western one close by, led

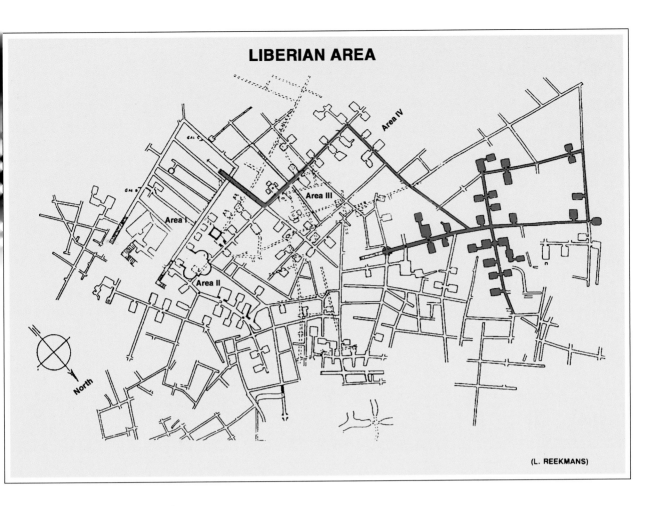

LIBERIAN AREA

Area IV

Area III

Area I

Area II

North

(L. REEKMANS)

Bosio to call this part of the Catacombs of St. Callixtus the "Cemetery of Mouths".

The few scattered frescoes in this area recall well-known themes: Christ the *pantocrator* (omnipotent), the monogram of Christ, "Oranti", Adam and Eve with the serpent (Original sin), Susannah accused by the elders, garlands...

Some of the clergy found here their last resting-place. Inscriptions reveal that some *cubicula* were those of deacons, such as Deusdedit, "who melted the hearts of the obstinate with his goodness. He was devoted to justice and led an upright life. He was rich to the poor and poor to himself" (ICUR, IV, 12601).

Deacon Tigridas "was distinguished for the austerity of his life. He was also a man of the old generation, diligent and watchful in observing the divine law" (ICUR, IV, 10228). Deacon Redemptus, as will be seen, "passed a youth worthy of praise and lived in innocence".

The deacons were close collaborators of the bishops. In Rome they assisted the pope. In the Church hierarchy they ranked next to the presbyters and in the Christian community they carried out liturgical and administrative functions, as well as charitable works...

3. SEPULCHRAL INSCRIPTIONS

Rather than confine ourselves to a detailed description of the *cubicula* or of a few frescoes in this area, it is preferable to draw one's attention to the epigraphs found here, which are numerous and very interesting.

The "Callixtian complex" has 3522 inscriptions, intact or fragmentary, as can be seen in the 4th volume of ICUR. Of them, 2378 belong to the Cemetery of St. Callixtus proper, while the remaining 1144 are in other catacombs of the "Callixtian complex" (see map on p. 22). It is quite a number!

A small anthology of these epigraphs follows[1].

4. THE STORY OF THOSE WHO "DO NOT MAKE HISTORY"

The kind of history we learn in our schools gives the names of illustrious persons and the dates of important battles. We get the impression that only the great and the powerful "make history".

The thoughts, feelings and the mutual affections of people who love one another, as well as everyday sufferings, are not generally told in official history. Those who are part of this reality are too poor, their social standing too low...

But the catacomb inscriptions hand down reminders of them and allow us to reconstruct all that humble world, which in so many ways resembles our own.

5. MARRIED LIFE

As Prof. Jos Janssens points out, "the epitaphs (in the catacombs) present marriage as a communion of souls and bodies. They underline the harmony of husband and wife as perennial companions and the joys of life together...

The early Christians thought of marriage as an exclusive union, as is evidenced by the eulogies paid to a departed wife. Her utter faithfulness and upright and chaste conduct were remembered, which witnessed a unique love. Of a departed husband, his honesty and stainless behaviour were recorded.

Marriage demands discipline, which calls the partners to persevere in faith and prayer, so as to set an example by their way of life.

In this way, Christians honour their marriage bond, but still more they discover the presence of God in it, as is seen in the exclamation of one Cyriacus, who turns to his dead wife saying:

"The Creator has given you to me as a holy gift"! (ICUR, 1, 1496).

On the preceding page.
Cubiculum of the Sacraments A5:
Jonah is resting under a vine
(1st half of 3rd century). See p. 83.

Adam and Eve
(the Original sin).
Reconstruction of the fresco.

Unforgettable wives

"They become one", is written in the Bible *(Genesis 2, 24)*. Tertullian speaks of married couples as brothers and sisters, collaborators, united in troubles, persecutions and hope *(Ad Uxorem)*.

Celsus Eutropius had lost his young wife when she was barely thirty, after eleven years of happy marriage. He wrote on her tombstone that the time he had spent with her had been a Paradise. How lucky he was!

"Celsus Eutropius to his wife... who lived always with me without even causing me any detriment to my soul and life (sine ulla lesione animi mei). *She lived for 31 years, 9 months and 15 days. She was buried 7 days before the Kalends of... She died on a Thursday. With loving memory in peace"* (ICUR, IV, 11241).

Love and tenderness is also in Flavius Crispinus' epitaph for his dear Aurelia:

FL CRISPINVS AYRELIAE ANIA
NETI BEN · M · COIVGE QVE VIXIT AN
XXVIII QVEM COIVCE HABYI AN
VIIII KARITATE SINE VLA ANIME MEI
LESIONE VALE MICHI KARA IM PACE
CVM SPIRITA XANTA VALE IN · ✠ ·

"Flavius Crispinus to Aurelia Aniane, most worthy wife, who lived 28 years. We were married for 9 years with love, and she never gave me cause for pain. Farewell, my dear. Be at peace with the holy souls. Farewell in Christ!" (ICUR, IV, 12566).

As again Jos Janssens points out, "the wish that she may be at peace 'with the holy souls' means that the husband believes her to be in heaven, with God, in full possession of happiness. The very fact of being among the just is considered as part of the state of beatitude. The company of other holy ones makes the soul rejoice; it contributes to the delight of each and the happiness of all. Blessedness, therefore, means to be with God and the Saints, to enjoy their presence and know that one is welcome among them.

Heaven is thus not seen as a place, but rather as a life in God and with God, a living in Christ who is light itself, rather than a luminous dwelling. More than living at rest, it is a living in peace which is God himself. The blessed life is more than a vision of God, it is a life of joy lived with God and the angels and the saints. The promise and the heavenly reward refer to a life in close union with God.

The true Christian message, then, is that the saints live in God forever. Such a life has a clearly personal character, because it is understood as an individual and intimate relationship with God, but at the same time it is essentially a 'church' (an assembly, a communion) as well, because it is lived in the company of the blessed".

Conjugal faithfulness

This is a virtue that has its roots in the Gospel. The Apologists, defenders of the truth of Christian faith, and the Fathers of the Church, the great bishops of the first centuries, exalt fidelity in their writings. Today it is also longed for by so many children and youths who are compelled to live in very painful family situations.

The tombstone described below concerns the faithfulness of a wife to her husband, but the same holds true for a husband to his wife.

Good Probilianus realized the importance of this virtue in married life and wanted to bear witness to it in praise of his wife.

"Probilianus to his wife Felicity, whose faithfulness, upright conduct and goodness were known to all our neighbours. In the eight years that her husband was absent she never betrayed him. She was then buried in this holy place on January 30" (ICUR, IV, 10953).

"One of the finest tributes a husband can pay to his wife – J. Janssens goes on – is to stress the integrity of her conduct, that is, her chastity. She keeps her body chaste for her husband. That Probilianus means not only the chastity of the body but also of the heart, is evident from the other virtues he underlines, such as her uprightness and probity, and the praise he gives to her decency as a way of life, and his insistence on her innocence.

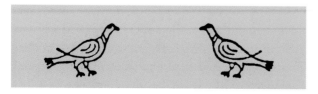

An ideal husband

If man and woman are the climax of a complex relationship, it is easy to understand what a derangement the death of a loved one may cause. Sorrow is born of love lived in depth, and there is no death more desolate than that for which no tears are shed. Only thus can we realize the pain of this young wife when her beloved Alexius died at the age of 31. They had been married very young and Alexius had loved her very much: fifteen years without the shadow of misunderstanding! Her husband had been a *lector* in his parish, called Fullonica, because it was near a wash-house *(fullonica)*. The *titulus Fullonicae* probably concides with the present church of SS. Marcellinus and Peter on the Via Merulana.

"To the most beloved husband Alexius, a most sweet soul, lector in the title of Fullonica. He lived with me for fifteen years. He was united with me in marriage at the age of sixteen. Virgin to a virgin (that is, they did not have pre-marital intercourse)*, from whom I never had any grief. Rest in peace with the Saints, with whom you have deserved (to live). Buried on 15th December"* (ICUR, IV, 11798).

"To live marriage as a communion of life means above all to live in harmony with each other... But premarital virginity is so often recorded on epitaphs so as to suggest that to remain virgin until one's wedding day was regarded as normal among the Christians. Pagans also held that in great esteem. But it seems that with the believers it had become an integral factor in their Christian concept of marriage" (J. Janssens).

Heartfelt regret

Sometimes the catacomb epitaphs witness genuine tragedies. Many wives died young because of difficulties in childbirth, but the death-roll among husbands was also high. Yet, among so much anguish, in Christian epigraphy it is hard to find a feeling of rebellion or despair. Faith always shed its comforting light on sorrowful human events. It was in this Christian vision of death that Aphrodite, Elia Capitolina and Cornelia Victorina mourned the loss of their husbands:

"For his unique love of his wife and his admirable charity, Aphrodite (made the tomb) for Antonius, her most beloved husband, who lived 25 years, 1 month and 7 days. In peace" (ICUR, IV, 11809).

Also the children join their bereaved mother in the sorrow and mourning for the departed father:

"To Quintus Ophellius Trophimus. Elia Capitolina made this inscription for her saintly husband together with her children, united with her (in remembering their father)" (ICUR, IV, 10059).

Or again:

"To Aurelius Macrobius. Cornelia Victorina to her dearest husband and the sons Aurelius Demetrius and Gennadius (erected this tomb) to their father. In peace" (ICUR, IV, 12574).

"Out of these and many other examples, if one wished to sum up the image of a husband as it emerges from those epitaphs, the conclusion would be: a good man, affable, a friend to all, cultivating friendship, amiable, intelligent and honest. People sought him out and respected him for his personal and professional qualities. He was admired for his faithfulness to traditional principles, for his integrity of mind, his upright conduct, his solid faith. A husband is everything to his wife, and speaks of her with respect and admiration" (J. Janssens).

An admirable couple

To end this first group of inscriptions devoted to married life, here is one, of uncertain origin and now unfortunately lost.

Children are the finest fruit of the conjugal love of parents and constitute their continuation after death. Each of us feels the need to go on living... The most precious legacy a married couple can leave to a son or daughter is the example of a life illuminated by love. And the profound harmony cultivated in their married life is a practical manifestation of it. Young Drusus was fully convinced of that and felt the need to hand on the memory on a tombstone:

"To Stephen and Generosa, most sweet parents, who lived long without ever quarrelling. The most unhappy Drusus made this tomb for the finest of parents" (ICUR, III, 9170).

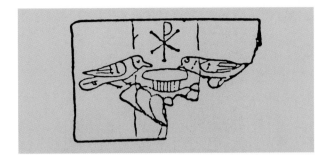

6. FAMILY LIFE

On the Christian idea of "family" as it is seen from the catacomb inscriptions, Jos Janssens' comment is again illuminating:

"Epitaphs tell us of families where the values of human warmth, benevolence, tenderness, serenity and peace were in great honour.

We meet parents who are attentive to their children: keeping an eye on their little ones at play and with their charming childish foibles. Their careful attention accompanies them as they grow and develop their qualities and talents, follows them through the first joys and sorrows when they get married. We notice sons and daughters who assist their elderly parents, grandchildren and grandparents who love each other, brothers and sisters who feel united by their family ties even in later years and look after one another.

The sense of family was deep, the ties between its members were close and affectionate. Families were also united in the faith. Children were brought up in the service of God and in the devotion to the Martyrs. Consecrated virginity and the service in the Church were valued. Prayer was an essential element in the reverence for the dead. The love of God was instilled into the children.

In Christian families, there also flourished such values as pre-marital virginity, matrimonial chastity, personal integrity, industriousness, friendship, social awareness, particularly in the care of abandoned children, defenceless and without help".

The epitaphs not only indicate young couples brusquely separated by death, but also children cut off from their parents at the dawn of their lives.

"True acceptance of death becomes possible only in a perspective which sustains life. The early Christians, like all mankind, have experienced that death in itself is brutal, because it took everything from us, removing us from everyone. How difficult must it be when it strikes the young, how shattering when it is sudden and unexpected. While pagans saw in death the inevitable and impersonal call of Fate, the Christians discerned the presence of God in it.

It is faith which makes death acceptable. That is possible because.., a believer dies in Christ, in the certainty that the same Christ, the conqueror of death, will be his guide towards eternal life" (J. Janssens).

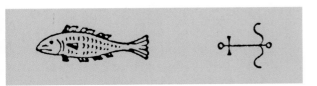

Junius, "a witty boy"

The natural endowments of Junius forecast a bright future. With his wit this boy had obviously won all hearts. Of course, he was the pride of his lucky parents.

But death is pitiless. It takes no account of age and plucked this tender flower just when it was beginning to bloom. There arises then a spontaneous cry of sorrow: "Why has God allowed this? Why must even the little ones, the innocent, the good, suffer and die? Why must we die?...".

Junius' parents did not ask themselves these questions. They simply give us the response of their faith. They do indeed speak of his being snatched away, certainly not wanting to deny the sorrow they feel at his unexpected loss, but they know that their little son goes on living and that one day they will find him again. Through death, little Junius, a lamb of goodness, has been offered to Christ. He has not been lost for eternity.

"...To Junius Acutianus, who lived about ten years.
Well deserving, in peace. Buried on...
In this tomb which you see rests a boy
witty of mind, despite his very tender age...
A lamb snatched from heaven and given to Christ" [2].

Augustine, "a dear youth"

This inscription is dedicated *"to the sweet repose, to the singular piety, to the innocence of life and the marvellous wisdom of a most dear youth, who chose his mother's religion. Worthy beyond all telling... Augustine lived fifteen tender years and three months. A most devoted mother to her sweetest son in eternal peace"* (ICUR, IV, 11823).

Poor mother! Augustine was her pride and the prop of her declining years. Now she was alone!

"The term 'innocent, applied by parents to their children — Jos Janssens points out — is to be understood primarily as a natural gift. If it is used for infants. It expresses a common human feeling insofar as infants harm no one and are free from malice. 'Innocent' thus comes to be a common qualification given to those who die before they are ten.

Later on, this common idea of 'infant innocence' allowed the Christians to give the term a religious hint, such as baptismal innocence, which, however, is rarely alluded to explicitly. The image of innocence, proper to infants, was also used to describe the good conduct of grown-ups", as in the above mentioned tombstone.

Macedonianus rests in the peace of the Lord

The early Christians realized that children are a precious gift of God.[3] Life was welcomed with respect and gratitude. They rejected every form of abortion and opposed the pagan custom of abandoning newborn babies. Rather, they gladly adopted these unfortunate children, offering them affection and help.

If the affection of parents for their children is to be gauged from the language of the epigraphs, we must conclude that it was truly boundless.

"To the dearest son Macedanianus,
sweeter than all sweetness of children,
who lived on this earth nine years and twenty days.
A parent raised this tomb to his loved one" [4].

From the inscription we gather that little Macedonianus was orphaned: whether of a father or mother we do not know. So this parent is doubly bereaved, having lost both his or her son Macedonianus, the fruit of married love, and his or her life's partner. Only in this context can we fully understand the expression "sweeter than all sweetness of children". What a void this boy filled in that house with his affection and presence!

The inscription is on the tablet at the centre of the lid. On the right is the bust of the child. Behind him, a banner held up by two "putti" is carved. On the left of the tablet the biblical Jonah appears, first thrown into the sea and then resting under a vine.

Secunda, "sweetest dove"

Above one of the steps of the staircase of the Liberian Area in its lower part, there is the little slab of Secunda, a wonderful girl who died when she was only twenty years. Her integrity of life and behaviour, the gentleness of her speech, her faith.., offer a rare example of an ideal fiancée and wife.

> MIRAE · BONITATIS SECVNDE
> QVAE VIXIT PVRA FIDE ANNOS
> VIGINTI PVDICA CESSAVIT
> INPACE ID VIRGO FIDELIS
> BENEMERENTI QVIESCET ID IVL
> PALVMBO SINE FELLE M ET N

"To Secunda, of admirable goodness, who lived twenty years with faith. She was of upright behaviour and always kept her virginity. She died in the peace of the Lord. A faithful virgin and well deserving. She went to rest on July 15, a dove without gall (without rancour in her speech), under the consulate of Mamertine and Nevicta" (AD. 362; cf. ICUR, IV, 9558).

Valentina, "sweet and so much loved"

It is proper to poetry to speak of death as "being snatched away", above all when it strikes the young. This sudden loss arouses consternation and rejection in one's parents. Not even the memories of the happiest hours, of the most affectionate conversations and smiles and kisses of their children can soften their grief. Valens and his wife experienced this separation in all its bitterness. Their only comfort was to know that their daughter, though taken away from them, went to heaven. Grief remained and brought affliction, but in their minds there was the certainty, founded on faith, that one day they would see Valentina again and God would give her back to them.

> *"...on the Kalends of April (April 1st)*
> *...(the wife) and Valens still living (made this tomb)*
> *to their most gentle daughter Valentina*
> *(now) in peace (of the Lord).*
> *O Valentina, sweet and so much loved,*
> *I am overcome by uncontrollable tears*
> *and I cannot utter a word.*
> *To those whom you endeared with your smile,*
> *this remains in their hearts;*
> *it adds more tears*
> *and cannot remove the sorrow.*
> *Heaven suddenly took you to itself".[5]*

Heliodora, a brave and grateful girl

It is not rare to find slabs in the catacombs which refer to *alumni* or *alumnae*. This does not mean students in the modern sense but adopted children.

As D. Mazzoleni explains, "in the Roman world exposure of the new-born was tolerated and they were left at the foot of a column in Rome, aptly called *Lactaria* (the suckling column), which stood in the *Forum Olitorium* (vegetable-market).

Anyone who found one of those unfortunate babies could adopt it or enslave it. This law remained in force until the time of Justinian (527-565), when full freedom was granted to adopted children and capital punishment was decreed for those who exposed them.

At the beginning of the 4th century, in order to prevent infants from being abandoned, Constantine bade that food and clothing be supplied to the destitute at the public expense. Later, St. Augustine assigned to consecrated virgins the task of collecting abandoned babies and having them baptized. Still, most of them faced death".

Epitaph of Leontius, an adopted child.

If the child survived, the Christian community provided for his or her welfare, offering him or her the warmth of a family *(alumnus,* from *álere,* to nourish). If death took the child, the "adoptive father" would indicate on the tombstone that the child had been adopted.

The contrary scarcely ever happened. A person who had been abandoned at a tender age generally gave no hint of his or her painful origin. It was too humiliating to admit it, but Heliodora Pascasia had no such inhibition. She had a double *loculus* excavated for herself and for Leo, as she wished to be in the company, even in death, of the man who had given her all the affection of a father:

"This is the tomb of Heliodora Pascasia whose foster-father died on the... of August... aged years"... (ICUR, IV, 11334).

---

[1] In the frequent theological, philosophical and ascetical reflections on the inscriptions in this selection I rely on the valuable study of Prof. JOS JANSSENS S.J., *Vita e Morte del cristiano negli epitaffi di Roma anteriori al sec. VII.* Università Editrice Gregoriana, Roma, 1981.

[2] ICUR, IV, 11328.

[3] Cf. *Psalm* 128, 3.

[4] ICUR, IV, 11946.

[5] ICUR, IV, 11444.

A gallery in the area called St. Miltiades.

XIII.
The Liberian Area

The Neighbour and God

1. LIFE IN THE SERVICE OF THE NEIGHBOUR

Christians, though they long for heaven, do not forget the earth and their everyday problems. They know that they are also called by God to work here below, for the benefit of their brethren.

A professor of Latin and Greek

In antiquity there were no state schools; only a few persons were lucky enough to receive an education. Teaching was done by masters who ran private schools or by tutors who lived with patrician families.

From the beginning, the Church concerned itself with that problem and set out to offer adequate instruction to the children of the people.

As Prof. D. Mazzoleni writes, "education was not prohibited to Christians as is evidenced by the presence, in various places, of inscriptions concerning masters, grammarians, and teachers of rhetoric. None of these activities enjoyed a worthwhile salary in the ancient world. Diocletian's edict of 301 fixed a fee of 200 *denarii* a month for every pupil, which was equal to four days wages for a skilled workman. This sum was not paid by the state but by the pupil who attended the lessons.

Christians received a classical education given in private schools; even the Fathers of the Church, such as St. Ambrose and St. Augustine..., acknowledged the value of secular scholarship.

The wax writing tablets of an Egyptian student of the 4th century were hardly distinguishable from the tablets used by an Hellenistic student. They had the same series of mythological names with which to practise writing, the same maxims and moral anec-

dotes. But on top of the tablets of a Christian pupil generally appeared the invocation: 'Blessed be God', or the monogram of the cross, which concealed the name of Christ".

The certainty of attaining eternal peace, to which teacher Deuterius alludes on his tombstone, allows us to assume that in life he had put his learning at the service of his neighbour.

PRISCORVM INTERPRES VATVM DOCTORQ · (ue bilinguis)
DEVTERIVS PLACIDA SECVRVS PACE QVIESCIT

*"Deuterius, interpreter of ancient seers (poets)
and teacher of Latin and Greek,
rests assured (of salvation)
in tranquil peace".*[1]

Theodulus, a brave soldier and an honest administrator

We know something about the lives of married couples, of Secunda, of Heliodora Pascasia, and of the teacher Deuterius, but also of the life of a much-decorated soldier, who later became an employee in the City Prefecture.

In his work, Theodulus was more concerned with being honest than using his position to make money. An example of a rare virtue, it is still valid today. The inscription is rhythmical and acrostic: uniting the initial letters of each line, the name "Theodulus"comes out, which means "servant of God". Here is a possible literal translation:

"His friends' memories keep the record of (Theodulus),
who died with military honours.
His loyalty was outstanding
among non-commissioned officers.
He was faithful to all fellow soldiers and friends.
Reputation declares him a servant of God
rather than of money,
and an upright non-commissioned official
of the City Prefecture.
If I were able I would sing his praises for ever
so that he may be granted
the promised gifts of light (i.e. Paradise)"...[2]

Now this inscription is to be seen on the wall of the exit staircase.

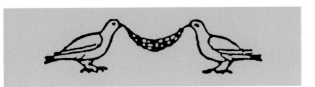

Redemptus, the deacon who loved music and sacred chant

Goodness, commitment and love for fellow creatures, the spirit of prayer, sacrifice, innocence of life, and fidelity in the ministry, particularly of a priest or a deacon, always leave a deep impression in the heart of a bishop and in the minds of the Christian people. The death of such men is for the whole church community a sad departure, as if they had lost a brother, a counsellor, a friend, a father. Thus was the deacon Redemptus mourned by his congregation and by Pope Liberius. Some decades later there was a desire to honour the memory of this faithful friend of God with a poem which interpreted the feelings of his people.

"O sorrow, dry your tears!
O holy people of God, do you ask about deacon Redemptus?
The kingdom of heaven suddenly called him.
He made delightful music, sang exquisitely
and celebrated with gentle harmony
the holy prophet David (singing the Psalms).
His life on earth was innocent.
His youth was praised.
He finally conquered evil
and it no more harms him.
Now Paradise welcomes him,
after snatching him away,
he who had won
so many victories over the enemy (the devil)".[3]

The inscription is found in the *cubiculum* where Redemptus was buried. This deacon probably died at the time of St. Liberius, but the poem was written by an imitator of Pope Damasus, perhaps during the pontificate of his successor St. Siricius (384-399).

The epitaphs in the catacombs also offer us some information about the social origins, education and spirituality of the clergy.

"Ideally it is desirable that their faith be genuine and rooted in their hearts. What attracts us to them is their love for Christ and for their neighbours. The former is shown in their faithful carrying out the divine precepts, their devotion to the service of the altar, their capacity for renunciation and detachment from the world. The latter is evident through their works of charity... In the pastoral care of the people of Christ we remember those who behaved with compassion and goodness to all and showed themselves zealous for the things of God" (J. Janssens).

Annius Innocentius, "apostolic nuncio"

"Acolyte" is one of the "minor orders" on the way to priesthood. The acolyte's task is to help the priests or bishop during liturgical celebrations. Annius Innocentius was a worthy servant of the Church of Rome. He knew Greek well. For this reason the pope entrusted him as his ambassador ("papal legate" or "apostolic nuncio", as we would say nowadays) on special missions.

"Annius Innocentius, acolyte, lived for 26 years. He laboured often on journeys by ecclesiastical command. Indeed he was sent twice to the provinces in Greece and in the regions of Campania, Calabria and Apulia in Southern Italy. On his last mission to Sardinia, he died. His body was translated to St. Callixtus. He sleeps (now) in peace, August 25th. Priest Annius Innocentius, his brother, with whom he worked well, prepared (this tomb for him)" (ICUR, IV, 11805).

The epigraph was discovered on Christmas Eve of 1908 in the original tomb of the acolyte, in the floor of a small *cubiculum* of the Cemetery of SS. Mark and Marcellianus, in the "Callixtian complex". A block of tufa, falling into the *cubiculum*, had split the slab into two unequal parts, the smaller of which had fallen into the sepulchre, crushing most of the friable bones.

The service of Annius Innocentius as an acolyte and "diplomat" probably coincided with the pontificate of St. Julius I (337-352) or St. Liberius (352-366). The Church was then going through difficult and troubled times in its struggle with the Arians, who denied the divine nature of Jesus and therefore refused the title of Mother of God given to Mary. There was often the need of sending messengers in order to convoke bishops to a synod, to communicate regulations to the various Churches, to summon to the See of Peter recalcitrant bishops or those suspected of heresy...

Annius Innocentius was one of such trusted and able couriers. But his health did not stand up to the strain of these repeated missions. His last journey, to Sardinia, was fatal. He died during the Summer, the worst period for malaria.

His brother and namesake, priest Annius Innocentius, was a person of some importance among the Roman clergy, as he was in charge of the Cemetery of SS. Mark and Marcellianus. He naturally chose this catacomb for his brother's last resting place, after bringing him back from Sardinia.

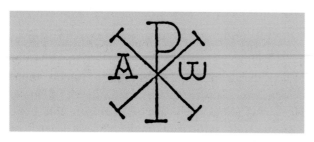

2. LIFE IN CHRIST

Several inscriptions tell us that the deceased was a "neophyte",[4] i.e. a recently baptized Christian. Perhaps we do not understand the importance of this, because nowadays Baptism is generally administered to babies and, as the saying is, one is born a Christian. Then to grow and mature in the faith is a life-long commitment.

For the early Christians the prospect was different. Those who were to receive Baptism (catechumens) were for the most part grown-ups. Baptism was the completion of a long journey which began with listening to sermons, undergoing a period of years of instruction before conversion, and moving towards a deeper understanding of one's Christian life. During this time the catechumens took part in the Church life, but not in all its manifestations, nor with full membership. With Baptism came the great day of one's encounter with God, the day of fulfilment of grace and of perfect communion with the brethren in the faith.[5]

Antonia Cyriaca, "having received the grace of God..."

"To the well deserving Antonia Cyriaca who lived for 19 years, 2 months and 26 days. Having received the grace of God (Baptism) she died on the 4th day, a virgin. Her father, Julius Benedictus, dedicated (this epitaph) to his most sweet and incomparable daughter. She was buried on November 20th" (ICUR, IV, 11806).

On the following page: A pleasant view of the Western Trichora.

The difference of surnames between father and daughter evidently indicates that Benedict had married a widow who had had Cyriaca by a previous marriage.

Felix, a neophyte

"To our most worthy son Felix, who lived for 23 years and 10 days. He departed this life a virgin and a neophyte. In peace. His parents dedicated this epitaph. He was buried on August 2ⁿᵈ" (ICUR, IV, 12459).

"In many epigraphs — Jos Janssens explains — the term 'virgin' refers to the physical integrity proper to an unmarried woman. The use of the word in this primary sense implies that the dedicators (parents) foresaw marriage as the obvious future for the dead girl.

On the other hand, applying the word 'virgin' to babies, youths and mature men meant that for Christians the term had an ideal 'force', attributable to both sexes. Virginity was thus understood not only as a physical value but a moral one as well".

The word "virgin", therefore, while retaining the meaning of an unmarried person, has a real overtone of praise and admiration. Indeed, for a youth and for a mature man this discipline of life calls for effort and implies personal merit. Such praise and admiration are also reflected in the description found in the epitaph of a husband and a wife as *virgo ad virginem*, which underlines that the man was a "virgin" too.

Three orphans and a desolate father

The following inscription tells us again of a family tragedy: a husband widower with three children. The mother is now in divine peace and goes on watching over and protecting her "broken" family, which is torn with grief but has the certainty of seeing her again one day.

"I was born in Rome. If you ask my name, it was Julia. I lived faithful to my husband Florentius to whom I left three living sons. Having just received divine grace, I was taken into the peace (of the Lord) as a neophyte" (ICUR, IV, 11927).

"In its Christian concept, death, enlightened by faith, is seen as a restitution of the soul to God, its creator. Death, then, becomes a welcome to heaven by God and by the Church.

God is seen as a Father who receives personally everyone who dies. The believer's confidence in the divine welcome is proved when he (or she) wishes such an encounter, and above all when the faithful, conscious of being a sinner, commits himself to God, in the belief that God has purified him through Baptism" (J. Janssens).

Irene, "a virgin consecrated to God"

In the "Callixtian complex" Pope St. Damasus had a mausoleum built for himself and his family. Beside him, in the sleep of death awaiting resurrection, lay his mother Laurentia, who died aged ninety, and his sister Irene.

Here is Irene's funeral eulogy written by Damasus himself. It shows deep affection and great esteem for his sister who was consecrated to God.

"In this tomb now rest limbs consecrated to God.
Here is Damasus' sister; if you seek her name: Irene.
When she was still living, she was promised to Christ,
so that holy modesty itself proved the merit of the virgin.
She had not yet reached twenty years of age;
but those years had already been lit up
by her oustanding way of life.
The girl's strength of mind and
the piety which was worthy of honour had
born magnificent fruit during her finest years.
The witness of our affection (our father), when he was
leaving this world, wished to give you, sister,
to me as a pledge of his integrity. And when the royal
palace of heaven (Paradise) resolved to take to
itself this pledge (Irene),
I had no fear of her death because
she was innocent and deserved heaven.
But I suffered, I confess,
because I lost the comfort she gave me here.
And now when the Lord shall summon me,
remember Damasus, O virgin,
so that by the grace of God
your torch may give me light".[6]

So, "virginity is prized by the Christians not only in view of marriage but also as a way of life... A virgin consecrates her body to God, as Damasus states, and therefore the spirituality of sacred virgins develops as a vision of spiritual nuptials with Christ" (J. Janssens).

"Christ will make Damasus rise from his ashes"

The poem composed by Damasus for his own tomb is an act of faith in the omnipotence of the Son of God, who has promised men the resurrection of the body. It is an inscription truly worthy of the catacombs!

Christians in fact decorated these cemeteries with frescoes, sculptures and mosaics not simply to offer us an illustration of the Old and New Testaments, but also to express the faith that their loved ones had professed in their lives and beseech for them everlasting reward.

In his inscription, after recalling some of Christ's miracles (his walking on the waters, the raising of Lazarus, his own Resurrection...), Damasus affirms with absolute certainty that Jesus Christ will one day raise him from his ashes.

"He who trod the tumultuous waves,
he who restores life to the seeds
which die in the earth;
he who could unloosen the lethal bonds of death
after darkness,
and restore life after three days
to Martha's brother,
will, I believe, make Damasus rise from his ashes".[7]

We have often dealt with this Pope, especially when describing the crypts of the martyrs. But who was St. Damasus really?

The *Liber Pontificalis* abounds in information about him. It tells that he belonged to the Roman clergy and was of Spanish origin *(natione hispanus)* on the side of his father Anthony. His election in 366 by the Roman clergy was particularly stormy. He was opposed by the schismatic faction, who elected presbyter Ursinus. The confrontation, carried to extremes by excited people, suddenly degenerated into a civil war, with dead and wounded.

Damasus' pontificate was very active. He summoned some local councils and was on excellent terms with the great bishop of Milan St. Ambrose. He also had a notable influence on the Eastern Churches.

The use of Latin in the Roman liturgy, instead of Greek, was a fact of great pastoral significance, a change which Damasus favoured with much eagerness. Moreover, he promoted scholarship by founding a library in his family home, and he chose the learned St. Jerome as his counsellor and "pontifical secretary".

But the work in which Damasus most distinguished himself was the cult of the martyrs. In the years when the Church had regained peace, the heroic accounts of the martyrs were told as Christian fireside stories. Damasus as a child had listened to those marvellous stories with the greatest interest. He confided later on, in one of his poems, how he had heard of the martyrdom of SS. Marcellinus and Peter from the very lips of their executioner.

Thus, from his earliest youth, he had felt deep affection and a particular devotion for those heroes of the faith. Hence he was eager to gather historical information about them and lovingly sought out their tombs in the cemeteries, transforming them into shrines.

Damasus understood how the Church was changing after the advent of Constantine. Imperial favour induced a great number of people to become Christians but there was little convictions behind the conversions. Egoism, ostentation of luxury and family prestige were noticeable, particularly in the mausoleums which now arose on the surface of the ancient cemeteries.

It became urgent to give Christians of his time authentic models of evangelical living, as the force of the earlier testimony began weakening. The best way to face this crisis was to look back to the primitive Church, to the pure springs of faith, that is, to the martyrs.

Damasus was the only person who really deserved burial alongside his beloved friends, the holy martyrs. He ardently wished for it. In fact in his poem for the Crypt of the Popes he wrote: "Here too I, Damasus, confess I would like to be buried". This man of God, however, was deeply humble. He felt unworthy of such a privilege and added: "...Were it not for the fear of disturbing the ashes of these holy persons." So, for the love of God and out of respect for his great Friends, St. Damasus had the heroic strength to forego that privilege.

Our loved ones pray for us

The death of a loved one is always very painful for everybody. Jesus himself wept for his friend Lazarus. Faith, however, reassures us that our loved ones have not left us forever.

"The human heart wants to keep alive the memory of a loved one, but even more does it wish a communion which goes beyond a mere affectionate memory. In the light of faith, this is possible through prayer and awaiting a final reunion in God.

This same hope that their loved ones are with God persuades the living to trust in their prayers. The fact that the dead pray for us, meant — so the early Christians thought — that they keep us in their minds and hearts, that they remember us and our needs. Prayer is seen, then, as a union of the living and the dead made possible by God" (J. Janssens).

The short quotation which follows is part of a funeral oration *(laudationes,* praises). The text which has come down to us in fragments, is not easy to interpret in some points.

The deceased was 17 years old. Very probably he was a young man, a relation or friend of the speaker. The fragments of this panegyric were found in the Crypt of deacon Redemptus.

> *"...You who are now dear to God, pray your Lord, because I do not deserve to be united with God... Obtain for me with your prayers the Lord's forgiveness of my sins. Live in peace".*[8]

Before God, the human being feels sinful and requests the prayers of the martyrs and the blessed, so as to obtain forgiveness. Union with God is impeded only by sin.

3. "OF DEAD PEOPLE SPEAK ONLY WELL"

The catacomb inscriptions bring out the positive aspect of the human mind and show its beautiful and most shining feelings. This ought not to arouse any surprise or suspicion. It is right that it is so.

Death, however evoked, brings us face to face with the transcendent, with all that which really counts and remains. By comparison, what is contingent, all human vicissitudes, shrink and fade away.

Death casts a new light upon the personality of the deceased, thanks to which, relatives and friends discover in them their deeper essential qualities. Hence their negative traits dim and their better qualities shine forth.

This process is most noticeable in family inscriptions, where the sentiments expressed spring from a closer and deeper tie of blood. But it can equally be seen in the early Christian communities, as the epigraphy abundantly testifies.

For that matter, also the wisdom of the pagans suggested the well-known saying: *"De mortuis nil nisi bene"*, "Of dead people speak only well".

---

[1] ICUR, IV, 10888.

[2] ICUR, IV, 11435.

[3] ICUR, IV, 10129.

[4] Neophyte from νέος, new and φύω, to generate. Hence "regenerated". The term in antiquity was applied to Christians after Baptism. The neophyte, reborn to the life of Christ, wore a white robe for a week, from Easter to the following Sunday when he took it off. Hence the Sunday after Easter is called: *In Albis... depositis.*

[5] Sepulchral inscriptions describe Baptism as a perception *(percipere)*, a receiving *(recipere)*, and an attainment of God's grace *(consequi)*. All this implies an activity on God's part as well as mans. Such a view of Baptism can refer only to grownups, capable of personal adherence to God.

[6] ICUR, IV, 12417.

[7] ICUR, IV, 12418.

[8] ICUR, IV, 10535.

Cubiculum of the Sacraments A5: Multiplication of the bread and fish, prefiguration of the Eucharist (1st half of 3rd century). See p. 79.

XIV.
The Crypts of Lucina

Description of the cemetery area

The Crypts of Lucina represent the very first nucleus of what grew to be the Catacombs of St. Callixtus. Chronological order would recommend then to be described first, but I have preferred to follow the ordinary route taken by the visitor.

1. ORIGIN AND DEVELOPMENT OF THE CRYPTS OF LUCINA

First period: the two independent hypogea

The Crypts of Lucina form part of an underground cemetery area which was developed along the Appian Way during the second half of the 2nd century, when both Christians and pagans excavated their *hypogea*.

According to de Rossi, they originated under a well-defined open-air cemetery: 30 metres by 15.

After the middle of the 2nd century, then, a *hypogeum* called "alpha", with its own staircase (A), was excavated under this area. It was reached by a path connecting the Appian Way to the Ardeatina.[1] This *hypogeum* was used for the benefit of a community. They must have been mostly humble people, as there are no table-tombs or *arcosolia*. From the finds, especially epigraphic, we note that Christian and pagan themes were present at the same time.

Shortly afterwards the "alpha" *hypogeum* was deepened and thus the two notable *Cubicula*, X and Y, were opened at a lower level, nine metres below. The latter, among all the Roman catacombs, is a real jewel for its frescoes.

At the beginning of the 3rd century a second *hypogeum* called "beta" was excavated, with a staircase (B) parallel to that of the "alpha". It developed northeastwards, as it was blocked to the south by the "alpha". Its extension was limited. It consisted only of Gallery B with its *cubiculum* C, Gallery G, and the short Gallery L with its *cubiculum*.

The main characteristics of this *hypogeum* is the presence of some *cubicula* and some table-tombs. It may originally have been a private *hypogeum* of very modest proportions, belonging to one or more related families.

Second period: transformation of the two hypogea into a catacomb

Between 253 and 257, in the "beta" *hypogeum*, in the short Gallery L, which was properly widened and deepened, the martyr Pope St. Cornelius was buried. The presence of a martyr's body in the Crypts of Lucina (of whom we shall presently speak) gave new impulse to the underground digging with a number of remarkable works.

The two *hypogea* were joined, creating a real catacomb. Their conjuction by means of Gallery U involved eliminating the lower part of the staircase of "beta". The whole level of this *hypogeum* was lowered by about 12 metres to link it with "alpha", and then *cubiculum* E was dug. During this period a lower floor was also begun with the excavation of Gallery b. The new access stair was placed right under the staircase of "beta".

The terminal part of Gallery b was walled off creating an ossuary. In Gallery A of *hypogeum* "alpha" a table was built to hold small lamps. In the early part of the 4th century, the Crypt of St. Cornelius also had its table for oils.

THE CRYPTS OF LUCINA

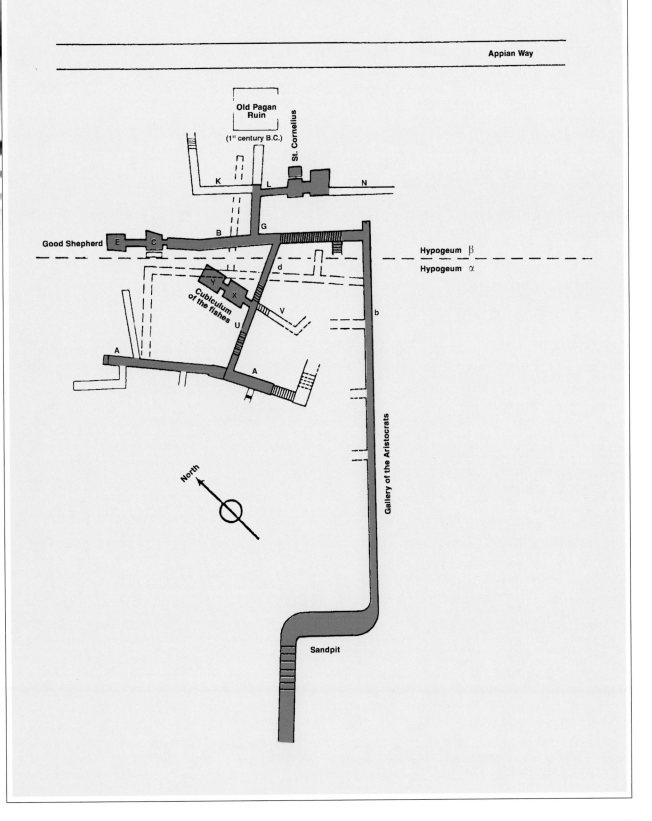

Third period:
the Crypts of Lucina become a shrine

The fact that the relics of St. Cornelius remained in the Crypts of Lucina for five centuries brought about other structural renovations of various sorts: the closing-up of some galleries, the opening of an underground passage to ease the way for the pilgrims coming from the Crypt of the Popes, the continued embellishment of the venerated crypt, and a monumental entrance from Gallery A into Gallery U... A staircase in Gallery K became necessary to allow the visitors to reach the Appian Way.

As we shall see in the next chapter, Pope Damasus played a prominent part in these works. By the end of the 4th century the Crypts of Lucina were already included in the area of expansion of the Callixtian cemetery. The galleries of the so-called "Labyrinth" extended at a higher level over the crypts, but we cannot speak of a true connection.

The only connection in the ancient period was by way of the sandpit or ossuary of Gallery b, called by de Rossi the "Gallery of the Aristocrats" when in the 4th century the underground route was opened to pilgrims.

2. THE NAME:
CRYPTS OF LUCINA

The "alpha" and "beta" *hypogea* were not originally called the Crypts of Lucina. Also the labels "alpha" and "beta" were given by modern scholars. De Rossi, basing himself on the legendary *Passio* of St. Cornelius, gave the name "Crypts of Lucina" to this cemetery area. From that edifying story of St. Cornelius' martyrdom, we learn that a noble Roman matron, Lucina, owned a *cubiculum* or crypt in this area, and that she had the body of St. Cornelius transferred to her family tomb.

This information was recorded in the *Liber Pontificalis:* "St. Cornelius also was beheaded in the above named place (by the temple of Mars near the "Porta Appia") and thus became a martyr. The blessed Lucina with the help of certain ecclesiastics collected the body of St. Cornelius by night to bury it in a crypt excavated on an estate belonging to her near the Cemetery of Callixtus on the Appian Way, September 14th".

In the *Passiones* of martyrs, written in the 4th and 5th centuries, we often meet a "pious Lucina", entirely dedicated to giving decent burial at her own expense to witnesses of Christ. By all accounts she was merely a literary creation, and so it seems to be also with the "Lucina" of this cemetery complex between the 2nd and 3rd milestones on the Appian Way.

3. 1835: AN ILL-OMENED YEAR FOR THE CRYPTS OF LUCINA

After the restoration of the Crypt and Basilica (built, it seems, in the 5th century) of St. Cornelius during the time of Leo III (795-816), the ancient literary sources make no further reference to the Crypts of Lucina or to their most sacred memorials.

During their excursions in the Cemetery of St. Callixtus the explorers of underground Rome (Bosio, Boldetti, Marangoni...) passed close enough to this area, but were unable to penetrate it because its entrances were obstructed by landslides. How can we explain that de Rossi found this area "barbarously" devastated? When was the part of St. Cornelius' inscription taken out of his crypt, to be found afterwards by de Rossi in the vineyard overground?

In 1835 a dig was conducted in order to extract "pozzolana" in the immediate vicinity of St. Cornelius' tomb. The wide shaft reached down to the lowest level of the cemetery. The digging led to the rediscovery of this area, which had previously remained inaccessible, but unfortunately it led also to its devastation. The proprietor of the sandpit and of the soil above, which was a vineyard, was at that time a Mr. Amendola, who took slabs of marble from the *hypogeum* for his buildings. Among those slabs was a small inscription of a Serpentius, who declared that he had bought the tomb next to the sepulchre of St. Cornelius.

The diggers of last century quickly took possession of the whole subterranean area discovered by the opening of the shaft. To gain access to the Crypts of Lucina a stair was excavated a few yards away from the primitive "beta" staircase. To find some way of paving the steps of that stair, they searched about for big slabs of marble, even rummaging among the rubble in the Crypt of St. Cornelius. Thus the fragment of

On the following page. Crypts of Lucina:
The Eucharistic Fishes (early 3rd century).

Crypts of Lucina:
Epitaph of Apuleia Crysopolis (3rd century).

St. Cornelius' sepulchral inscription with the letters ... NELIVS MARTYR came to light.

This is precisely what happened, as de Rossi learnt from Giovanni Zinobile, the old foreman of a gang of diggers. He was the very man who had dismantled that staircase, which became useless when that part of the underground area (under de Rossi's guidance) was joined up with the Cemetery of St. Callixtus. Once he had broken up that stair, Zinobile left the marble slabs, which had been used for the steps, lying about on the ground, and among them the fragment containing St. Cornelius' name.

The new owner of the vineyard, a Mr. Molinari, collected those marble slabs and piled them up outside his farmhouse, which is now the Eastern *Trichora*. There de Rossi found them in 1849. The recovery of St. Cornelius' sepulchral inscription marked the happy beginning of the rediscovery of the Catacombs of St. Callixtus.

4. A VISIT TO THE CRYPTS OF LUCINA

There are two ways of reaching this area. The first is from above ground by the staircase probably built under Pope Leo I (440-461), re-utilizing the old staircase of the "beta" *hypogeum*.

The second, more impressive and exciting, is to follow the underground route used by the ancient pilgrims (see map on pp. 50 and 155). After praying at the tombs of the martyr Popes and of St. Cecilia, they then crossed the so-called Area of St. Miltiades as far as the "four pilasters". This reference is to a gallery-crossing which had already been consolidated in the first centuries and is found near the *Cubiculum* of Sophronia. Having passed along a short gallery, they reached a staircase which goes down to the sandpit located on the third-floor level. Here the old *fossores* dug the "pozzolana" they needed to make mortar for sealing the *loculi*. At a later date that sandpit was used as an ossuary, in order to have space for new tombs for the burial of the faithful.

Past that sand bed ossuary, the pilgrims entered the lowest part of the "alpha" *hypogeum*, which is a third floor 18.24 metres below ground.

5. THE CHRISTIAN ARISTOCRACY OF ROME

Here begins a very distinctive gallery, which de Rossi labelled "the Gallery of the Aristocrats". There are in it some of the oldest and finest epitaphs of the Callixtian cemetery, dating back to the 3rd century. They bear only names and some symbols.

The epigraph of ΕΣΠΕΡΟΣ (Hésperos), with an anchor, has remained *in situ*. The beautiful inscription of VRBICA has the name written on a small boat

between an anchor and a dove intent on breaking off an olive twig with its bill: a clear reference to the soul that has achieved peace sustained by the hope in Christ's cross.

The inscription ΡΟΥΦΙΝΑ ΕΙΡΗΝΗ (Rufina Irene) is also written in Greek letters and has the cross, with equal arms, engraved under the name. The slab of FAVSTINIANVM is rich in symbolism: under the name is the image of a dove with an olive twig in its claws, of an anchor in the form of a cross and of a lamb at rest (ICUR, IV, 9484, 9453, 9499, 9399).

6. THE NOBILITY OF WORK

"Some Christians, and for that matter their pagan neighbours, also wanted to be remembered after death by having carved the picture of the trades they had practised in their lives: blackmiths, greengrocers, boatmen, carters, coopers, bakers... on their tombs. Even the *fossores*, as we have seen in the *Cubicula* of the Sacraments, followed this usage at times.

The Gospel and the search for truly eternal riches did not make the early Christians forget the earth with

**Crypts of Lucina:
Epitaph
of Valerius Pardus
(3rd century).**

145

its honest pleasures and its everyday problems. We might almost think that they were proud to remind their survivors and friends that a trade, well practised, had been for them a means of reaching heaven" (L. de Bruyne).

Here, then, is a little inscription dedicated to Valerius Pardus. Felicissima, his wife wanted to commemorate her good husband (a market - gardener or a farmer) with a sickle or a pruning hook in one hand and vegetables in the other.

"Here lies Valerius Pardus. Felicissima put up this inscription to her excellent husband" (ICUR, IV, 9450).

7. A FORMER SLAVE DEVOTED TO THE LADY OF THE HOUSE

It is rare nowadays to find good feeling between managers and workers between masters and servants. It is equally rare to find signs of gratitude after such work relations are over.

It was not so for Secundus, who felt not so much gratitude but sincere affection for the mistress of his household, to the point of caring for her tomb. Rufina, a good Christian, had not only given her slave his liberty, but had treated him like a son. And Secundus behaved like a son to such a good mother.

"D. M. For Marcia Rufina, a worthy lady of the house, the freedman Secundus prepared this tomb" (ICUR, IV, 9415).

The initials D. M. *(Dis Manibus)* refer to the Manes, deities who protected the dead. As Prof. C. Carletti explains: «the initials *d(is) m(anibus)* and the corresponding Greek θ(εοῖς) κ(αταχθονίοις), the ordinary dedications of pagan funerary inscriptions from the middle of the first century, are frequently seen also in titles which are assuredly Christian, especially from the 4th century onwards. Examples can be found even in the 7th century.

The presence of this classical invocation *(adprecatio)* is not so much a sign of religious syncretism[2] as a legacy[3] from a rooted secular tradition, which tends to be preserved longer, especially in the epigraphic practice. Here stereotyped expressions, such as *Dis Manibus*, crystallize and in time become anachronistic, gradually losing their peculiar original meaning.

In the Christian inscriptions the D.M. was evidently adopted because of its value as a distinctive sign of a funerary text, and therefore as an indication of the juridical right (the *ius*) marking the tomb as a religious object *(res religiosa)* and therefore inviolable.

It can be verified that sometimes Christians bought marble slabs from funeral workshops with the D.M. already carved. In such cases it was either kept, or sometimes scratched out and replaced by a specifically Christian sign, like the fish, or by a generally decorative subject".

Two tools, which are difficult to interpret, were also carved on Marcia Rufina's slab. One may be a millstone or a container for grain, probably an implement used by Rufina and Secundus. The other looks like a hammer with a long handle which seems to have been transformed into a palm leaf.

8. HE LOVED HER TOO MUCH NOT TO FEEL THE CALL FROM HEAVEN

At the end of Gallery b, or "of the Aristocrats", the inscription of APVLEIA CRYSOPOLIS, a child just seven years old, welcomes us with the graceful carving of the Good Shepherd and an olive tree (ICUR, IV, 9384).

We then climb a narrow staircase, already in use in the 4th century for pilgrims. In front of *Cubiculum X* we come upon the slab of Pàrdale and Justin.

The loss of a life's companion is painful and bitter, particularly when marriage has been lived with deep and sincere affection. Then the wish to mend that broken unity steadily grows stronger.

This is what happened to Justin when his wife died. He loved her too much not to feel the call from heaven, and so he joined her only eight months after her departure.

Crypts of Lucina: "Eucharistic Fish" with the basket of bread and the cup of red wine (Cubiculum Y, early 3rd century).

"In the year in which the two emperors were consuls, Honorious for the eighth time and Theodosius II for the third, eight days before the Ides of April (6th April), Pardale was laid to rest in peace. Ten days before the Kalends of January (23rd December) her husband Justin was laid to rest in peace". It was 409 A.D. (ICUR, IV, 9378).

"Death particularly affects the feelings of married couples and parents. It takes away a person who was so much a part of their lives.

Sometimes the blow is so great that it seems impossible to survive such a painful separation. The memory of the affections they shared makes the absence of the loved one more acute. It is like a wound in the heart which remains open and will not heal. The greater love is, the harder the parting" (J. Janssens).

9. TWO FISHES AND A MYSTERIOUS BASKET

Coming up from the third to the second floor by the "pilgrims' staircase" (B), after a few paces in Gallery U, the communicating *Cubicula* X and Y are seen on the right. They date back to the end of the 2nd century. The frescoes in these two *cubicula* are very ancient and are the very first representations of Baptism and of the Eucharist.

The Baptism of Christ

Cubiculum X, unfortunately, was almost completely redone by de Rossi and preserves only the scene of the Baptism of Jesus on the front wall, over the door eading into Y: St. John the Baptist helps the Lord out of the Jordan. The dove above Christ symbolizes the Holy Spirit *(Matthew 3, 13-17)*. As we know, the theme of Baptism was very dear to the early Christians.

"Eucharistic" fishes

The most lovely surprise is to be found in the twin *Cubiculum* Y. Here, in the vault, we admire a decoration in the classical style, made up of ornamental heads, putti, birds and garlands.

At the centre is Daniel in the lions' den and, symmetrically at the four sides, are two figures of the Good Shepherd and two "Oranti".

"We realize that the Christian art is here at its beginnings. While it was entirely intent on selecting and creating biblical representations, it did not yet concern itself with additional ornamental decorations of its own, but took them from pagan classical art" (de Rossi).

On the wall in front of us two fish face each other, each bearing on its back a wicker basket full of loaves.[4] This scene, of course, refers to the miracle of the multiplication of the loaves and fishes worked by Jesus. And there is more. Each basket contains a glass of red wine among the loaves. The Eucharistic symbolism could not be clearer or more explicit: the bread and the wine consecrated in the Mass, become ΙΧΘΥΣ (fish),

Crypts of Lucina: Ceiling of Cubiculum Y (early 3rd century).

Crypts of Lucina: Ceiling of the Cubiculum of the Good Shepherd (1st half of the 3rd century).

that is, the body and blood of "Jesus Christ, Son of God, the Saviour". Jesus, then, offers himself to the Christians as food, to make them gain eternal life. St. Ignatius of Antioch (middle of the 2nd century) defines the Eucharist as a "medicine of immortality, antidote against dying" *(Ephesians* 20, 2). Biblical scenes from the cycle of Jonah are painted on the other walls.

10. A SPLENDID POLITICAL CAREER

Leaving the twin *Cubicula* X and Y and passing through a modern opening ("busso") we enter the "beta" *hypogeum*. On the right is the steep staircase of St. Leo the Great, while on the left begins the short Gallery B, which ends in the two *cubicula* C and F. In the higher part of the gallery some tombs of the first period of the "beta" *hypogeum* can be seen. Some of them are "a mensa" tombs (table-tombs).

In this gallery and in its vicinity de Rossi found a number of fragments of sarcophagi, mostly from lids, with inscriptions relating to noble Roman families of the 3rd and 4th centuries. Those fragments were originally above ground, and some are undoubtedly pagan. Here are the epitaphs of Pompeia Octavia Attica Caeciliana, of senatorial rank,[5] of Quintus Caecilius Maximus, a child also of the senatorial order, and of Pomponius Graecinus... (ICUR, IV, 9431, 11233, 10669).

Tiberius Pomponius Bassus' epitaph, written in Greek, is very interesting. It relates his *cursus honorum*, that is, his political career.

"To Pomponius Bassus... of the senatorial order, twice consul ordinary, prefect of Rome, vice-master of the pontiffs (a pagan priestly office), *auditor* (corrector) *of the local finances for all Italy, official of the imperial court* (comes Augusti), *proconsul".*

"To Pomponia Cratidia, devoted to her husband...

For all the benefits received..." (the dedicator made the inscription for both). Cf. ICUR, II, 2 - N. 904.

In the *Fasti Consulares* (list of consuls) the name Tiberius Pomponius Bassus appears twice, in 259 and in 271 A.D., as is also implied in his dedicatory epitaph. Needless to say, it is a pagan, not a Christian inscription.

Referring to those illustrious people, who were inter-related, Prof. Enrico Josi writes:

"The ties of relationship between the *Caecilii*, the *Pomponii*, the *Attici*, the *Bassi*, inferred from the inscriptions found here, reminded de Rossi of the celebrated Pomponia Graecina, wife of Aulus Plautius and a contemporary with Nero, a woman held to be a Christian from the description given by Tacitus in Book XIII of the Annals".

11. THE GOOD SHEPHERD WITH A PAIL OF MILK

At the end of the short Gallery B we enter *Cubiculum* C. In its vault there is a fresco of the Good Shepherd between two sheep and an olive tree. The *cubiculum* was excavated after the "beta" *hypogeum* was begun. At the time when "beta" was deepened, the *cubiculum* was lowered and *Cubiculum* E was then added.

The vault, slightly groined, of this *Cubiculum* is all decorated. At the centre a splendid Good Shepherd stands out. With his left hand he holds a lamb on his shoulders and with his right he holds a pail of milk and a stick. Beside the Good Shepherd are two other sheep. The familiar dove decorates the four lunettes at the corners of the vault.

Here there is a new development, an enrichment in the theme of the Good Shepherd, as he is represented concretely in his everyday tasks. The art of sculpture was to develop this theme further.

Then the heavenly setting around the Good Shepherd would take on the aspect of a true country scene where the sheep are at play, where farmers come home from their fields, where other shepherds guard the flock, pat their dog, milk some of the ewes... A similar bucolic image can be admired on the left of the entrance wall of the Eastern *Trichora*.

Looking at the image of the Good Shepherd with the pail of milk, one is reminded of a well-known passage from St. Paul's *First Letter to the Corinthians:* "I could not talk to you as I talk to people who have the Spirit; I had to talk to you as though you belonged to this world, as children in the Christian faith. I had to feed you with milk, not solid food, because you were not ready for it" (3, 1-2). The fresco dates back to the second half of the 3rd century.

A few yards away we see the shaft excavated in 1835, which caused serious damage to the Crypts of Lucina, as we have already mentioned.

12. NOT EVEN DEATH COULD PART THOSE FRIENDS

"The sense of friendship which is so often expressed appears to be almost a distinctive feature of the epitaphs dedicated to men. To be agreeable, friendly to all and devoted to friendship, is evidence of a serene and trusting character, which is open to one's own neighbour, and it perfectly fits the ideals proper to Christianity. It echoes the celebrated biblical examples of friendship between David and Jonathan (*1 Samuel* 18, 1-4), between Christ and Lazarus (*John* 11, 1-44)", (D. Mazzoleni).

I have already spoken of the more important inscriptions in the Crypts of Lucina. Another which deserves mention is that of Januarius, bound by close ties of friendship to Severinus. Not even after death did he wish to be far from his friend, and he felt the need to show his affection for him even on his tombstone: *"Januarius wanted to be buried together with his friend Severinus"* (ICUR, IV, 9408).

As Jos Janssens points out: "the friendship which is mentioned in the epitaphs, is a quality of the young and of the mature man as well. It is cultivated as something

152

valuable, and care is taken to keep it. Relations with others are defined in terms of friendship, which means a kindly disposition towards everybody and the certainty of being accepted and welcomed by all.

The constant and faithful friend is admired, the sincere and upright friend is sought after, the serene and cheerful friend is loved. A friend is a support and a counsellor. Friendship brings with it gentleness and affability".

13. DIONYSIUS, PHYSICIAN AND PRIEST

As has already been noted, the oldest inscriptions in the Crypts of Lucina are laconic. Only names appear and, occasionally, a symbol or a very brief expression of faith: "Peace be with you", "In peace...". Unfortunately we do not know much about the very early Christian communities. The same can be said of their ecclesiastical organization.

In these crypts de Rossi found only three inscriptions which refer to priests. One of them is at the beginning of Gallery B: *"Dionysius, physician priest,"* buried in this *hypogeum* probably in the first half of the 3rd century. The epigraph is in Greek.

Dionysius, while exercising his priestly mission, followed the medical profession, which was much valued in antiquity as an effective means for apostolate. This is more or less what our missionaries often do today: promote welfare and at the same time announce the message of salvation (ICUR, IV, 9483).

---

[1] For the topography of the Crypts of Lucina see map on p. 141.

[2] A sometimes incoherently made blend of mythological, cultural and doctrinal elements from various religions.

[3] A spiritual inheritance or patrimony which comes from ancestors.

[4] Strangely enough, some scholars think the baskets do not rest on the fishes' backs, but on the grass of a meadow in front of the fishes.

[5] According to de Rossi, the parents of Pompeia Octavia Attica Caeciliana, who died a few months after her birth, were Octavius Caecilianus and Pompeia Attica. Their epitaphs are in the Crypt of St. Cecilia.

On the preceding page: The Good Shepherd (detail from the cubiculum of that same name).

XV.
The Crypts of Lucina

The Crypt of St. Cornelius

1. "AT THE SIGHT OF THESE PAINTINGS I EXULTED WITH DELIGHT..."

"In March 1852 — writes de Rossi — our excavators came upon the opening of an ancient staircase which went down into the Crypts of Lucina. There were high hopes of finding a new access to an unexplored zone of the cemetery. Having taken out the earth which blocked the entrance, they realized that the staircase had never been completed by the ancients. The diggers wanted to go on and thus reached the second floor of the Catacombs of St. Callixtus in the area called the 'Labyrinth', very close to the Crypts of Lucina. By means of two modern 'bussi' (links),[1] they connected this passage with the two *hypogea* below... Passing by way of this staircase one day with Fr. Marchi, I pushed my way into Gallery N, which was blocked with earth. We went on crawling and creeping through the gallery. When we reached the end we saw a modern hole in the tufa. We looked through it and saw a big room half-full of rubble, not deposited by the ancient *fossores* but fallen down from above through a skylight. My readers well know that all this is an excellent clue in searching for martyrs' tombs.

Modern excavators have the habit of retreating before these ruins; instead we look for the crypts buried beneath the rubble which had come down from the skylight, the stairs and the collapsed roofs.

We quickly saw an arch built in fine 'laterizia' (brick work), a sure sign of alterations and restorations of the primitive crypts. Then, below the arch, we discovered some paintings. They were images of two saints done in the Byzantine style, a sure sign that this was a famous and historic crypt.

At the side of the first figure was written: $\overline{\text{SCI}}$ CORNELI $\overline{\text{PP}}$, while beside the second these letters were traced: ...IPRI...N... (CIPRIANI). Here were Cornelius and Cyprian in a historic crypt of the Cemetery of St. Callixtus, far away from those of St. Sixtus and St. Cecilia. At the sight of these paintings I exulted with delight. It was the first time I had come upon the monuments of a papal crypt in the underground cemeteries. I had no doubts about identifying the sepulchre beside those paintings: it was St. Cornelius' tomb!

On the other side of the sepulchre we saw the image of two other saints in priestly dress. The name of the first was intact: $\overline{\text{SCS}}$ XVSTVS $\overline{\text{PP}}$ ROM. The name of the second was not legible.

The tomb, placed between these two groups of images, was open and without its marble slab and inscription. But a fragment of marble remained in place at the top right corner of the tomb, and on it were a few letters carved in the style of Damasus.

In front of the tomb was a second fragment, part of a large inscription. The letters were of monumental form and proportions, and the calligraphy resembled the style of Damasus. But neither fragment offered any hint of a name.

However, what was missing from the few surviving letters of these inscriptions, I found in the tomb itself. There at the bottom lay the other part of the inscription of Cornelius. This mutilated slab, joined with that which I had found three years earlier in the vineyard, tallied exactly and gave me the whole inscription: CORNELIVS · MARTYR · EP(iscopus). This illustrious and invaluable piece of evidence, made up of

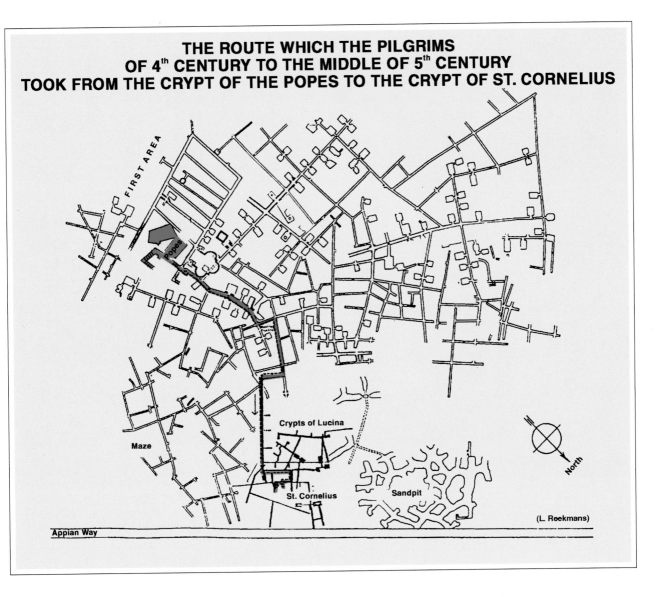

THE ROUTE WHICH THE PILGRIMS OF 4ᵗʰ CENTURY TO THE MIDDLE OF 5ᵗʰ CENTURY TOOK FROM THE CRYPT OF THE POPES TO THE CRYPT OF ST. CORNELIUS

two parts, found at different times and added to a third fragment still fixed in place, perfectly closed the tomb..." (R.S.C., I, pp. 277-279).

2. THE MARTYR POPE ST. CORNELIUS

There is little and dubious information about Cornelius in the *Liber Pontificalis*. What is said of him in the letters of his contemporary St. Cyprian, bishop of Carthage, is more reliable.

St. Cornelius was a Roman and came from the noble family *(gens)* of *Cornelii*. As a priest he belonged to the clergy of Rome. After St. Fabian's death, the see was vacant for 14 months because of the persecution of Decius. Cornelius was elected in March 251. "Cor-

nelius had many merits", wrote Cyprian. "Having passed through all the grades of the hierarchy, he was elected to the supreme pontificate not through his own initiative but because of his humility, prudence and goodness".

That election was contested by an intransigent minority led by the priest Novatian. They accused Cornelius of having betrayed the faith during Decius' persecution. Novatian had himself elected antipope and as such appeared among the Christian community of Rome "as though hurled into our midst from a catapult", as Cornelius himself wrote to bishop Fabius. Gradually, however, the situation returned to normal, though Novatian remained uncompromising.

Cornelius at once showed himself a zealous pastor. He took care of the organization of the Church. From

155

Crypts of Lucina: The Crypt of the martyr Pope St. Cornelius.

one of his letters we know that the ecclesiastical hierarchy of Rome was made up of forty six priests, seven deacons and seven subdeacons. The minor orders were also numerous and efficient. The Pope had forty two acolytes at his disposal and, between exorcists, readers and doorkeepers he could count on fifty two ecclesiastics.

The spontaneous offerings of the Roman faithful enabled the Church to provide for 1500 persons every day and among these were widows, orphans and the destitute.

In June 252, as we have noted, emperor Trebonianus Gallus, successor to Decius, suddenly launched a persecution, exiling bishops, priests and deacons. Cornelius was immediately arrested. As soon as the news spread among the Christian community of Rome. many faithful rushed to accompany him to the trial. Thus the Pope, as St. Cyprian wrote, had many "companions in the glory" of suffering for Christ and "was a leader to his brethren in openly confessing the faith".

Cornelius was condemned to exile at Civitavecchia *(Centumcellae)*, where he died the following year in June 255. Even if this Pope did not die a violent death, his confinement was hard and caused him much suffering. St. Cyprian on several occasions described him as a martyr, a title confirmed in his epitaph.

The Church of Rome celebrated the date of St. Cornelius' new burial in the Cemetery of St. Callixtus on 14th September. This date coincided with the commemoration of the bishop of Carthage, the martyr St. Cyprian. Thus these two heroes, inseparable opponents of the schismatic Novatian and his sect, were commemorated on the same day in the Catacombs of St. Callixtus from the first half of the 4th century.

The *Liber Pontificalis* tells us that St. Leo I (440-461), called "the Great", had a basilica built near St. Cornelius' tomb. It was probably Paul I (757-767) who removed the relics of the Pope martyr to the Basilica of Santa Maria in Trastevere, which is also called the Basilica of St. Callixtus and St. Cornelius.

3. THE CRYPT OF ST. CORNELIUS

On the right side of Gallery G a small corridor opens (L) which ends in a spacious burial chamber with an unusual form. It originated with the "beta" *hypogeum* and was deepened at the time when St. Cornelius was buried in the catacomb. This burial chamber was always soberly decorated: the walls were not covered with marble and there were no ornamental columns.

The crypt (see map on p. 141) is divided into three sections. First there is an entrance corridor, no longer than three and a half metres, which widens towards the interior. There is then an intermediate space, a little wider, but for its limited size we cannot call it a *cubiculum*. It was here, in the left (eastern) wall that the tomb of St. Cornelius was dug. One then passes into the crypt proper, which is of an irregular shape.

Following the burial of the martyr Pope, the crypt was at various times embellished, reinforced and restored. The primitive walls were covered with stucco. The tombs were given a border of red paint.

Towards the end of the 3rd century a first group of *formae* were dug in the floor, and some more at the beginning of the 4th century. During this period the walls of the short corridor were also painted with a coat of white lime.

The most important structural renovations were done at the time of St. Damasus, when the crypt was transformed into a shrine. At the sides of the tomb two pilasters reinforced the structure. The walls were covered with a new layer of stucco and the primitive light-shaft was widened, making it a double skylight. Imposing brick arches strengthened the vault against possible collapse.

On the walls are numerous graffiti made by pilgrims during the five centuries of uninterrupted visits.

4. THE TOMB OF THE MARTYR POPE

The place chosen for St. Cornelius' burial in the Crypts of Lucina may be regarded as privileged: it was the biggest space available in the "beta" *hypogeum* at the moment of the martyr's translation from Civitavecchia.

His bones were placed in a tomb excavated under the primitive light-shaft, in the lower part of the eastern wall. The tomb is not a simple *loculus* dug in the tufa, but an arch of unusual proportion. The upper part of the sepulchre is slightly curved like a bow, shaped like a trunk lid.

The inside is completely covered with white stucco and on the vault there is some illegible writing traced with the smoke of a candle flame, made by some of the modern researchers who preceded de Rossi. The front wall of the tomb is in tufa. Being thin and friable, it was reinforced by the ancients with a little wall made with bricks and small solid pieces of tufa ("tufelli").

The Greek "hymettus" marble slab sealing the tomb was not fixed to the sepulchre horizontally, but vertically and rested directly on the little wall.

We know the troubled story of this famous inscription, by which the Cemetery of St. Callixtus came to be identified. It is cut in Latin letters:

> ## CORNELIVS · MARTYR · EP
> ### Cornelius - Bishop - Martyr

The original inscription consisted of only two words: one written in full (Cornelius), the other abbreviated (Episcopus). They were placed symmetrically in the centre of the slab and coloured red.[2] To make things easier for the engraver, two horizontal lines were traced with a chisel, between which the letters were carved.

The title "Martyr" is a later addition. As Mons. J. Wilpert points out, "papal inscriptions, except that of St. Gaius, originally indicated only the name and the episcopal dignity. The title 'Martyr' was added later to the epitaphs of Pontianus and Fabian, in the form of the first three consonants of the Greek word Μάρτυς.

Since the epitaphs of martyrs are rare, it would be hard to say for certain when that word was added... The early Christians thought it quite natural to testify to their faith in their Redeemer even by sacrificing their lives...

Nevertheless, it can be assumed that the Greek letters MPT for M(ά)PT(υς), in the inscriptions of Pontianus and Fabian, and the full word in Latin (Martyr) in the epigraph of Pope Cornelius were carved only after the middle of the 3rd century, perhaps during the time of Pope Eutychian" (275-283).

Why was St. Cornelius not buried in the Crypt of the Popes together with his illustrious predecessors? And why is his inscription written in Latin, while those of his contemporaries are in Greek?

Several scholars have tried to give an anwer to these questions. beginning with the great de Rossi, but the real reason escapes us. Perhaps some light may be offered by the account in St. Cornelius' *Passio*, even though it is in part legendary. St. Cornelius was buried in the Crypts of Lucina because there — as we shall see — were buried some martyrs (Cerealis, Sallustia...) probably associated with him in the dispute with the Novatianists and executed during Decius' persecution or that of Trebonianus Gallus.

If this hypothesis, adopted by Prof. L. Reekmans, is sound, we can understand why, at the moment of Cornelius' burial in this crypt, the two *hypogea* ("alpha" and "beta") were conjoined, so as to facilitate the visits of pilgrims.

5. POPE DAMASUS' EULOGY

St. Damasus not only embellished and restored the crypt, but wished to place his own poem of seven hexameters above Cornelius' inscription. The slab with that poem has come down to us mutilated. It was sculpted by St. Damasus' friend Filocalus. De Rossi restored the text. Here is a translation:

"The staircase built and the darkness banished,
You may now at last contemplate the monuments
in honour of Cornelius and his venerated tomb.

This work was, completed by the zeal of Damasus,
though he was ill, making the way easier for the people
who implore the help of the Saint.

Ah! pray you also with sincere heart
that Damasus may recover his health.
This he desires
not for an attachment to life
but because of the heavy engagements of his ministry".[3]

Immediately below St. Cornelius' epitaph, a monumental marble slab with a second inscription of four lines was placed. Only fragments of it survive, with very few letters: S and PIA... MEMBRA. From a detailed analysis, Prof. L. Reekmans deduced that this marble slab was put in front of the tomb at the same time as Damasus' poem. The "almost Damasian" calligraphy

of this inscription is assignable to a hand which was not of Furius Dionysius Filocalus. Perhaps the work was done by one of his pupils. The slab hints at some other works carried out by Damasus in this area.

6. THE TABLE FOR THE OIL LAMPS

On the right of Cornelius' tomb there is a round table, made at the beginning of the 4th century. It was used to support the oil lamps which burned in honour of the martyr pope. It might also have served for celebrating Mass by pilgrim priests or perhaps for receiving the offerings of the faithful.

On the wall near the table there are graffiti by some ecclesiastics: "LEO $\overline{PRB}$ (= PResByter, priest), PETRVS PRB, + TEVDORVS PrB, + SERGI(us)[4] $\overline{PRB}$, KyPrIANVS dIACONVS (deacon)"... (ICUR, IV, 9373).

7. THE FRESCOES OF ST. CORNELIUS' CRYPT

At the beginning of the 7th century the Crypt of St. Cornelius was newly decorated with frescoes in the Byzantine style, painted on the two pilasters beside the tomb. The four figures represent two Popes, Cornelius

and Sixtus II, and two African bishops, the martyr St. Cyprian of Carthage and St. Optatus bishop of Vescere in Numidia.

The four figures have haloes round their heads and are tonsured. Their features are different but the vestments and attitudes are the same.

They are shown in pontifical robes. Over a sleeved tunic they wear a dalmatic which reaches to the ankles, and over that they wear a grey chasuble. The *pallium*, sign of episcopal power, is on their shoulders.

With the left hand each of them holds a book decorated with precious stones, the Gospel, while their right hand is raised in the recognized gesture of teaching. They wear *campagi*, a particular type of liturgical shoes.

They are not realistic portraits, but idealized. The main colours used are black and red, while the writing is in white.

Cornelius and Cyprian

Above the table, on the right pilaster, are the images of Pope St. Cornelius and bishop St. Cyprian. The first is painted with a moustache, while the second is beardless. Next to the two figures their names are written vertically and are now unfortunately lacking some letters.

S(an)C(t)I + CORNELI(i) P(a)P(ae)
S (an)C(t) I + (c)IPRI(a)N(i episcopi)

Image of "Saint Cornelius Pope".
Image of "Saint Cyprian (Bishop)".

159

In the frieze above the figures were written the words from Psalm 116, verse 12: + QVID RE-TRIBVAM D(omi)N(o pro om)NIBVS QVA(e re-tribuit mihi?). *"What can I offer the Lord for all his goodness to me?"* (ICUR, IV, 9371).

Cornelius had a wrytten correspondence with the most renowned bishop of Carthage, Cyprian. They had difrences of opinion concerning the problems of the *lapsi:* St. Cyprian being more rigorous, and St. Cornelius more willing to pardon after appropriate penance.

We have already remarked that the ancient Liturgical Calendar of the Church of Rome venerated Cornelius and Cyprian together as early as the 4th century.

Sixtus II and Optatus

On the left pilaster by St. Cornelius' tomb were painted the images of the martyr Pope Sixtus II and of the African bishop Optatus: the first beardless, the second with a small beard. Their names appear near their haloes.

The unknown pilgrim, wishing to commemorate a martyr, had begun to write in capitals and in the singular, but then went on writing in small letters, citing not only one name but an entire group.[5]

The honorific title of "saint" and the twenty one anonymous companions clearly refer to martyrs. The wording is concise, as is usual in the Martyrologies. However, neither Martyrologies nor *Itineraries* mention this group of martyrs.

The only information about them comes from the *Passio* of St. Cornelius, which, as we have pointed out, is late and legendary, dating from the 5th century. The story reads: "On the same day, together with the most blessed Pope Cornelius twenty one persons, men and women, were beheaded; and also Cerealis and his wife Sallustia, on September 14th. The same night some ecclesiastics came with the blessed Lucina and her family and seized the bodies of the holy Martyrs and buried them in her estate, in a crypt of the Cemetery of St. Callixtus, where today prayers are offered in their praise...".

> ## S(an)C(tu)S + XVSTVS P(a)P(a) ROM(anus)
> ## S(an)C(tu)S + OPTAT(us) EPISC(opus)
>
> *"St. Sixtus, Roman Pope".*
> *"St. Optatus, Bishop".*

On the frieze above their images the passage from Psalm 59, verse 16 is written: EGO AV(tem) CANTABO BIRTVTEM (virtutem) TVAM ET EXALTABO MANE MISERICORDIAM TVAM QV(i)A FACTVS (e)S ET SVSCEPTRO (susceptor) MEVS ET REF(u)G(ium) MEVM I(n) DI(e tribulationis meae). *"But I will sing about your strenght; every morning I will sing aloud of your constant love. You have been a refuge for me, a shelter in my time of trouble"* (ICUR, IV, 9370).

8. CEREALIS, SALLUSTIA AND THEIR TWENTY ONE COMPANIONS

Beside the images of Sixtus and Optatus there is a graffito which is particularly interesting.

The agreement between the graffito and the information given by that legendary *Passio* is perfect. It is reasonable to suppose that the latter derives from the graffito in the Crypt of St. Cornelius. It is unlikely that the mention of these Martyrs buried in the Catacombs of St. Callixtus is just the fruit of the hagiographers' fantasy, because the presence of their tombs could be ascertained by the numerous visitors to that cemetery.

The graffito in the Crypt of St. Cornelius was written after the pilgrim had seen those Martyrs' tombs and not simply because he remembered reading their *Passio.*

From all this it may be concluded that Cerealis, his wife Sallustia and their twenty one Companions truly existed, and their tombs were already venerated at the

> ## SCS Cerealis et Sal(l)ustia cum XXI [hic sunt]
> *"(Here are buried) SS. Cerealis, Sallustia and twenty one Companions".*

end of the 4th century. Moreover, there must have been a topographical connection in the Crypts of Lucina between St. Cornelius' tombs and those of the twenty one.

Their burial place has yet to be located and it is hard to do so with precision, given the present state of the monuments. Despite their importance, we have only clues at the moment.

In the Crypts of Lucina three places deserve particular attention as possible tombs of martyrs: the Crypt itself of St. Cornelius, *Cubiculum* C, Gallery A in the "alpha" *hypogeum* (see map on p. 141).

a) *Again the Crypt of St. Cornelius*

In the crypt of this Pope there are two *loculi* for which particular care was taken. They are in the upper part of the wall facing the Martyr's tomb. They are separated by a bridge built in masonry as a reinforcement.

The higher *loculus* is accurately cut, even though it is behind the reinforcement. The lower one on the other hand, is exceptionally deep, and a marble slab, quite excessively large for a normal *loculus*, was placed in front of it.

Simple clues, but they might indicate tombs of martyrs.

b) *Cubiculum C*

This *cubiculum* originated with the "beta" *hypogeum*. It contains, among other sepulchres, a table-tomb. This is now in the upper part, because the *cubiculum* was deepened at the time when the two *hypogea* were joined. It is the main tomb of this sepulchral chamber.

In front of this tomb a large marble slab was placed, which did not form part of the original decoration of the *cubiculum*. The imprint it left on the wall suggests that it was not a simple tomb slab but rather a monumental commemorative inscription.

Other details are worth noting. After the deepening, when the upper part of the entrance to this *cubiculum* C was walled up, two small windows were opened to let light into the upper part of the burial chamber.

This work led even de Rossi to suppose that *cubiculum* C had been a venerated place. True, there are no graffiti and only two *formae* on the floor, but there is nothing contrary to the idea that this was a *cubiculum* of particular and ancient interest, since a sarcophagus was put there at a later period.

c) *Gallery A in the 'alpha' hypogeum*

One last place deserves consideration, as it shows some circumstantial evidence which is more solid than anywhere else.

At the end of Gallery A there is a spacious tomb in the form of a *loculus* with abnormal proportions. The surrounding walls were covered with slabs of marble.

Because of its position, dimensions and decorations, this tomb appears undoubtedly as the most important in Gallery A.

Beside the tomb there are still the remains of a table for oil lamps. It is surprising that the table is not inside a *cubiculum*, its usual place, but in a gallery. Furthermore, that table was constructed at a later period, during the middle of the 3rd century.

Under the table for the oils, and in its vicinity, an ossuary was dug, in the same way as occurred near the tomb of St. Cornelius. Ossuaries like this are normally found next to the tombs of martyrs.

Moreover, the walls of Gallery A were coated with lime plaster, something which is uncommon in the catacombs. The passage from Gallery A to Gallery U was monumentalized. All that remains today is a semi-cylindrical column covered with stucco, which must have supported a triumphal arch. The pilgrims were thus invited to proceed in this direction to reach the sepulchre of St. Cornelius.

There are numerous *formae* both in the floor of Gallery A and in the neighbouring galleries. A sarcophagus was also placed in this area.

The monumental entrance to Gallery U, the re-making of the stairs, the coating of the walls with lime plaster, etc., all bear witness to an initiative which was

not private but ordered by the competent Church administrators.

We should also consider the reinforcement of a wall in Gallery A, carried out between the 6th and 7th centuries. This means that the gallery was still being visited at a late period, when the staircase (B) built under St. Leo the Great (440-461), had made that passage obsolete to reach St. Cornelius' tomb.[6]

We find these characteristics together in all the Roman catacombs near the tombs of martyrs, and they can only be explained by a continuous public veneration.

We are thus led to believe that some martyrs (Cerealis, Sallustia...) were buried in the exceptionally large *loculus* at the end of Gallery A. If we then take into account the fact that the table for the oil lamps was constructed at the time when St. Cornelius was transferred to the "beta" *hypogeum*, we have a link between the principal tomb of Gallery A and the sepulchre of the martyr Pope.

9. THE CULT OF THE MARTYRS

After the martyrdom of its bishop Polycarp and eleven faithful believers (in 156, or in 167 A. D.), the Church of Smyrna (in modern Turkey) informed "the Church of God which is pilgrim at Philomelius (in Phrygia) and all the communities of the holy universal Church" of their glorious deaths, and added:

"We worthily venerate the martyrs as disciples and imitators of the Lord and for their supreme fidelity towards their King and Master; and may it be granted to us also to become their companions and fellow-disciples...

Having collected the bones of Polycarp, more precious than rare gems and purer than the finest gold, we laid them to rest in the appointed place. And meeting in this place in exultation and gladness whenever we can, the Lord will allow us to celebrate the anniversary of his martyrdom, remembering all who have faced the same struggle and in practice and preparation for those who will face it in the future" (*Martyrium Polycarpi* XVII, 3; XVIII 2-3; P G V, 1042. 1044).

The faithful in Rome, however, were not less enthusiastic than their brethren of Smyrna in their devotion to the Holy Martyrs. The Crypt of the Popes, the Crypts of St. Cecilia, St. Eusebius, SS. Calocerus and Parthenius, and St. Cornelius, described in this book, are a clear proof of how much our early brothers and sisters loved those champions of the faith. The Christians of the first centuries were sure that whoever honours the Martyrs in this world will have them as advocates in heaven. This is confirmed by the good Serpentius already mentioned, who "bought a grave from Quintus the fossor next to St. Cornelius":

SEREPNTV
S EMIT LOC
M A QVINTO
FOSSORE AD
SANTVM CO
RNELIVM

Here are the letters in order, supplying the missing ones: "*Serpent(i)us emit loc(u)m a Quinto fossore ad san(c)tum Cornelium*" (ICUR, IV, 9441).

10. POPE ST. MARK

The grave of Pope St. Mark is not in the Crypts of Lucina, but we want now to mention him in order to complete the biographical notes on the popes buried in these catacombs.

He was Roman. He was elected on 18th January 336, and governed the Church until October 7th of that same year. The *Liber Pontificalis* ascribes to him the building of places of worship both within the city and in the catacombs. During his pastoral ministry the first liturgical calendar of the Church of Rome was laid out with the compilation of the *Depositio Martyrum* and the *Depositio Episcoporum*.

He was buried in a basilica above the Catacomb of Balbina in the "Callixtian complex".

In early September 1991, Tarcisio Gazzola, a Salesian brother, while working in the lucerne fields between the Catacombs of St. Callixtus and the "Quo Vadis?" Church and Card. Pole's small Oratory on the Appian Way, noticed some interesting marks (a different colour of the lucerne) of what seemed to be the foundation of a basilica, shaped like a circus 66 metres long by 27 metres wide. Although the archaeological excavators will draw the final conclusions, this is probably the basilica built by Pope St. Mark in 336, the same year when he was also buried there.[7]

11. A GOOD WISH

I wish to conclude this Introduction to the Catacombs of St. Callixtus with the little epitaph of Veneriosa, which has the flavour of a good omen:

"Veneriosa, your soul lives among the Saints" (ICUR, IV, 9451).

"The content of the good wishes and prayers for the deceased persons indicates the welcome given to the soul by God, by the Martyrs and by the departed Saints. The wish that the loved one may be found with God tells us of a disposition of faith and hope among those who survive... It shows that the living still love their dear ones, and express the desire of remaining still closely bound to them by their common faith" (J. Janssens).

12. CONCLUSION

The Catacombs of St. Callixtus are very extensive. We have covered only a part of the second floor or level, which is the most important, because of the presence in it of crypts of undoubted historic value: the Popes', St. Cecilia's, St. Eusebius', St. Cornelius'... Of course there is much more in the Catacombs of St. Callixtus.

It has been a short visit for devotion and study, but it is enough to give an idea of this great underground cemetery of the first centuries of Christianity, and of its importance for its legacy in iconography and inscriptions.

It is a cemetery where everything speaks of life, more than of death. When the early Christians came to these tombs to pray, they looked beyond a sealed tomb or a marble slab. Through the images painted in the *cubicula* or *arcosolia* and, most of all, through the inscriptions, the loved ones spoke to the living: *"I am in peace. I remember you. I am waiting for you. I pray for you..."* and the living to the loved ones: *"Rest in Christ. Live with the Holy Souls. Remember your husband and children. Pray for us...".*

Friends and relatives, though with tearful eyes revealing an intense love they felt for their departed, went home in peace, in the assurance that they had not lost them forever. One day they would rejoin them in their Father's house, to reunite again the family that earthly vicissitudes had parted.

This is the finest message left to us by our early fellow Christians.

165

[1] Modern links between two ancient galleries.

[2] ICUR, IV, 9367.

[3] ICUR, IV, 9368.

[4] Probably the future Pope St. Sergius I (687-701). The *Liber Pontificalis* writes that "when he was a priest he often zealously celebrated solemn masses in the catacombs in honour of the martyrs".

[5] ICUR, IV, 9372. In trying to locate the tombs of these martyrs its the Crypts of Lucina, I follow the study of Prof. L. Reekmans: *"La tombe du pape Corneille et sa region cémétériale" (Roma Sotterranea Cristiana, IV)*, Città del Vaticano, 1964, pp. 222-225.

[6] This is the stairway still used today to go down into the Crypts of Lucina. It replaced the earlier stairs of the "beta" *hypogeum*.

[7] See V. FIOCCHI-NICOLAI: *Rinvenuti nei pressi del "Quo Vadis?" i resti di una Basilica paleocristiana*, in *L'Osservatore Romano*, 20th September 1991, p. 4.

...The Geta was vigilant. The angel entered:
[PEACE!
he said. And in the infinite city of the mighty
he heard that only. And closed his eyes in
[peace.
He alone heard, and he repeated it to the dead,
and the dead to the dead and the tombs to the
[tombs.
And the seven hills in rapture did not know what
you knew, o catacombs!

GIOVANNI PASCOLI
From: "La Buona Novella - In Occidente" (1904)

**Glass or terracotta objects
used by the early Christians
in the catacombs: vessels, phials,
oil lamps, amphorae ...**

Appendix

I. VERY INTERESTING LETTERS

In telling the story of the Catacombs of St. Callixtus we have met personalities of the highest order: the martyr Popes Fabian, Cornelius, Sixtus II... The bishop of Carthage St. Cyprian has also been spoken of.

The Church of Rome and that of Carthage were often in contact. It is interesting to know the content of some letters, in order to be acquainted with what those great Pastors talked about and how they judged their times, which were anything but tranquil.

1. The Church of Rome to the Church of Carthage

The Church of Rome, during the persecution of emperor Decius, offered to the Church of Carthage the following testimonial of its faithfulness to Christ.

Rome, early 250

"The Church resists strong in the faith. It is true that some have yielded, being alarmed at the possibility that their high social position might attract attention, or from simple human frailty. Nevertheless, though they are now separated from us, we have not abandoned them in their defection, but have helped them and keep close to them so that by penance they may still be rehabilitated and pardoned by Him who can forgive. Indeed if we were to leave them to their own resources, their fall would become irreparable.

Try and do the same, dearest brothers, extending your hand to those who have fallen, that they may rise again. Thus if they should be arrested again, they may this time feel strong enough to confess the faith and redress their former error.

Allow me also to remind you of what course to take on another problem. Those who surrendered in the time of trial, and are now ill and have repented and want communion with the Church, should be helped. Widows and other persons unable to present themselves spontaneously, as also those in prison or far from home, ought to have people ready to look after them. Nor should catechumens who have fallen ill remain disappointed in their expectation of help.

The brethren who are in prison, the clergy and the entire Church, that watches so carefully over those who call on the Lord's name, salute you. In return we also ask you to remember us" (*Letter* 8, 2-3; CSEL III, 487-488).

2. The Bishop of Carthage to the Church of Rome

When Cyprian was informed of Pope Fabian's death, he wrote this letter to the priests and deacons in Rome.

Carthage, early 250

"My dear Brothers,

news of the death of my saintly fellow bishop was still uncertain and information doubtful, when I received your letter brought by subdeacon Crementius, telling me fully of his glorious death. Then I rejoiced, as his admirable governing of the Church had been followed by a noble end.

For this I share your gladness, as you honour the memory of so solemn and splendid a witness, communicating to us also the glorious recollection you have of your bishop, and offering us such an example of faith and fortitude.

Indeed, harmful as the fall of a leader is to his subjects, no less valuable and salutary for his brethren is the example of a bishop firm in his faith... My wish, dearest brothers, is for your continued welfare" (*Letter* 9, 1; CSEL III, 488-489).

3. Cyprian, bishop of Carthage, to Pope Cornelius

Carthage, Autumn 253

"Cyprian to Cornelius, his brother bishop.

We know, dearest brother, of your faith, your fortitude and your open witness. All this does you great honour and it gives me so much joy that I feel myself part of, and companion in, your merits and undertakings.

Since indeed the Church is one, and one and inseparable is love, and one and unbreakable is the harmony of hearts, what priest singing the praises of another does not rejoice as though they were his own glory? And what brother would not feel happy at the joy of his brethren? Certainly none can imagine the exultation and great joy there has been among us here when we have learnt such fine things, like the proofs of strength you have given.

You have led your brethren to testify to their faith, and that very confession of yours has been strengthened further by that of the brethren. Thus, while you have gone before the others in the path of glory, and have shown yourself ready to be the first in testifying for all, you have persuaded the people too to confess the same faith.

So we cannot decide what to praise more in you, your prompt and unshakeable faith or your community's indivisible fraternal charity. In all its splendour, the courage of the bishop leading his people has been manifested, and the fidelity of the people in full solidarity with their bishop has been a great and shining example. Through all of you, the Church of Rome has given a magnificent testimony, entirely united in one spirit and one voice.

In this way, dear brother, the faith which the Apostle recognized and praised in your community, has shown forth. We may say that he, then, already foresaw prophetically and celebrated your courage and your indomitable fortitude. Even then he recognized your merits which were to make you glorious. He exalted the deeds of the fathers, foreseeing those of their sons.

With your complete harmony and strength of spirit, you have given all Christians a shining example of constancy and unity.

Dear brother, the Lord in his Providence forewarns us that the hour of trial is at hand. God in his goodness and eagerness for our salvation gives us helpful promptings for the coming struggle. So, in the name of that charity which binds us together, let us help one another, persevering with the entire community, with fasts, vigils and prayer. These are for us the heavenly arms which keep us firm and strongly united, and make us persevere. These are the spiritual weapons and the divine arrows which protect us.

Let us remember one another in harmony and spiritual brotherhood. Let us pray for each other at all times and in all places, and let us try to lessen our sufferings with mutual charity" (*Letter* 60, 1-2; CSEL III, 691-692. 694-695).

4. Cyprian announces the death of Pope Sixtus II

Carthage, August 258

"My dear brother,

I was unable to send you a letter earlier because none of the clergy of this Church could move, because they were object of persecution, which however, thank God, found them inwardly most ready to pass at once to heaven. I now send you what news I have.

The envoys I sent to Rome have returned. I sent them to verify and report the decision taken by the authorities concerning myself whatever it may be, and so put an end to all the speculations and uncontrolled gossip which circulated. And now here is the truth, duly ascertained.

Emperor Valerian has sent the Senate his rescript by which he has decided that bishops, priests and deacons shall immediately be put to death. Senators, notables and those who have the title of Roman knighthood shall be deprived of all these, as well as of their possessions. If they are obstinate in professing Christianity, even after the confiscation, they will be condemned to capital punishment.

Christian matrons will have all their goods confiscated and then be sent into exile. All imperial functionaries who have professed the Christian faith or should do so now, will suffer the same confiscation. They will then be arrested and registered for forced labour on the imperial estates.

Valerian also adds to the rescript a copy of a letter he has sent to the provincial governors concerning myself. I expect this letter any day and hope to receive it quickly, keeping myself firm and strong in faith. My decision in the face of martyrdom is quite clear. I am waiting for it, full of confidence that I shall receive the crown of eternal life from the goodness and generosity of God.

I have to report that Sixtus suffered martyrdom with four deacons on 6th August, while he was in the 'Cemetery' area (in the Catacombs of St. Callixtus).

The Roman authorities have a rule that all who are denounced as Christians must be executed and their goods forfeited to the imperial treasury.

I ask that what I have reported be made known to our colleagues in the episcopate, so that by their exhortations our communities may be encouraged and ever more prepared for the spiritual combat. This will stimulate them to consider not so much death as the blessings of immortality, and to consecrate themselves to the Lord with ardent faith and heroic fortitude, to delight in and not to fear at the thought of testifying to their faith. The soldiers of God and of Christ know very well that their immolation is not so much a death but a crown of glory.

To you, dear brother, my greetings in the Lord" (*Letter* 80; CSEL III, 839-840).

5. The martyrdom of St. Cyprian

It would have been very useful and edifying to have the reports of the trials of the martyrs Pontianus, Fabian, Cornelius, Sixtus II, Eusebius, Cecilia... Unfortunately, during the tremendous persecution of Diocletian the archives of the Church of Rome were destroyed.

But the reports of St. Cyprian's trial have come down to us. The Acta were read in the Christian communities for the glory of the Martyr in order to strengthen others in the moment of their ordeal. We can therefore assume that the reports of the trials of the other martyrs just cited were written in much the same way.

Carthage, 14th September 258

"On the morning of September 14th a large crowd gathered at Sesti by order of proconsul Galerius Maximus. And the same proconsul Galerius Maximus bade that Cyprian should be brought to the hearing which he conducted on that same day in the Hall of 'Sauciolus'. When bishop Cyprian stood before him, the proconsul said to him:
— 'Are you Tascius Cyprianus?'
Bishop Cyprian answered:
— 'Yes, I am'.
Proconsul Galerius Maximus said:
— 'Are you the one who has presented himself as the leader of a sacrilegious sect?'.
Bishop Cyprian answered:
— 'I am'.
Galerius Maximus said:

— 'The most holy emperors bid you to sacrifice'.
Bishop Cyprian said:
— 'I will not do it'.
Proconsul Galerius Maximus said:
— 'Think it over'.
Bishop Cyprian said:
— 'Do what you have been ordered to do. In such a just cause there is nothing to think over'.

Galerius Maximus, after conferring with the college of magistrates, pronounced this sentence with difficulty and unwillingly: 'You have long lived sacrilegiously and have gathered many in your criminal sect, and set yourself up as an enemy of the Roman gods and of their religious rites. The pious and most holy *Augusti* emperors Valerian and Gallienus, and Valerian most noble *Caesar*, failed to bring you back to the observance of their religious ceremonies. Therefore, since you have been seen to be the instigator of the worst of crimes, we shall make an example of you before those whom you have associated with yourself in these wicked actions. The respect for the law will be sanctioned by your blood'. Having said this he read out in a loud voice from a tablet the decree: 'I order that Tascius Cyprianus be punished by being beheaded'. Bishop Cyprian said: 'Thanks be to God'.

Following the sentence, the crowd of Christian brethren said: 'We want to be beheaded with him'. At this there was great agitation among the brethren and a large crowd followed him. Thus Cyprian was led into the countryside of Sesti, and there he took off his cloak and hood, knelt on the ground and prostrated himself in prayer to the Lord. He then removed his dalmatic and gave it to the deacons, leaving himself only in his linen garment, and so waited for the executioner.

When the latter arrived, the bishop ordered his own followers to give the executioner twenty-five gold pieces. Meanwhile his brethren held out pieces of cloth and handkerchiefs (to receive the blood as relics). Then the great Cyprian with his own hands bandaged his eyes, but since he could not tie the corners of the handkerchief; presbyter Julian and subdeacon Julian went to help him.

Thus bishop Cyprian was martyred and his body, because of the curiosity of the pagans, was laid in a place nearby where it was hidden from their indiscreet eyes. It was then carried away at night with lighted flares and torches and accompanied as far as the cemetery of procurator Macrobius Candidianus, which is in the Huts Road near the Baths. A few days later, proconsul Galerius Maximus died.

The holy bishop Cyprian was martyred on September 14th under emperors Valerian and Gallienus, but in the reign of our Lord Jesus Christ, to whom all honour and glory be forever. Amen!" (From the *Acta Proconsularia*, 3-6; CSEL III, CXII-CXIV).

6. The "identity card" of the early Christians

In a document dating back to the end of the 2nd century and beginning of the 3rd, called the "Letter to Diognetus", there is a kind of true "identity card" of the early Christians. Here are the main points:

They are men like others

"Christians are not different because of their country or the language they speak or the way they dress. They do not isolate themselves in their cities nor use a private language; even the life they lead has nothing strange.

Their doctrine does not originate from the elaborate disquisitions of intellectuals, nor do they follow, as many do, philosophical systems which are the fruit of human thinking. They live in Greek or in barbarian cities, as the case may be, and adapt themselves to local traditions in dress, food and all usage. Yet they testify to a way of life which, in the opinion of many, has something extraordinary about it".

They dwell on earth but are citizens of heaven

"They live in their own countries and are strangers. They loyally fulfil their duties as citizens, but are treated as foreigners. Every foreign land is for them a fatherland and every fatherland, foreign.

They marry like everyone, they have children, but they do not abandon their new-born. They have the table in common, but not the bed. They are in the flesh, but do not live according to the flesh. They dwell on earth, but are citizens of heaven.

They obey the laws of the state, but in their lives they go beyond the law. They love everyone, yet are persecuted by everyone. No one really knows them, but all condemn them. They are killed, but go on living.

They are poor, but enrich many. They have nothing, but abound in everything. They are despised, but in that contempt they find glory before God. Their honour is insulted, while their justice is acknowledged...".

They are in the world as the soul is in the body

"In the way the Christians are in the world, so the soul is in the body. As the soul is diffused in all parts of the body, so Christians are spread in the various cities of the earth. The soul lives in the body, but is not of the body; so Christians live in the world, but are not of the world. As the invisible soul is imprisoned in a visible body, so Christians are a reality quite visible in the world, while the spiritual worship they give to God is invisible.

As the flesh hates the spirit and fights against it, though not receiving any offence from it, but only because the spirit hinders it in its savouring of harmful joys and pleasures; so the world hates the Christians who have done it no harm, merely because they oppose a way of life based on mere pleasure.

As the soul loves the body and its limbs, which hate it in return, thus Christians love those who hate them. The soul, though it sustains the body, is enclosed in it. So Christians, though they are a support to the world, are confined in the world as in a prison. The immortal soul lives in a mortal tent, so Christians live like strangers among corruptible things, awaiting the incorruptibility of heaven.

By mortifying itself in food and drink, the soul is refined and strengthened; so Christians, maltreated and persecuted, grow in number every day. God has assigned them such a high state that they must not ever abandon" *(Sources Chrétiennes, 33 bis, 62-67).*

II. HOMAGE TO THE TOMBS OF THE MARTYRED POPES BY THEIR SUCCESSORS

After de Rossi had identified the Catacombs of St. Callixtus and discovered the Crypt of the Popes, Pius IX paid homage to his glorious predecessors in a memorable visit.

His example was followed by John XXIII, Paul VI and John Paul II, pilgrims "to the springs". Here are some notes on their visits.

1. Pius IX pays homage to the Crypt of the Popes

Pius IX's visit to the Crypt of the Popes on 11ᵗʰ May 1854 is described by P.M. Baumgarten, who had heard about it by word of mouth from de Rossi.

An unexpected invitation to dinner

"When the land of the vineyard was bought, de Rossi was able to start work. In a short time he discovered several historic crypts and the news came to the Holy Father's ear.

Though Pius IX had no great interest in the study of archaeology, he was impressed to learn that de Rossi's predictions about the Catacombs of St. Callixtus being under that vineyard had proved true. So, on May 10ᵗʰ he sent a message to the celebrated archaeologist stating he would like to visit the catacomb on the following afternoon. On that same day the Pope invited him to dinner at Santa Maria del Priorato, the villa of the Knights of Malta on the Aventine Hill.

On the 11ᵗʰ several cardinals, prelates, ministers and ambassadors met in the beautiful hall of Villa Malta. Among them was de Rossi, who was given a place at table some distance from the Pope.

During that dinner Pius IX spoke of archaeology, and said loudly that he did not believe much in it, because he thought archaeologists were dreamers and poets and wove fantasies about so many things that few could understand. These and similar things were said so that de Rossi could hear them. But the great archaeologist kept quiet.

After dinner, while coffee was being served in the garden, the Pope sent Mons. de Merode to tell de Rossi not to he offended by those words spoken at table. He had said them only for fun, wanting to provoke him to speak up in favour of 'poor archaeology'.

De Rossi replied: 'I quite understood what the Pope meant, so there was no danger of my being offended. On the other hand, it was impossible for me even to speak in the presence of so many distinguished gentlemen, cardinals and diplomats. Soon, in the catacomb, I shall make the monuments do the talking. Down below, the science of Christian antiquities will defend itself' ".

De Rossi's incredible discovery

"A few days before this visit de Rossi had discovered the famous Crypt of the Popes and some of their epitaphs, which were partly broken. Among these was the very important poem by Damasus. Thus, while the Pope's visit was imminent everything was still in rather a mess, because there had not been enough time to clear the crypt of the rubble and put the inscriptions in place. So de Rossi was forced to spend the entire night with his workmen making a way for the Pope to enter the crypt...".

The visit of Pius IX

"In the afternoon Pius IX went by carriage from Villa Malta to the Appian Way where de Rossi was waiting for him. He received the Pope at the entrance to the catacomb and briefly explained the importance of his recent finds, and in particular he mentioned the valuable help he had received from the evidence of the ancient *Itineraries*.

As proof he showed the Pope the verse inscription by St. Damasus. When he read this out, the Pope said, in a loud voice:

— 'But is all this true? Is there no possible illusion here'?

— 'Here, Holy Father, no illusion is possible. We have even discovered the epitaphs of some of the holy successors of the Prince of the Apostles (St. Peter). If Your Holiness would be pleased to put these pieces together, you will find the names of the popes whom Damasus — that tireless devotee of the martyrs of the catacombs — mentions in the lines I have just explained'.

Pius IX took the marble slabs in his hands and read the names, greatly astonished. He went red in the face with excitement at seeing the names of his predecessors. Deep emotion brought tears to his eyes and he said in a loud voice:

— 'Are these, then, really the epitaphs of my predecessors who were buried here'?

De Rossi felt very happy at seeing his beloved Pontiff so moved and delighted. At that moment there came back to his mind the Pope's words about the dreams of archaeologists; innocently and without malice, his thoughts on the triumph of archaeology, he could not resist saying:

— 'But they're all dreams, Holy Father, all archaeologists' dreams'!

— 'O de Rossi, you are naughty!', replied the Pope. He warmly congratulated him on his success and thanked him for the service he had rendered the Church and the Holy See through archaeology.

This marvellous and important visit made a deep impression on Pius IX. De Rossi always enjoyed the esteem and protection of the Pope, who defended him when anyone ever tried to hinder his excavations or even do him harm".

2. John XXIII visits the Catacombs of St. Callixtus

A promise kept

On 19th September 1961, after a lapse of 107 years. another Pope, John XXIII, made a devotional visit.

A month before, on August 23rd, the Pope had told the superior of the Salesian Fathers, responsible for the Catacombs of St. Callixtus: "I want to come to the catacombs. I will come as a pilgrim, to pray as so many visitors do". But he added: "I don't want any people, otherwise it is the end. I'm only coming to pray".

A visit of intense prayer

On the morning of September 19th, at 7,45 a.m., Pope John's car stopped in the square in front of the catacombs. He was accompanied by his private secretary Mons. Capovilla and his chamberlain Mons. Nasalli Rocca. To greet them were only the director of the Catacombs of St. Callixtus, Rev. Virgilio Battezzati, and the inspector of the Pontifical Commission for Sacred Archaeology, Prof. Enrico Josi.

The Holy Father at once went down the "Staircase of Damasus" to the Crypt of the Popes. From the outset the visit was more devotional than cultural. Indeed, as

Pope John XXIII visits the Catacombs of St. Callixtus accompanied by Prof. E. Josi.

soon as he entered the Crypt he knelt down reverently and recited the Litany of the Saints with the Salesians working in the Catacombs. Psalm 70 was sung with the proper antiphon for the martyrs. Then John XXIII recited the *oremus* of the martyr popes and that of the common of martyrs and gave his apostolic blessing. It was a gathering of faith and prayer and most moving.

The intentions of the Pope's prayers

The Pope then said a few fatherly words: "Don't you want the Pope, who has come after the last visit of Pius IX over a century ago, to leave a record or reveal his reason for this pilgrimage?

Here it is: the problems of the universal Church and the peace of the world, and that the Lord may grant peace and unity to all Christian peoples".

As the Pope wished, this visit was to serve as an example to all the faithful of Rome. They were to come, exhorted by their Pastor, not only to love but to know and venerate these sacred places: as a support to generous resolutions and encouragement through their lives.

On the tide of memory

John XXIII liked to recall that he had visited the Catacombs of St. Callixtus for the first time in 1900. Later on, as a student at the Lateran Seminary, he enjoyed the lectures of the distinguished archaeologist Orazio Marucchi and appreciated his deeply Christian spirit. In this connection he remembered one shocking episode. Prof. Marucchi was a member of the Council of the capital City. A staunch Catholic, he was steadfast in his defence of religious principles. For this reason one day he was treacherously maltreated and struck during a session of the City Council.

Following this incident, when he returned to lecture at the Lateran, he was welcomed by the clerical students and the entire teaching staff as in triumph and with such enthusiasm that he remembered it for all his life. Angelo Roncalli, the future Pope John XXIII, was one of those enthusiastic students...

"The history of the Church", the Pope went on, "is one of strife, but also of victories. We, consecrated persons, know this better than anyone. Serene confidence, then, in spite of everything: God is with us. The Church of today will surely triumph, as did the Church of the catacombs".

Pilgrim to the tombs of the martyrs

After visiting the Crypt of the Popes, John XXIII stopped at the Crypt of Cecilia and at the *Cubicula* of the Sacraments. He then walked the long 3rd century gallery, pausing at the tombs of the popes SS. Gaius and Eusebius and of the martyrs Calocerus and Parthenius.

He went as far as the *cubiculum* of deacon Severus. At the reading of his epitaph, John XXIII was struck by the deacon's phrase describing his *cubiculum* as "the house of peace". He asked his secretary Mons. Capovilla to transcribe it.

During his pious visit, though he was listening to Prof. Josi, the Pope remained deep in prayer and spoke very little.

3. Another pilgrim, Pope Paul VI

On the eve of the last phase of the Ecumenical Council Vatican II, Pope Paul VI came to two famous shrines of the Roman martyrs, the Catacombs of Domitilla and then of St. Callixtus.

Visit to Domitilla and the Ardeatine Caves

On Sunday September 12th 1965, he went to the underground basilica of SS. Nereus and Achilleus in the Cemetery of Domitilla on the Via delle Sette Chiese to celebrate Mass. From the basilica he went on to the Ardeatine Caves to pray for the repose of the souls of those who died in the massacre of March 1944... He laid there an olive branch, tied with the papal colours, and lit a lamp, his own gift, which from that time burns in the place as a symbol of peace and hope.

Visit to the Catacombs of St. Callixtus

Going on to the Catacombs of St. Callixtus, Paul VI descended to the second level where the Crypt of the Popes is located. He was accompanied by Prof. Sandro Carletti, inspector of the Pontifical Commission for Sacred Archaeology.

The latter said: "Holy Father, in this area nine popes of the third century were buried".

Paul VI remained silent for a moment then uttered, almost to himself: "Nine popes!".

They showed him the lines of St. Damasus dedicated to the martyrs of the crypt and of the cemetery. He read them himself and when he came to the line "Here lies the pope who lived in a long peace", he pointed out:

— "Damasus probably meant Pope Fabian".

Prof. Carletti agreed, adding that five of the fourteen years of Fabian's pontificate (236-250) coincided with the reign of Philip the Arabian (244-249) and of his son Philip II, co-emperor with his father.

— "Yes", said Pope Paul, "it is said that they were Christians. Anyway they were not persecutors. But perhaps the reference is to Dionysius".

Dionysius, in fact, was pope from 259-268, under the rule of Gallienus, during a period of complete peace for the Church.

The poem ends with the following lines: "Here too I, Damasus, confess I would like to be buried were it not for the fear of disturbing the ashes of these holy persons".

Prof. Carletti pointed out that Damasus gave up the idea of being buried in the crypt and arranged that he should be interred with his mother and sister in a basilica on the Via Ardeatina, which unfortunately archaeologists have not yet been able to find.

— "Not even with excavations?", asked the Pope.

— "Not even with excavations", replied Prof. Carletti somewhat discouraged.

— "But you'll find it in the end", was the encouraging answer of the Pope.

Pope Paul VI then read the five Greek epitaphs of Pontianus, Antherus, Fabian, Lucius and Eutychian. He stopped to pray before the altar of the Crypt of the Popes, as well as at the tomb of the martyr St. Cecilia in the nearby crypt. He then went back into the open-air.

Paul VI, a member of the "Collegium Cultorum Martyrum"

Paul VI had been a member and patron of the Collegium Cultorum Martyrum and had taken part in its celebrations in the catacombs, as well as in the Lenten Stations of the Cross. On 29th June 1976, the feast of SS. Peter and Paul, addressing the faithful at noon in St. Peter's Square, he spoke of the Martyrs in the Catacombs and added:

"We would he glad if the study and devotion for the memory of the Apostles and Martyrs, who make up the unique glories of this Christian City, still had today many faithful followers... There still exists a 'Collegium Cultorum Martyrum' open to all who have an understanding and affection for the monuments of Rome's Christian history. We hope it will always promote pious and edifying meetings, with new and youthful members, a perennial flowering of religion and cultural life over the tombs of the martyrs of the faith...".

Paul VI's gift to the Catacombs of St. Callixtus

On the night of Christmas 1975, during the closing of the Holy Door at the Vatican Basilica, Paul VI lit an artistical bronze lamp. It was intended for the Western

Trichora of St. Callixtus, where young people particularly attend "pious and edifying meetings" near the shrines of the martyrs.

4. John Paul II takes part in the first Lenten Station of St. Callixtus

John Paul II came to the Catacombs of St. Callixtus on Ash Wednesday 1984. It was the late afternoon of March the 7th. He had made a date with the young people of the Roman parishes for the first Lenten Station.

After Mass, celebrated in the olive grove, he went down into the catacomb as a pilgrim. He was accompained by Rev. Umberto Fasola, secretary of the Pontifical Commission for Sacred Archaeology. In the Crypt of the Popes he knelt down in prayer, which was so intense and prolonged that his guide did not dare interrupt with any word of explanation.

Then John Paul II got up and went into the Crypt of St. Cecilia. Here too he paused all absorbed in a thoughtful silence. Then, turning to the guide, he asked: "Is it quite certain that the Martyr was buried here, where the statue is now?". Prof. Fasola confirmed that it was so. As a proof he also mentioned that de Rossi, during the excavation, had read on the wall of the sepulchre a graffito about St. Cecilia. This graffito, due to the deterioration of the plaster, has now completely vanished.

As it was very late, Pope John Paul II could not prolong his devotional visit any further, and he left.

Paul VI praying in the Crypt of the Popes.

III. MORE PILGRIMS

Visitors to the catacombs of Rome have always been numerous: people of every age, social condition and faith: saints, illustrious personages, as well as a multitude of ordinary people. Many have even written their impressions and memories. It may be a useful addition to this book to note a few.

The poet Francesco Petrarca made a pilgrimage to the Catacombs of St. Sebastian in 1337, and left an interesting description in a letter. St. Brigid of Sweden and her daughter St. Catherine came for the Holy Year indulgence in 1350. St. Philip Neri (1515-1595) spent entire nights in prayer in these catacombs. So did St. Charles Borromeo (1538-1584) before becoming archbishop of Milan.

St. Maria Domenica Mazzarello (1837-1881) came to pray at the Catacombs of St. Callixtus in November 1887. She had come to Rome with a small group of Sisters, who were received by Pius IX before leaving for their missions in Uruguay. It was in these catacombs that the Saint performed a charming act of charity. During the visit she noticed that a cleric was suffering from fever. Taking off her shawl and approaching the sick man, with firm gentleness she told him to put it round his shoulders. The poor young man was rather embarrassed and reluctant, but the insistence of Mother Mazzarello and his shivers forced him to accept...

1. The 'ecstasy' of Don Bosco

St. John Bosco (1815-1888) came to the Catacombs of St. Callixtus probably on 13th April 1858, on the same day after visiting the Catacombs of St. Sebastian. This is how his biographer J. B. Lemoyne describes his visit:

"Whoever enters these places feels emotions which can never be forgotten. Don Bosco was absorbed in holy and loving thoughts as he walked through these underground passages.

Here the early Christians heard Mass, prayed together, sang psalms and prophecies, went to Communion, listened to the words of bishops and popes. Here they found the necessary strength for the martyrdom which awaited them.

It is impossible to look with dry eyes at those *loculi*, which once contained the torn bodies of so many heroes of the faith, and at the tombs of fourteen popes, some of whom gave their lives in witness to what they taught.

Don Bosco observed the very ancient frescoes and symbols which represented Jesus Christ, the Eucharist and Mary, the Mother of God with the Child on her knees. He was enchanted and enraptured by the feeling of simplicity and authenticity that those images communicate.

Here, the early Christian art had been able to represent the incomparable beauty of the soul, the high ideal of moral perfection attributed to the Madonna. There were also other figures of saints and martyrs.

The Saint came out of the catacombs at six o clock in the evening having entered at eight in the morning. He had had a little lunch with the Franciscan Fathers, custodians of those catacombs".

2. "Little Thérèse of Lisieux"

St. Thérèse Martin ("Little Thérèse", 1873-1897) came to Rome with her father and her sister Celine on 14th to 20th September 1887. They were part of a French pilgrimage to Italy. Thérèse was only fourteen and ardently wanted to meet Pope Leo XIII and ask him a favour: that she might realize the dream she kept in her heart of consecrating herself to God despite her young age.

During her six days in Rome she visited the Catacombs of St. Callixtus. She left an account of this in her autobiography: *The Story of a Soul*.

"The catacombs left a delightful impression upon me. They are just as I imagined from reading their description in the Lives of the Martyrs. Having stayed there for most of the afternoon, it seemed as if I had gone down for only a few minutes, so much does the atmosphere surrounding you seem imbued with holiness.

We had to take away some special memento of the catacombs, so we let the others go on ahead. Then Celine and I stretched down for a little while where the primitive tomb of St. Cecilia had been, and took also some of the earth sanctified by her presence.

Before going to Rome I never felt any special devotion to this Saint. But visiting her house (in Trastevere), turned into a church, as well as the place of her martyrdom, I learnt that Cecilia had been proclaimed the queen of harmony (patroness of music) not so much for her beautiful voice and musical talent, but in memory of the virginal chant she made to her heavenly spouse Jesus) hidden in her heart. I then felt for her, more than devotion, the true 'fondness of a friend'.

Cecilia became my favourite saint, my confidante. Everything about her enraptured me, especially her 'abandonment', her boundless trust, which made her capable of fascinating, by her virginity, souls which had only wished the joys of this present life".

3. A Martyr of the "Church of silence"

On 6th October 1971 a real martyr of modern times, Cardinal Josef Mindszenty (1892-1975), primate of Hungary, came to pray in the Catacombs of St. Callixtus.

Arrested in 1948, after tremendous psychological and bodily tortures and a farcical trial, he was condemned to life imprisonment. He spent 8 years in jail, and 15 as a refugee in the United States Embassy in Budapest, following the Hungarian revolt against the communist government on October 1956.

When he came to the Catacombs of St. Callixtus as a pilgrim, he had just been freed and was in Rome as a guest of the Vatican. His liberation championed by Paul VI, cost him very dear: the renunciation of his episcopal see and perpetual exile from his native country.

He wrote in the Distinguished Visitors Book at St. Callixtus: *"Plenus emotionibus fidei prim. suae Ecclesiae. Card. Josef Mindszenty, primas Hungariae"* (Deeply moved by the faith of his Church of the beginnings. Cardinal Josef Mindszenty, primate of Hungary). The Cardinal spent the remaining four years of his life as an exile in Austria.

IV. THE GREAT ADVENTURE

In 1892 Giovanni Battista de Rossi celebrated his 70th birthday. Forty years had passed since his first sensational discoveries at St. Callixtus.

That same year, on April 20th the great master was honoured with the unveiling of a bust placed in the Eastern *Trichora*.

The reader knows something already about his story; but, on that occasion de Rossi recounted his admirable adventure at St. Callixtus with such feeling and so many new details that it is worth reporting:

"It was the Summer of 1844..."

"... It was the Summer of 1844. With my ten-year-old brother Michele Stefano, I was walking through the vineyards which extended from the Appian Way to the Via Ardeatina. I was looking for ruins of monuments and epigraphs.

I had entered the vineyard from the gate which faces Via Ardeatina, when my eye was attracted by two ancient buildings, each with three apses. One had been turned into a farm house. The other was being used as a cellar. Its three apses were full of barrels of wine. The structure and architectural style of each building made me think they were of paleochristian origin and had been used by the early Christians.

The ground surrounding the two buildings was strewn with fragments of stone, very different from the thin marble slabs found in the underground tombs. Among the fragments were pieces of consular inscriptions dating back to the 4th and 5th centuries.

Finally, I singled out three very interesting marble pieces: they were carved in the style of Damasus and bore incomplete hexameters. One of them made an explicit reference to an altar. These pieces of marble lay close to the corner of the door of this former cellar. Now, in the place of the door you have erected my bust. The clues were more than sufficient to convince me of the sacred and historic character of these two triapsidal buildings...".

The capital importance of the topographical documents

"Day by day, I collected and organized the precious fragments, hitherto largely forgotten, of the Christian monuments of this suburban area. But a scientific method for reconstructing those monuments demanded that every fragment, every relic should be catalogued and identified in its exact place, or at least in the group of roads close together in the same area.

**From de Rossi's family album:
Giovanni Battista, his brother Michele Stefano
and his sister Teresa (3 May 1857).**

In the main group, at the centre, the greater number of the 3rd century popes had been buried. The crypt was called 'of St. Sixtus', after Sixtus II who was killed in 258. His name was given to that crypt because of the solemn and historically certain circumstances of his martyrdom.

Alongside them, St. Cecilia ought to have been buried. Above that ground the little church called SS. Sixtus and Cecilia was built, certainly because it stood above their sepulchres. In separate and distant crypts Cornelius and Eusebius were also buried. These were the three groups in the Cemetery of Callixtus. which were singled out in the topographical documents of the *Itineraries*".

A difficult task

"From the centre of this aisle, in 1844, one entered the catacombs by a rudimentary staircase recently built. The stairs led to some parts of the nearby *hypogea*. These places had been turned into cool cellars for keeping the wine in summertime, and nothing seemed to be of any importance. Everything had been broken and buried under the earth or rubble.

The *Itineraries* are not enough for finding the precise location of the monuments that they mention. Hence, I did not dare give its historical name to this triapsidal building with absolute certainty. I did not even dare pronounce the historical names of the martyrs who had once been buried in the tombs hidden here underground, and now enveloped in ruin and rubble under the wine barrels.

Nevertheless, I fearlessly insisted, in the face of the scepticism of my best friends, that this had been one of the most outstanding sanctuaries of the true Cemetery of St. Callixtus: probably, I stated, the shrine of Sixtus and Cecilia.

One day in 1850, however, I let myself go. I was then an excited and impatient youngster, and I could not overcome the obstinate incredulity of an old Professor who was benevolent towards me and condescending. I grabbed him by the arm and dragged him underground with me. To enter the catacomb you had to lower yourself through the opening of the skylight a long distance from here, at the place where the abbey of the Trappists is now located (today's St. Tarcisius Salesian Institute).

I already saw clearly what there was in the Appia-Ardeatina groups of roads. Along the Appian Way we had to distinguish three very ancient underground cemeteries. Each of them had its historic monuments above and below ground. I maintained that the most famous cemetery of all, that of Callixtus, where lay the precious tombs of the 3rd century popes and the sepulchre of the most celebrated martyr Cecilia, was not in the underground area next to the Basilica of St. Sebastian, but in this vineyard, in the place where we are now gathered.

Late medieval tradition had located it near the Basilica of St. Sebastian. But it was not the right place.

By the comparison and cross-reference with ancient topographical texts, I had learnt something important. In the Cemetery of Callixtus, the most famous and venerated sepulchres had been divided into three groups.

We walked the apparently inextricable maze of the cemetery galleries. After twists and turns in the underground network, I came as near as possible to the area under this building and with a firm and resolute voice I shouted: 'One day they'll listen to me! When all these heaps of rubble are taken away, below we shall find the tombs of Sixtus. Cecilia and all their noble companions, just as history tells us and the topographical documents attest'.

I was taken for a madman. He told me to calm down and not to risk exposing myself and archaeology to ridicule. And yet the Crypt of the Popes and that of St. Cecilia were really here below. That of St. Cornelius was a hundred yards on my left. That of Eusebius was even closer on my right. The indisputable proofs by now have been under everybody's eyes for about forty years.

I will now recall in a few words how we arrived at these great discoveries and at fulfilment of my boldest prophecies".

A conclusive find

"In 1849, in this vineyard, I saw a fragment which had just been pulled out of the ground. In a beautiful lettering, much older than that of St. Damasus' style, it read: ...NELIVS MARTYR. It was easy to complete the name CORNELIVS. I was now sure that the tomb of the famous Pope who bore this name was to be found here and not somewhere else. In that marble slab I saw the primitive epitaph of that tomb and I held it as a sure sign that my topographical insights were accurate. However, no one believed me.

In 1852, however Pius IX, whom I have called with good reasons the 'second Damasus' created the Commission for Sacred Archaeology. It was entrusted with the scientific direction of the excavations of the underground cemeteries. I then proposed that a new series of explorations and research had to be started in the galleries below these vineyards. The proposal was accepted.

The first fruit was the discovery of the tomb of St. Cornelius and of the fresco of his portrait and St. Cyprian's. Near that tomb was uncovered the missing piece of the epitaph which I had found in the vineyard. The two pieces fitted together and sealed the opening of the tomb perfectly; it read: CORNELIVS MARTYR EP(iscopus).

I do not want to mention here all the other historic epitaphs found in that same crypt. I was already certain that this was the Cemetery of Callixtus, in which, according to history, the martyr St. Cornelius had been buried".

The great Benefactor

"This discovery was decisive and made all the rest easy. I persuaded the Commission for Sacred Archaeology to make a proposal to the Pope for the purchase of the vineyards which covered the immense necropolis. They belonged to different owners and extended into the woods beyond the fork of the Appian Way and the Ardeatina.

I remember that Pius IX called me to a private audience with special affection. He told me playfully that my archaeologist's dreams were behind the Commission's proposal. I replied, trying to inspire him with confidence, but also telling him the complete truth.

I confessed that I was sure of the existence of illustrious monuments under those vineyards, but that it was impossible for me to forecast in what state they would be found. In the Crypt of St. Cornelius we had made very important finds, but I did not know whether in the other crypts we would also discover 3rd century inscriptions, 4th century eulogies in the style of Damasus, frescoe paintings done during the time of peace, or visitors' graffiti. In spite of his playful diffidence, the Pope said to his household: 'De Rossi is sure of what he says and promises. He is right'.

The Pope ordered the land to he bought, and the Commission for Sacred Archaeology went on with the excavations unhindered. The discoveries exceeded my expectations and triumphantly confirmed every forecast".

Glory be to God...

"Having happily reached the much desired goal, I must express my thanks. I raise my eyes and my mind upwards and thank Divine Providence for all its goodness. Certainly I would not have been able to prove the historical truth of these monuments if the *hypogea*, invaded by the vine growers and reduced to summer wine cellars, had been despoiled of their historic riches by rough and greedy hands...

If that had happened, my undertaking would have failed, and my studies would have been judged an ingenious hypothesis or just an archaeologist's dream.

But, fortunately, under the wine barrels no greedy hand had rummaged among the earth and rubble, no one had completed the damage and plunder begun centuries earlier. Hidden and broken in this earth lay four Greek sepulchral epitaphs of the popes belonging to the 3rd century, 130 fragments of historic poems by Pope Damasus, historic frescoes, entire walls covered with graffiti, columns, sculptured marble, inscriptions of every kind, and memories of the clan of the Christian *Caecilii* near the venerated tomb of their Heroine.

After so great a number of monuments eagerly searched for with love, before the inestimable riches of this unique discovery, I feel it my duty to thank God, the author of all good...".

Pope Pius IX praying in the Crypt of St. Cecilia.
In the corner on the right: Giovanni Battista and Michele Stefano de Rossi (19th century print).

Chronological Table

I. POPES[1]

1. St. Peter	(†) 67
2. St. Linus	67-79
3. St. Anacletus	79-90
4. St. Clement I	90-99
5. St. Evaristus	99-107
6. St. Alexander	107-116
7. St. Sixtus I	116-125
8. St. Telesphorus	125-136
9. St. Hyginus	136-140
10. St. Pius I	140-154
11. St. Anicetus	154-166
12. St. Soter	166-174
13. St. Eleutherius	174-189
14. St. Victor	189-199
15. ST. ZEPHYRINUS	199-217
16. St. Callixtus I	217-222
17. St. Urban I	222-230
18. ST. PONTIANUS	230-235
19. ST. ANTHERUS	235-236
20. ST. FABIAN	236-250
21. ST. CORNELIUS	251-253
Novatian	251-258
22. ST. LUCIUS I	253-254
23. ST. STEPHEN I	254-257
24. ST. SIXTUS II	257-258
25. ST. DIONYSIUS	259-268
26. ST. FELIX I	269-274
27. ST. EUTYCHIAN	275-283
28. ST. GAIUS	283-296
29. St. Marcellinus	296-304
30. St. Marcellus I	307-308
31. ST. EUSEBIUS	309
32. ST. MILTIADES	311-314
33. St. Sylvester I	314-335
34. ST. MARK	336
35. St. Julius I	337-352

36. St. Liberius	352-366
Felix II	355-365
37. ST. DAMASUS I	366-384
Ursinus	366-367
38. St. Siricius	384-399
39. St. Anastasius I	399-402
40. St. Innocent I	402-417
41. St. Zosimus	417-418
42. St. Boniface I	418-422
Eulalius	418-419
43. St. Celestine I	422-432
44. St. Sixtus III	432-440
45. St. Leo I	440-461
46. St. Hilarius	461-468
47. St. Simplicius	468-483
48. St. Felix II	483-492
49. St. Gelasius I	492-496
. . . . .	
53. St. John I	523-526
. . . . .	
61. John III	561-574
. . . . .	
92. Stephen II	752-757
93. St. Paul I	757-767
94. Stephen III	768-772
95. Adrian I	772-795
96. St. Leo III	795-816
97. Stephen IV	816-817
98. St. Paschal I	817-824
99. Eugene II	824-827
100. Valentine	827

[1] The popes buried in the "Callixtian complex" are printed in capital letters.

II. ROMAN EMPERORS

The Julio-Claudian Dynasty (27 B.C. — 68 A.D.)

Augustus	27 B.C. - 14 A.D.
Tiberius	14-37
Caligula	37-41
Claudius	41-54
Nero	54-68
Galba - Otho - Vitellius	68-69

The Flavian Dynasty (69-96)

Vespasian	69-79
Titus	79-81
Domitian	81-96

Adoptive Emperors (96-192)

Nerva	96-98
Trajan	98-117
Hadrian	117-138
Antoninus Pius	138-161
Marcus Aurelius	161-180
Lucius Verus	161-169
Commodus	180-192
Pertinax - Didius - Julian - Clodius - Albinus - Pescennius - Niger	193

The Severian Dynasty (193-235)

Septimius Severus	193-211
Caracalla	211-217
Geta	211-212
(Macrinus)	217-218
Elagabalus	218-222
Alexander Severus	222-235

Military Anarchy (235-268)

Maximin (the Thracian)	235-238
Gordian I & II	238
Pupienus & Balbinus	238
Gordian III	238-244
Philip (the Arabian)	244-249
Trajan Decius	249-251
Trebonianus Gallus	251-253
Emilian	253
Valerian	253-260
Gallienus	253-268

The Illyrian Emperors (268-282)

Claudius II	268-270
Aurelian	270-275
Tacitus	275-276
Florian	276
Probus	276-282
Carus	282-283
Carinus & Numerian	283-284

The Tetrarchy (284-305)

Diocletian	284-305
Maximian (the Herculean)	286-310
Constantius Chlorus	292-306
Galerius	292-311

Civil War (306-324)

Severus	306
Maxentius	306-312
Constantine (the Great)	306-324
Maximin Daia	307-313
Licinius	307-324

After the unification of the Empire

Constantine (the Great)	324-337
Constantine II	337-340
Constans	337-350
Constantius	337-361
Julian (the Apostate)	361-363
Jovian	363-364
Valentinian I	364-375
Valens	375-378
Gratian	378-383
Valentinian II	375-392
Theodosius	379-395

Emperors of the West

Honorius	394-423
Valentinian III	423-455
Maximus	455
Avitus	455-456
Majorian	457-461
Severus	461-465
Ricimer	465-467
Anthemius	467-472
Olybrius	472
Glicerius	473-474
Julius Nepos	474-475
Romulus Augustulus	475-476

III. MARTYRS AND SAINTS BURIED IN THE CATACOMBS OF ST. CALLIXTUS

Martyred Popes

1. St. Pontianus: buried in the Crypt of the Popes.

2. St. Fabian: buried in the Crypt of the Popes.

3. St. Sixtus II: buried in the Crypt of the Popes; the exact place of his tomb has been identified.

4. St. Eusebius: buried in his Crypt; the exact place of his tomb has been identified.

5. St. Cornelius: buried in the Crypts of Lucina; the exact place of his tomb has been identified.

Popes declared Saints

1. St. Zephyrinus: buried above ground, perhaps in the Western *Trichora*.

2. St. Antherus: buried in the Crypt of the Popes.

3. St. Lucius: buried in the Crypt of the Popes.

4. St. Eutychian: buried in the Crypt of the Popes.

5. St. Stephen I: buried in the Crypt of the Popes.

6. St. Dionysius: buried in the Crypt of the Popes.

7. St. Felix I: buried in the Crypt of the Popes.

8. St. Gaius: buried in his Crypt; the exact place of his tomb has been identified.

9. St. Miltiades: buried in the Cemetery of St. Callixtus.

Bishops Saints

1. St. Urban: perhaps buried in the Crypt of the Popes.

2. St. Numidian: perhaps buried in the Crypt of the Popes.

3. St. Optatus: perhaps buried in the Crypt of St. Gaius.

4. St. Laudiceus: buried in the Cemetery of St. Callixtus.

5. St. Polycarp: buried in the Cemetery of St. Callixtus.

6. St. Julian: buried in the Cemetery of St. Callixtus.

7. St. Mannus: buried in the Cemetery of St. Callixtus.

Martyrs

1. St. Tarcisius: buried above ground, perhaps in the Western *Trichora*.

2. St. Cecilia: buried in her Crypt; the exact place of her tomb has been identified.

3. SS. Calocerus and Parthenius: buried in their Crypt. The wall (now remade in concrete by de Rossi) containing their tombs has been identified.

4. Eleven Martyrs died with Sixtus II. Among them four deacons: Januarius, Magnus, Vincent, Stephen. They are buried in the Cemetery of St. Callixtus.

5. SS. Cerealis and Sallustia with their 21 Companions: buried in the Crypts of Lucina.

6. St. Polycamus: buried in the Cemetery of St. Callixtus.

IV. MARTYRS AND SAINTS BURIED IN THE "CALLIXTIAN COMPLEX"

Popes declared Saints

1. St. Mark: buried above ground in the Cemetery of Balbina.
2. St. Damasus: buried above ground in the Cemetery of Basileus.

Martyrs

1. St. Soter: buried in her Cemetery.
2. SS. Mark and Marcellianus: buried in the Cemetery of Basileus.

3. Greek Martyrs: Maria, Neon, Hippolytus, Adria, Pauline, Martha, Valeria, Eusehius and Marcellus: buried in the "Callixtian complex".

Summing up:

In the Cemetery of St. Callixtus proper were buried: 44 Martyrs (of whom 5 were Popes) and 16 Saints (9 Popes and 7 Bishops).

In the "Callixtian complex" were buried: 2 Popes and 12 Martyrs.

These figures, though reliable and based on ancient sources, are probably underestimates.

Sunset at the Catacombs of St. Callixtus.

Selected Bibliography

BARUFFA ANTONIO, *Giovanni Battista de Rossi*, Libreria Editrice Vaticana. Città del Vaticano, 1994.

BRANDENBURG HUGO, *Überlegungen zu Ursprung und Entstehung der Katakomben Roms*, in "Vivarium", Festschrift Theodor Klauser zum 90, Geburtstag, Münster, 1984, 11-45.

CARLETTI CARLO, *Iscrizioni Cristiane a Roma. Testimonianze di vita cristiana* (Secoli III- VII), Nardini Editore, Firenze, 1986.

CARLETTI SANDRO, *Le antiche chiese dei martiri cristiani* (Le Chiese di Roma illustrate 122-123), Edizioni "Roma", Roma, 1972.

DE ANGELIS D'OSSAT GIOACCHINO, *La geologia delle catacombe Romane* (Roma Sotterranea Cristiana III), Città del Vaticano, 1938-1943.

DE BRUYNE LUCIEN, *L'arte cristiana nella Roma sotterranea*, in "Roma Nobilis", Edizione Edas, Roma, 1953.

—, *L'Initiation Chrétienne et ses reflets dans l'art paléochrétien*, in "Revue des Sciences Religieuses", 3-4, Strasbourg, 1962, 27-85.

DE ROSSI GIOVANNI BATTISTA, *Inscriptiones Christianae Urbis Romae septimo saeculo antiquiores*, I, Roma, 1857-1861.

—, *La Roma Sotterranea Cristiana*, t. I-III, Roma, 1864-1877.

DUCHESNE LOUIS, *Liber Pontificalis*, t. I-II, Parigi, 1886-1892. Re-edited with a third volume by C. Vogel, Parigi, 1955-1957.

FASOLA UMBERTO, *Les Catacombes entre la légende et l'histoire*, in "Les Dossiers de l'Archéologie" 18, Dijon, 1976, 51-64.

—, *Indagini nel sopratterra della Catacomba di San Callisto*, in "Rivista di Archeologia Cristiana" 56, Città del Vaticano, 1980, 221-278.

—, *Orme sulla roccia. Pietro e Paolo a Roma*, Vision Editrice, Roma, 1980.

—, *Scoperta di nuovi dati monumentali per lo studio dell'Area prima callistiana*, in "Rivista di Archeologia Cristiana" 59, Città del Vaticano, 1983, 257-273.

—, *Santuari sotterranei di Damaso nelle Catacombe Romane. I contributi di una recente scoperta*, in "Saecularia Damasiana" XXXIX, Città del Vaticano, 1986, 175-201.

FERRETTO GIUSEPPE, *Note storico-bibliografiche di archeologia cristiana*, Città del Vaticano, 1942.

FERRUA ANTONIO, *Epigrammata Damasiana* (Sussidi allo studio delle antichità cristiane II), Città del Vaticano, 1942.

—. *Inscriptiones Christianae Urbis Romae septimo saeculo antiquiores*, Nova series, vol. IV: *Coemeteria inter vias Appiam et Ardeatinam*, Città del Vaticano, 1964.

—, *Lavori a San Callisto*, in "Rivista di Archeologia Cristiana" 51, Città del Vaticano, 1975, 213-240.

—, *Ultime scoperte a San Callisto*, in Ibidem 52, Città del Vaticano, 1976, 201-219.

—, *Cimitero di San Callisto*, in Ibidem 57, Città del Vaticano, 1981, 7-24.

FIOCCHI NICOLAI V., BISCONTI F., MAZZOLENI D., *The Christian Catacombs of Rome. History, Decoration, Inscriptions*. Schnell & Steiner, Regensburg, 1999.

GATTI GIUSEPPE, *Inscriptiones Christianae Urbis Romae*, suppl. I/1, Roma, 1915.

GUARDUCCI MARGHERITA, *L'etimologia del toponimo "Catacumbas"*, in "Mélanges de l'Ecole Française de Rome", t. 98, Roma, 1986, 840-842.

JANSSENS JOS, *Vita e morte del cristiano negli epitaffi di Roma anteriori al sec. VII*, Università Gregoriana Editrice, Roma, 1981.

JOSI ENRICO, *Il Cimitero di Callisto*, in Collezione "Amici delle Catacombe" of the Pontificio Istituto di Archeologia Cristiana, Roma, 1933.

MAZZOLENI DANILO, *L'Arte delle Catacombe*, in "Archeo-Dossier", Istituto Geografico De Agostini, 8, Novara, 1985, 1-68.

—, *Vita quotidiana degli antichi cristiani nelle testimonianze delle iscrizioni*, in Ibidem 28, Novara, 1987, 1-68.

—, *II lavoro nell'epigrafia cristiana*, in "Spiritualità del lavoro nella catechesi dei Padri del III-IV secolo", cur. Sergio Felici, Libreria Ateneo Salesiano Editrice (LAS), Roma, 1986, 264-271.

NESTORI ALDO, *Repertorio topografico delle Pitture delle Catacombe Romane* (Roma Sotterranea Cristiana V), Città del Vaticano, 1975.

—, *La Basilica Anonima della Via Ardeatina* (Studi di Antichità Cristiana XLIII), Città del Vaticano, 1990.

PIETRI CHARLES, *Roma Christiana. Recherches sur l'Eglise de Rome, son organization, sa politique, son idéologie de Miltiade à Sixte III (311-440)*, 2 v., Rome, 1976.

REEKMANS LOUIS, *La tombe du pape Corneille et sa région cémétériale* (Roma Sotterranea Cristiana IV), Città del Vaticano, 1964.

—, *L'oeuvre du pape Damase dans le complexe de Gaius à la Catacombe de S. Callixte*, in "Saecularia Damasiana" XXXIX, Città del Vaticano, 1986, 259-281.

—, *Le complexe cémétérial du pape Gaius dans la Catacombe de Callixte* (Roma Sotterranea Cristiana VIII), Città del Vaticano, 1988.

SAINT-ROCH PATRICK, *Sur la tombe du pape Damase*, in "Saecularia Damasiana" XXXIX, Città del Vaticano, 1986, 283-290.

STYGER PAUL, *Die Römischen Katakomben*, Berlin, 1933.

TESTINI PASQUALE, *Le Catacombe e gli antichi Cimiteri cristiani in Roma*, Cappelli Editore, Bologna, 1966.

—, *Ancheologia cristiana*, Edipuglia, Bari, 1980.

VALENTINI R. - ZUCCHETTI G., *Codice topografico della città di Roma*, 4 v., Roma, 1940-1953.

WILPERT JOSEPH, *Le Pitture delle Catacombe Romane*, 3 v., Roma, 1903.

—, *La Cripta dei Papi e La Cappella di Santa Cecilia nel Cimitero di Callisto*, Desclée e C., Roma, 1910.

—, *I Sarcofagi cristiani antichi*, 5 v., Pontificio Istituto di Archeologia Cristiana, Città del Vaticano, 1929-1936.

"St. Callixtus" Salesian Institute seen from the archaeological area.

Contents

V. The Area of the Popes and of St. Cecilia

The Crypt of the Popes

VI. The Area of the Popes and of St. Cecilia

The Crypt of St. Cecilia

VII. The Area of the Popes and of St. Cecilia

The Cubicula of the Sacraments

VIII. The Area called St. Miltiades

XIII. The Liberian Area

The Neighbour and God

XIV. The Crypts of Lucina

Description of the cemetery area

XV. The Crypts of Lucina

The Crypt of St. Cornelius

APPENDIX

I. Very interesting Letters

II. Homage to the tombs of the martyred Popes by their Successors

III. More Pilgrims

IV. The great adventure

Chronological Tables

Selected Bibliography

Contents

VATICAN PRESS